Temporal Matters
in Social Psychology

Temporal Matters
in Social Psychology

Examining the Role of Time
in the Lives of Groups
and Individuals

Joseph E. McGrath and
Franziska Tschan

American Psychological Association
Washington, DC

Published by
American Psychological Association
750 First Street, NE
Washington, DC 20002
www.apa.org

To order
APA Order Department
P.O. Box 92984
Washington, DC 20090-2984
Tel: (800) 374-2721; Direct: (202) 336-5510
Fax: (202) 336-5502; TDD/TTY: (202) 336-6123
Online: www.apa.org/books/
E-mail: order@apa.org

In the U.K., Europe, Africa, and the Middle East, copies may be ordered from
American Psychological Association
3 Henrietta Street
Covent Garden, London
WC2E 8LU England

Typeset in by Goudy by Page Grafx, Inc., St. Simons Island, GA

Printer: United Book Press, Inc., Baltimore, MD
Cover Designer: Naylor Design, Washington, DC
Technical/Production Editor: Rosemary Moulton

The opinions and statements published are the responsibility of the authors, and such opinions and statements do not necessarily represent the policies of the American Psychological Association.

Library of Congress Cataloging-in-Publication Data
McGrath, Joseph Edward, 1927-
Temporal matters in social psychology : examining the role of time in the lives of groups and individuals / Joseph McGrath and Franziska Tschan.
    p. cm.
   Includes bibliographical references and index.
   ISBN 1-59147-053-6 (alk. paper)
   1. Time—Sociological aspects. 2. Social psychology. 3. Social groups.
  4. Social interaction. I. Tschan, Franziska. II. Title.

HM656.M34 2003
304.2′3—dc21

                                        2003007762

British Library Cataloguing-in-Publication Data
A CIP record is available from the British Library.

Printed in the United States of America
First Edition

CONTENTS

PREFACE

Almost 20 years ago, the first author (McGrath) began writing about the importance of time and its neglect as a topic in social psychology and related social and behavioral sciences. That work has been done with a number of splendid collaborators and coauthors, among them Linda Argote, Holly Arrow, Terry Beehr, Jennifer Berdahl, Janice Kelly, Kathleen O'Connor, Nancy Rotchford, and Ellen Shupe, all of whom have contributed crucially to the ideas in this book. During the past decade, the second author (Tschan) has been tackling the difficulties of dynamic processes in groups from a background in action theory, also with collaborators, especially Mario von Cranach. After we completed a recent collaborative chapter on groups as complex action systems, we realized that between us we had done a lot of work on time but that much of it was scattered in bits and pieces. So we decided to try to pull together all of these ideas about time in social psychology and, if we could, extend and elaborate that material. This book is the result of that decision.

The content of the book has been driven and constrained by three sets of factors. First, we tried to reflect as much as possible the theoretical and empirical research that has been done on temporal issues in social psychology. Second, we tried to focus on temporal aspects of various social psychological phenomena. So the book focuses on those phenomena for which we can see clear temporal connections and does not try to cover other interesting phenomena that seem to us not to be particularly temporal. At the same time, to talk about temporal effects on social psychological phenomena, we often had to describe those social psychological phenomena in some detail, including aspects that are not especially time related, so that we might then discuss how they are affected by temporal matters. Thus, not every passage in the book is tightly tied to time. Third, inevitably, we have given more emphasis than other scholars might to the particular domains of our own research interests and experience. In our case, that includes emphasis on three particular areas in which we have both done research: groups, stress, and research methodology. Given these driving and constraining forces, we have done our best to weave this material into a coherent, cogent, and readable whole.

Besides those past collaborators we have noted above, this book owes a debt to a number of others. These include the many graduate students at our academic institutions, the University of Illinois at Urbana–Champaign and the University of Neuchatel, Switzerland, respectively. We have generated and honed many of these ideas in discussions with them. We want to thank three valued colleagues—Linda Argote, J. Richard Hackman, and Janice Kelly—for providing thorough reviews and helpful critiques of an earlier version of the manuscript. We also want to thank Norbert Semmer for his review and critique of the material on time and stress.

We want to thank Lansing Hays at the American Psychological Association (APA), acquisitions editor, for his encouragement and helpful advice in early stages of this project. We also want to thank two anonymous APA reviewers and APA development editor Kristine Enderle and production editor Rosemary Moulton for their thoughtful and helpful comments. We owe a special thanks to Dr. Patricia Taylor for her careful and helpful analysis of the final version of the manuscript. The comments and suggestions of all of those reviewers have helped us make this a substantially better book.

Finally, we wish to give special thanks to our spouses, Marion McGrath and Norbert Semmer, for the support they gave us. That support, in myriad ways, sustained us during our struggles to generate the materials in this book.

Temporal Matters

in Social Psychology

1

INTRODUCTION

Time matters. Temporal factors affect individual personality and motivation, moods and emotion, judgment and decision processes, stress and coping processes, and even the construction of the self. The growth and development of individual humans follows a temporal course. The formation and development of groups, and sometimes their demise, are inherently temporal processes. The task performances of individuals and groups take place in a dynamic temporal context and are characterized by cyclical and phasic patterns throughout. When individuals and groups act in organizational contexts, all of these temporal factors are in play, along with some additional crucial temporal issues raised by the need for effective collective action. All of these time matters are the topic of this book.

This book catalogues many of the ways in which temporal matters affect how individuals, groups, and larger collectivities behave. It focuses on temporal matters and behavior of individuals and groups in organizational and other embedding contexts. In the past, temporal matters have not been given very much attention within social psychology or within other areas of social and behavioral sciences (e.g., Doob, 1971; Fraser, 1975; Hall, 1983;

3

McGrath & Kelly, 1986; Michon, 1988; Slife, 1993; Young & Shuller, 1988). That neglect has led to serious questions about the limitations of our extant bodies of evidence, about the validity of conclusions drawn from them, and about theoretical formulations founded on them (cf., Colquhoun, Blake, & Edwards, 1968; Kelly & McGrath, 1988; McGrath & Kelly, 1986; Slife, 1993; Tasto, Colligan, Skjei, & Polly, 1978). In recent times, there seems to be an increased concern with temporal matters in some areas (e.g., Bennett, 2000; Block, 1990a, 1990b; Bluedorn & Denhardt, 1987; Brown & Paulus, 1996; Dabbs, 1982; Das, 1991, 1993; Friedman, 1990; Hesse, Werner, & Altman, 1987; McGrath & Kelly, 1986; Robinson & Godbey, 1997; Zerubavel, 1981), although time matters seem still to be a relatively neglected topic in many areas.

This book will note those areas of neglect, but it is not about that neglect of time matters. Rather, the book is about those temporal issues themselves: how they arise, what we know about them, and above all, how further study of those temporal matters can aid our understanding of the behavior of individuals, groups, and collectivities.

The first section of this chapter outlines a conceptual framework for the ways in which temporal matters enter into social psychological phenomena. It also includes a brief discussion of a number of temporal parameters that are part of the temporal matters that we wish to explore. (In Appendix A, we present a series of assumptions and definitions of those temporal parameters, as a step toward providing a common "language" for talking about temporal matters in social psychological theory and research.) The second section of the chapter sketches out the organization of the rest of the book, and indicates how various chapters relate to that conceptual framework.

TIME AND THE STUDY OF SOCIAL PSYCHOLOGY

Temporal matters play a part in human behavior in many different ways. They are involved in the conceptual, the substantive, and the methodological *domains*. Temporal factors operate at different system *levels*. They play different *functions* or *roles* in social psychological phenomena and study. And they involve different types of social psychological *processes*.

Domains

All systematic, scientific inquiry entails a blending of information from three domains: conceptual, substantive, and methodological. Time matters are involved in all three of them. Time issues arise in the conceptual domain in a number of ways: for example, all postulated processes, or cause–effect relations, take some finite amount of time. Time is a feature of all aspects of the substantive domain, and is implicated in all empirical information we can gather about any of the substantive areas of our field. And all of our research strategies and methods by which we obtain such empirical information also contain numerous crucial temporal features.

Levels

Time needs to be considered as it plays into social psychological phenomena at many different levels, macro, micro, and in between. Those different levels encompass not only different sized units of time, micro, meso, and macro, but also different sized acting systems—individuals, groups, and larger collectivities—and different sized "chunks" of behavior (specific actions, extended multiperson processes, long-term strategic plans). Moreover, the levels are often overlapping, and usually are intertwined. That is another way of saying that human behavior can be regarded as hierarchically and sequentially patterned in complex ways. We deal with such hierarchical and sequential patterning in a number of places in the book, notably in chapters 3, 4, 5, 6, and 7.

Functions or Roles

Moreover, there are at least four different roles that temporal factors can play in social psychological inquiry. That is, temporal issues arise in four different functional relations to the substantive phenomena of social psychology.

1. Virtually all social psychological effects have important temporal properties. That is, some temporal factors are descriptive of the states and actions of the focal system itself, and constitute effects, consequences, or dependent variables (e.g., frequency or periodicity of a given type of activity).
2. There are important temporal properties of most if not all *causes*, or contextual conditions. That is, some temporal properties arise from the embedding contexts of the social systems being studied and constitute parameters of the causes, or antecedent conditions, or independent variables (e.g., the rate or timing of environmental events).
3. There are important temporal properties of many so-called intervening variables—variables that function as mediators or as moderators of cause–effect relations (e.g., some events have different impacts depending on the history or stage of development of the system).
4. There are also important temporal features embedded in the research process itself—in our strategies, designs, measurements, and experimental operations (e.g., time between occurrence of cause and measurement of outcomes). These function as meth-

odological features of all of the empirical research information that we acquire.

Types of Processes

In addition to these differences in level or scope, and in the role of temporal variables within social psychological inquiry, time matters also differ in the types of processes that they entail. Some temporal issues have to do with changes that arise out of *developmental processes* inherent in the systems being studied. Some are generated by changes that arise from the system's own experience; that is, *learning processes*. Some are *adaptational processes* generated by the system's response to (actual or anticipated) changes in the embedding contexts. Furthermore, the system's own operation as it carries out its projects entails complex *operational processes* that are hierarchically and sequentially related. There are temporal processes involved in strategic planning, in operational or tactical planning, and in execution. These sets of processes, at different hierarchical levels, are intricately related in recurrent execution and feedback cycles, each with different cadences and temporal patterning.

To some degree, these types of temporal processes are interdependent with one another. For example, processes considered as "cohort effects" often are the interaction of system developmental forces and system adaptations to contextual forces, both of which are parallel for systems of the same cohort operating in the same set of embedding contexts.

These types of temporal processes are also interdependent with both scope and role. That is, the processes sometimes have different faces as they play out at different levels or in different functional roles. But at every level, temporal issues are implicated in change processes that stand in different relations to the substantive systems under consideration. These four types of processes are considered at various places in the book, but most extensively in our discussions of group and collective action in chapters 6 and 7.

TEMPORAL PARAMETERS

In our view, parameters of temporal patterns include a relatively wide span of features of situations in which humans behave, not just the simple reckoning of clock time and calendar date. Of course, temporal factors do include features having to do with location of events and actions in *historical time*, as reckoned by some clock and calendar such as Greenwich Mean Time and the Gregorian calendar. But they also include the location of events or actions in one or more *situational times*, such as years of tenure in an organization, time before the end of some specific season, or time before some performance deadline.

Moreover, time matters also have to do with the *duration* of events and actions, and with the *durations of intervals* between successive re-occurrences of events or actions of a particular kind, or between two or more notable events of different kinds.

Time is a component of *rate* and *frequency*—that is, of the number of repetitions of an event or action of a certain kind within a given total time interval. Time is also an aspect of the order relations (*sequence* or *simultaneity*) of two or more notable events or actions of same or different kinds.

At a more complex level, temporal processes are reflected in the rhythms of cyclical events or actions—that is, in the regularity or similarity of the durations of the intervals between successive multiple occurrences of events or actions of a certain type. Time is also a key aspect of cause–effect relations—that is, of the regularity of occurrence, and of the interval before occurrence, of events or actions of a given type (taken to be effects) following the occurrence of an event of a specific different type (taken to be a cause). Finally, time is an aspect of the synchronization of multiple cycles (i.e., of entrainment) of the same system, or of different but interacting systems, or of a system in response to external pacing events.

It is important to try to keep all of those temporal parameters clearly distinguished from one another as we consider a range of temporal issues in this book. In Appendix A, we lay out a set of fairly straightforward definitions of all of these temporal parameters (rate, frequency, periodicity, and so on). To make those parameter definitions clear, we need to assume some arbitrary units of time and to state what we mean by events, observations, amplitudes, and the like. Those assumptions and definitions are also presented in Appendix A. We will use these terms as carefully as we can throughout the book.

ORGANIZATION OF THE BOOK

As the preceding discussion suggests, there is a very wide range of temporal issues inherent within social psychological theory and research. The facets of our framework, discussed in the previous section, do not by any means provide a comprehensive metatheory for our consideration of all of those temporal issues. The organization of chapters and the connections and distinctions among them, however, are founded on and to some extent illustrate the facets of that framework. Those facets consist of the following:

- domains (conceptual, substantive, methodological)
- levels (individual, group)
- functional roles (time as dependent, independent, intervening variable and as methodological factor)
- types of temporal processes (developmental, adaptational, experiential, operational)

At the broadest level, we have organized the book around three domains that are involved in all scientific study of phenomena: Conceptual, Substantive, and Methodological. Each domain subsumes some major topics and many smaller ones. Those domains and topics are, of course, quite intertwined, but they can be separated for purposes of discussing them more clearly. We have tried to choose topics within those domains so that, on the one hand, collectively they cover as much as possible of the relevant domain, and on the other hand, they offer the reader more manageable "chunks" of material to deal with.

The overall organization of the chapters of the book reflects the three domains: Chapter 2 deals primarily with conceptual issues regarding the nature of time. Chapters 3, 4, 5, 6, and 7 deal with a series of substantive areas of social psychology within which time matters are important. Chapters 8 and 9 are primarily methodological in focus. (See Figure 1.1.)

The Levels distinction is mainly reflected in our distinction between substantive topics dealing with individual and group or collective levels.

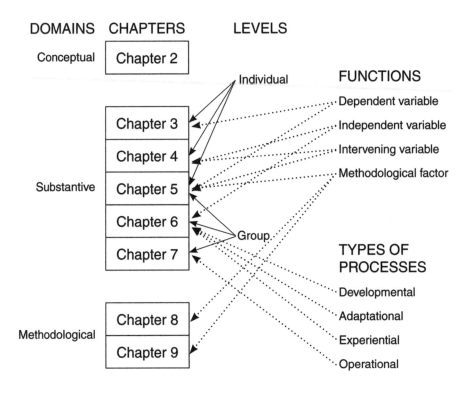

Figure 1.1. Organization of the Book

Chapters 3 and 4 are at the individual level. Chapters 6 and 7 are at the group and collective action level. Chapter 5, on stress and coping processes, spans those two levels.

The distinction regarding Functional Roles is also reflected in differences among those substantive chapters. The two chapters on individual level issues, chapters 3 and 4, are differentiated from each other in that the topics dealt with in chapter 3 primarily treat time as dependent variable whereas those dealt with in chapter 4 primarily treat time as independent and intervening variable. The topics treated in chapter 5 deal with time in all four of its functional roles: as independent, intervening, and dependent variable. Chapters 8 and 9 deal with time as methodological factors. So, too, do chapters 6 and 7 on groups.

The distinction regarding Types of Temporal Processes is reflected most clearly in the division between the two chapters dealing with groups. Chapter 6 deals with developmental, adaptational, and experiential processes, and chapter 7 deals with operational processes.

We have identified and examined a number of temporal issues in each of the areas covered by the various chapters, and we have tried to connect and integrate those topics partly via the facets of that framework. But we clearly have not been able to construct a totally integrated treatment of time in social psychological matters. In part, that is because those different areas of social psychology are themselves quite disparate and not totally integrated in their underlying metatheories.

CHAPTER-BY-CHAPTER ORGANIZATION

After this brief introductory chapter, the book begins with the conceptual domain: a discussion of the nature of time in people's lives. That formulation, in chapter 2, provides a discussion of how time has been and is conceptualized, experienced, and measured, both in our culture and in others, and both now and in the past. That chapter offers a discussion of the culturally dominant conceptual paradigm of time—a modified Newtonian conception—along with several alternative conceptions that have been dominant in other cultures and other times, and that are still relevant in particular subcultures and situations. An analysis of the dimensions underlying those clashing cultural conceptions of time points up a number of aspects of the nature of time that complicate how people deal with temporal issues in their lives. These matters are discussed in somewhat more detail in Appendixes B and C.

That conceptual chapter is followed by five chapters treating five different sets of substantive issues. Chapters 3, 4, 5, 6, and 7 deal with different substantive areas. The first two of those (chapters 3 and 4) are at the level of individual behavior; the latter two (chapters 6 and 7) are at the level of group and organizational behavior. The middle one (chapter 5) deals with stress and coping processes and bridges the group and individual levels.

Chapter 3 treats a number of areas in which temporal issues affect the everyday lives of individual humans, including matters such as how people use time, how they judge its passage, how the pace of life differs in different times and places, and how individuals differ in their persistent temporal orientations. These are mainly matters of "time as dependent variable." Chapter 4 deals with how time plays into individual motivation, goals and action, how temporal issues affect human cognitive processes such as decision making and problem solving, and how various time-related aspects of emotion such as boredom and impatience arise in relation to temporal matters (e.g., waiting). These are mainly matters of time as independent and intervening variable.

Chapter 5 examines a set of processes that have been much studied, although not always with temporal issues in mind: stress and coping processes. That chapter deals both with temporal aspects of single stress event cycles and temporal aspects of persistent, recurrent, and long-term stress and coping cycles. These processes not only span individual and group level considerations, they also deal with time in all four of its functional roles—as independent, dependent, and intervening variable, and as methodological factor in the research itself.

We then consider temporal matters at the level of groups and collectivities. Chapter 6 deals with temporal factors in the formation and development of the group itself, as a functional social entity. That chapter also discusses the idea of an ordered set of stages of group development—a temporal issue of long standing in social psychology. This chapter also deals with the impact of the dynamic interplay between the group and the multiple contexts—physical, social, organizational, and technological—within which groups are embedded, and also with temporal matters regarding how groups change as a function of their own experience (i.e., how they learn). Thus, chapter 6 deals with three of the four types of temporal processes noted earlier.

Chapter 7 examines temporal patterning in the behavior of individuals and groups when they attempt to carry out collective action within their embedding physical, temporal, and social contexts. It begins with a formulation of three key temporal issues that arise inevitably in all attempts at collective action: temporal scarcity, temporal ambiguity, and temporally conflicting interests and demands. Temporal scarcity leads to the need for strategic planning and allocation of resources. Temporal ambiguity leads to the need for scheduling and structuring of task processes (i.e., who will do what when). Temporally conflicting interests and demands lead to the need for coordination of actions of multiple social units. These three sets of needs get reflected in activities that are both hierarchically nested and sequentially patterned, and that involve recurrent cycles of orientation, execution, feedback, and modification.

The book then moves on to deal with a range of methodological considerations that arise if one considers how time matters play into social psychological phenomena and into theory and research on those phenomena. Chapter 8 discusses some of the main temporal issues that create problems within the research process and thereby make difficult the analysis and interpretation of substantive information about social psychological phenomena. These include temporal issues embedded in our logic of causality, issues of time in relation to the assessment of validity of findings, issues of time in relation to our theory of measurement and error, and the differences in time scale underlying various research strategies.

Chapter 9 is an attempt to suggest some of the theoretical, substantive, and methodological tools we will need in social psychological inquiry if we are going to develop a more time-sensitive discipline. In that chapter we examine the problem of a lack of temporal consideration in our theories, and what we might do about that serious omission. A second part of the chapter considers some methodological tools and approaches we will need to enable future social psychology to take temporal factors more fully into account. The final part of the chapter lists a set of topics for which we think future empirical research would be especially fruitful.

CONCLUDING COMMENTS

The overview in the preceding section makes clear that this book's coverage of social psychological issues is broad; but it is of course not totally comprehensive. As noted in the preface, our inclusion of material has been affected by at least three factors. First, we tried to cover areas in which there has been a lot of research regarding temporal matters—even if some of those areas are not central areas of social psychology (e.g., perceptions of the passage of time, in chapter 3).

Second, we tried to focus tightly on temporal issues involved in each topic. Consequently, there are many issues related to every one of our topics, some of them very interesting and important ones, that we do not cover because those topics do not seem to have very strong or direct connections to temporal matters. At the same time, because we are attempting to discuss time in relation to social psychological phenomena, we sometimes need to describe these phenomena in some detail and in nontemporal terms, so that we can then discuss how temporal matters affect those phenomena. Thus, not every single passage in the book is tightly related to temporal matters.

Third, as scholars often do, we have emphasized areas and topics that are within our own areas of scholarly specialization. Thus, we have given extensive treatment to groups, stress, and research methodology, and we probably have given less adequate coverage than other scholars might to some other areas of social psychology.

We end this introductory chapter, and each of the others, with some brief "Afterthoughts" in rhyming form. We hope these rhymes will amuse readers and perhaps even provide insights into the time matters being discussed.

AFTERTHOUGHTS

Why Study Time?

There's some sign of time in everything,
Some facet of time in all.
Each new topic leads back to time
Like summer leads to fall.

All of life is dynamic,
Everything grows—and dies.
Change over time is pandemic,
And all in the future lies!

Everyone thinks they know about time,
But actually—nobody knows!
So, studying time is wondrous play:
Just about anything goes.

Yes, studying time is wondrous work,
You can roam where your instincts guide.
And besides, it gives you one wondrous perk:
Time's always on your side!

2

THE COMPLEX NATURE OF TIME

What is time? It is now more than half a millennium since Saint Augustine made his classic comment about time: We know what time is until someone asks us, but when we are asked what time is we cannot adequately explain it. That comment still stands as an apt expression of the complex nature of our conceptions of time, now and throughout history.

This age-old question has been of concern to humans in many cultures, for both philosophical and practical reasons, for at least several millennia. And the answers generated to that question have varied considerably across history and cultures.

Most people in our culture take time for granted, in at least two senses: First, they usually do not pay much attention to it. They assume it is "there" and "make use" of it as they go. Second, they do not consider the nature of time or its measurement as problematic. In other words, to borrow Heidegger's terms (Slife, 1993), people tend to treat time as "ready to hand" in their everyday lives, and a part of the normal flow of events.

But philosophers and other scholars have spent a lot of time considering the nature of time, and how we ought to conceptualize it (that is, they treat time as "present at hand"). Moreover, engineers, scientists, and other practitioners (e.g., navigators) have taken as problematic the accurate, robust measurement of time. If we want to examine time as it plays out in social psychology we need to consider all three of these views: time as *experienced*, time as *conceptualized*, and time as *measured*. That is the subject of this chapter.

SOME UNRESOLVED PHILOSOPHICAL ISSUES ABOUT TIME

In Western culture, people are accustomed to considering time in a very particular way. But over history and across cultures, there are a number of different aspects of time about which humans have not always agreed (Gould, 1987; Heath, 1956). We state some of these matters below in very abstract terms and in the form of questions with dichotomous, alternative answers. We discuss them more concretely and in more detail throughout the chapter.

1. Is the essence of time succession and simultaneity or is time a matter of pure duration?
2. Is time an abstract dimension, independent of objects and events, or is time concrete and an integral part of events?
3. Is time absolute or is time relative to the location of observers and objects?
4. Is time continuous or is time a succession of discrete units?
   a. If time is continuous, can it be divided into smaller, contiguous units or is it indivisible?
   b. If time is a series of discrete units, what is the minimum sized unit and can there be lacunae between those units?
   c. In either case, are all parts of time homogeneous, or is time epochal, in that different instants have qualitatively different significances?
5. Is time linear or cyclical in its flow?
   a. If time is linear, is it bidirectional (as in Newton's and Einstein's conceptualizations), or is it unidirectional (as in thermodynamics and the progressive idea of history)?
   b. If time is cyclical, are the cycles strictly recurrent (circular) or are they approximately recurrent, and perhaps progressive (hence, spiral-like)?
6. Is time measurable solely in quantitative terms, or does time encompass qualitative aspects that are not captured in any numbering arrangement?

These questions are, essentially, unresolved—and indeed, unresolveable—philosophical issues regarding the nature of time and its measurement.

In different cultures and in different times, some sharply divergent conceptions of time have been built by accepting different sets of answers to these questions. These philosophical issues are discussed in some detail in a number of sources (Aveni, 1989; Heath, 1956; McGrath & Kelly, 1986; Slife, 1993) which we draw upon here.

For example, over the past several millennia, philosophers have considered the complex relations among time, space, motion, and change. In one view, proposed by the Greek philosopher Heraclitus, space, motion, and change are fundamental, and time is derivative. In another view, held by Aristotle, Newton, and others, time and space are fundamental, and motion and change are derivative. The latter view has predominated throughout modern Western cultures, although by no means can all aspects of motion and change easily be construed within that formulation.

Moreover in the Newtonian view, which is the fundamental one for modern conceptions of time in the lay culture, both space and time are dimensions independent of one another and of events and objects. In contrast, the Einsteinian view, which is important for certain parts of advanced physics and astrosciences, holds that time and space are both parts of a multidimensional space–time continuum, and that motion and change are relative to location in that space–time continuum.

The Newtonian view also holds that measures of time are on an abstract dimension measuring time in absolute terms, independent of persons and events. The Einsteinian view holds that, although measures of time are abstract, time is relative to the location of people (i.e., the observer) and of events (i.e., the observed). In still other views, time is relational in that its meaning inheres in the relations between persons and events. Some other views regard time not as abstract but as concrete, an integral part of events—either having real effects (such as erosion or forgetting) or being a medium within which those effects occur.

There are also some unresolved issues about the flow of time. The Newtonian view treats the abstract dimension of time as bidirectional and linear. One can reckon it from any given starting point, either forward or backward, and in either case it "flows" uniformly. Both modern notions of thermodynamics and the progressive view of human history, however, regard time as flowing only forward—albeit uniformly or linearly. Although this latter view recognizes that an abstract dimension of time could be calculated in either direction, they hold that "real" time can only run forward, inexorably and at a uniform rate.

Still other views hold that time is, in many contexts, circular or cyclical rather than linear. That idea is often incorporated into examinations of development and life cycles of living systems. Sometimes—in conceptions that McGrath and Kelly (1986) refer to as *transactional*—the idea of cyclical time is combined with the idea of progression, holding that time tends to spiral forward in its cyclical path, rather than to be strictly circular or recurrent in its movement.

There is the related question of whether time is singular, or whether perhaps there are multiple times. The idea of singular time fits with the Newtonian conception of an abstract and absolute dimension. The idea of multiple times seems compatible with the Einsteinian idea of relativity, though it does not seem to fit with the Einsteinian idea of an inseparable space–time continuum.

There also is a further question of whether time is holistic, not capable of being subdivided, or instead can be divisible into smaller and smaller units. If it is divisible, there is the further question of whether there is some ultimately minimal unit (a quantum of time!) and, if so, whether there can be spaces between those units of time. A related question is whether time is homogeneous or epochal: that is, are all "pieces" of time the same, or are some pieces of time qualitatively different from others?

This set of questions can be viewed as an array of possible assumptions one can make about the nature of time. Any "complete" conception of time must take a stance with respect to each of these issues—that is, the conception must choose to assume one or the other, or perhaps both, of the dichotomous choices that they involve. So we should be able to characterize every conception of time in terms of a profile of positions on these issues.

Two relatively recent treatments of time and psychological phenomena have grappled with many of these questions in considering the role of time in psychological and social psychological theory and research. One is a treatment by Slife (1993), which identifies five key aspects of time (objectivity, continuity, universality, linearity, and reductivity) that are central to the Newtonian conception that is dominant in our cultural treatment of time, space, and movement. Slife pointed out a number of anomalies that arise in psychological theory and evidence when the Newtonian position is adopted; and he compared the Newtonian treatment of time with two alternative conceptions of time (organismic holism and hermeneutic temporality) in terms of those anomalies for psychological study. Slife's treatment of these matters is presented in more detail in Appendix B.

The second is a treatment by McGrath and Kelly (1986) that identified four clusters of temporal issues, each defined in terms of a combination of two of the questions noted earlier in this chapter, treated dichotomously. Those four clusters have to do with (a) the structure of time, (b) the flow of time, (c) the reality of time, and (d) the validity of measures of time. McGrath and Kelly discussed the meaning of each of the four quadrants of each cluster, and associated each of four different broad conceptions of time with one quadrant within each of the four clusters. Those four broad conceptions of time are (a) a Newtonian view, (b) a view associated with the "new physics," (c) a conception characteristic of some eastern mystical religions, and (d) a conception arising from a transactional view of social psychological phenomena. The McGrath and Kelly conceptualization is discussed in some detail in Appendix C, and we draw on aspects of it, often implicitly, throughout the book.

OUR CURRENT CONCEPTION
OF TIME

It is certainly clear that more than one of the quadrants in each cluster of the McGrath and Kelly conception of time has some credence within our ongoing conceptualization, experience, and measurement of time. In other words, even though there is a culturally dominant conception of time—basically, the Newtonian conception modified by the idea of time as irreversible—there are also a number of variant conceptions of time that are part of our experience and action.

It is important to note that our current conception of time in modern Western culture has been shaped not only by celestial and biological factors but also by religious, economic, political, and social factors. Moreover, it is reasonable, we think, to posit that for many of the aspects discussed in this chapter, time can be regarded as having both of the opposed dichotomous alternatives rather than just one or the other. With that in mind, we think one can state the current culturally shared conception of time roughly as follows:

As of the year 2003, we in Western cultures regard time as having to do both with succession and duration. We regard time as a continuous quantity, but capable of being measured, quantitatively, in discrete units, with the microscopic size of those units arbitrary and limited only by the level of precision of our current time-reckoning technology (and with no lacunae between the units). Time as measured is clearly an abstract dimension, and we regard it as a medium within which events occur rather than as having concrete effects (except, perhaps, for some aspects of geology). We regard time as absolute.

Yet, in some situations time is relative. For example, for certain aspects of advanced physics, time is regarded as relative to the position of the observer. Also, for many aspects of cultural life, time is reckoned not only in absolute terms but also in terms relative to some situational context (e.g., the life span of an organization or a person, the progression of an athletic contest or a school term or the seasons of the year, the stages of a developmental or production process). We regard that abstract, absolute time as linear and directional (although because it is abstract, it can be reversed, conceptually, if we so desire). But we recognize that lived time (time as experienced by humans in their lives) also has cyclical aspects, both recurrent and near recurrent (i.e., spiraling). We regard abstract time as homogeneous (i.e., every bit of time is like every other bit), but we recognize that lived time is epochal (i.e., some moments in time are more significant than, hence different from, other moments).

OUR CONCEPTION VERSUS OUR EXPERIENCE OF TIME

Our conception of time, and our experience of it, are intimately inter-twined but are not the same thing. Let us begin with the premise that time, as we ordinarily understand it, is the time of the abstract dimension as measured by our currently most accurate and reliable clocks and calendars. Though our measures of time are ultimately arbitrary (see discussions in Aveni, 1989; Doob, 1971; Landes, 1983; McGrath & Kelly, 1986; Moore, 1963), we have learned to measure that abstract time with great accuracy. At the same time, we experience time in our lives in many different ways, not all of them totally consonant with our formal measures of it.

Starting with a basically Newtonian view, we examine many features by which humans have interpreted temporal patterns in the past (as indicated in the questions listed earlier in this chapter). In social psychology, we make some use of 11 of the 16 quadrants laid out by McGrath and Kelly. Regarding time's structure, we recognize both succession and duration as key aspects of time and also regard it as epochal in experience. In regard to time's flow, we recognize both linear flow—time's arrow—and phasic aspects of time. We also recognize that the abstract dimension of time can be run in reverse, in principle. Regarding time's reality or existential status, we regard it as math-ematical. We also regard it as experiential, and we recognize time's relational aspects. Regarding validity of measures of time, we see time both as a single independent dimension and as encompassing multiple constructs. These aspects are described in more detail in the following section.

Although we conceptualize time as homogeneous, it is easy to make the case that time is experienced as epochal. Any one instant can be given meaning with respect to many clocks and calendars of different contexts. It represents a juxtaposition of (a) events within one's own life course (e.g., my 21st birthday or 10th wedding anniversary), (b) events in the secular history of the culture (e.g., Memorial Day, or the day Kennedy was shot), (c) events within some organizational setting (e.g., the final week of instruction of a semester), (d) events within some episode that is partially nested within and confounded with one or more of those other contexts, (e.g., the due date for a term paper). Although many moments in time are not special on any of those calendars and clocks, some are special moments for one, or sometimes more than one, of them. So, for example, dawn is not just another instant in a ho-mogenous 24-hour (or $24 \times 3600 = 86,400$ seconds) day. Nor is Christmas or my birthday or the first day of school just another day in the (approximately) 365.25 day year. Those examples are all special instants in time, defined in terms of human experience—the first for humans at a particular location on the planet earth, the others in terms of historical and religious beliefs, personal life courses, or practices of a particular institution. Whatever the case for the abstract measurement of mathematical time, time is certainly epochal as experienced.

In our experience of time, and certainly in our measurement of it, time flows linearly and forward. But because our measures of it are along an abstract dimension, if we so choose we can consider it, abstractly, in a backward direction as well (as did Newton). It has often been argued that time is cyclical or near-cyclical rather than or in addition to being linear. That argument builds on the observation that many celestial, biological, and psychological processes exhibit cyclical or near-cyclical forms over time, each with its own identifiable periodicity. The sun rises, moves overhead, sets, and then rises again at almost the same place where it rose before. The stars and other celestial bodies move in a similar way. At the same time, many biological and psychological processes—body temperature, arousal and attention, the flow of hormones—wax and wane and wax again in particular and relatively precise temporal patterns.

Note, however, that it is not time that rises and sets, waxes and wanes, increases and decreases. Rather, objects (e.g., the sun) or processes (e.g., the flow of a hormone) wax and wane along a linear directional flow of the abstract temporal dimension. Indeed, we make use of the regularity of these cyclical patterns of objects and processes to define the units of time that "march" linearly and forward. Early on, we defined the day and year in terms of the apparent movement of the sun around the earth (or, later, of the earth on its own axis, and of the earth around the sun). We used the movement and appearance of the moon in the skies to define the month. For a while, we used the near recurrent movements of a pendulum to define the passage of linear and directional units of time smaller than a day. In modern times, we use the oscillations of certain materials, such as quartz crystals and cesium atoms, to define the passage of very tiny units of time as those units flow linearly and forward. But in our conceptualization, time itself—the thing we measure—is by definition an abstract concept; and it is a concept that is defined as linear and directional. The observable events by which we measure that abstract conception, time, may be oscillatory in their patterns over time (as per the examples above), or may be linear–directional (as in some measures of time that map it to spatial distance). But the conception that is being measured—time itself—is defined as linear and directional.

Time is both abstract and concrete, in certain ways. For measurement purposes, we adopt an abstract conception of time, but in other ways time is very concrete in the lives of humans, or at least is the "carrier" of very concrete effects. Time, both as we reckon it abstractly on a clock or calendar and as we experience it in our lives, is absolute: It passes inexorably and uniformly as reckoned on any given timekeeping instrument. At the same time, the meaning of time is relative to the multiple situational contexts of observers. Abstract time is regarded as homogeneous: All "pieces" of it are alike. Yet, as described previously, time as experienced is clearly epochal; that is, some points in time or units of time, specified in terms of particular cultural circumstances and assumptions, have special significance to the humans in those circumstances.

Although our conception of time sees time as a singular independent dimension, it is also easy to make a case that time in our experience is *multiple* in some senses. There are many situations in everyday life in which we operate within a context shaped by multiple "clocks" and "calendars." Consider a basketball game as an example. A basketball game is scheduled with reference to the standard Gregorian calendar and Newtonian clock (but also within a concocted "season"). It is played out with reference to both a game clock (noting time remaining) and a play clock (noting time left to get off a shot or else lose possession of the ball), and of course, also within the ongoing Newtonian time of that locality. Time is also "seasonal" within the game, in certain respects. There is a major rest period after two quarters and smaller ones after the first and third quarters. Some features start over again every quarter (e.g., the number of team fouls), some start over only every half. Certain rules about shooting fouls and ball possession hold only during the closing minutes of each half.

We take this example, which is trivial in some senses, because in the world of competitive sports all rules (including those about timing) are explicit and designed to cover all contingencies. In "real-life" events, the norms and rules about timing as well as other matters are often implicit. There is not a two minute warning, nor a formal half-time rest, in most on-going life events. Nonetheless, people behave in ways that make it clear that they are aware of, and take into consideration, time deadlines and other temporal contingencies. Gersick (1988, 1989) found, for example, that all of her groups made a major reorientation in their work patterns at approximately halfway to their deadlines, even though those deadlines varied for different groups from a matter of hours to a matter of months.

One can make a similar case for many of the other 16 temporal quadrants. Often, however, the "credibility" of a particular quadrant in one cluster depends on one's view about time in the other clusters. So, for example, whether one is willing to regard time as potentially bidirectional or reversible may depend on whether one regards time as totally an abstract dimension (in which case, it can be run, abstractly, backward as well as forward), or whether, instead, one regards time as a dimension with concrete effects (in which case, it is harder to buy into the idea of a reversible time).

FUNCTIONS OF DIFFERENT AND CONFLICTING
CONCEPTIONS OF TIME

Some of the conceptions and experiences of time are clearly contradictory. How can time be seen both as a homogeneous succession of instants and as epochal, as both absolute and relative at the same time, and as linear and cyclically recurrent?

The different conceptions of time serve different human purposes. For most of our day-to-day purposes, we experience time as a dimension separate from and independent of any of the three familiar spatial dimensions. Yet for certain purposes (e.g., certain considerations in advanced physics and cosmology) time can be viewed as an inseparable part of a four (or higher) dimensional space–time continuum. For other purposes (e.g., certain considerations in some mystical religions) time can be viewed as pure duration without dimension, or as being entirely illusory, solely a function of human perception and, hence, immeasurable.

We understand time to be a continuum, even though we often choose to divide it into arbitrarily small units—with the size of those units limited only by our measurement technology and our purposes, and with no space between units. Yet for some purposes we can regard time as a series of discrete though contiguous units of a certain size (e.g., seconds until blastoff; days until Christmas). And for some other purposes (e.g., some analogies with quantum physics) we can regard time as ultimately being a series of temporal quanta, of some specific though infinitesimal size, which we experience in succession, and which may or may not have infinitesimal lacunae between them.

People live their lives within contexts that are shaped by multiple conceptions of time. Sometimes, we are enmeshed in situations that are shaped by multiple conceptions of time that seem incompatible with one another. For example, people sometimes are under pressure to work on a day that is just another work day for the secular calendar but that their religion defines as holy and not to be worked on. In another example, when a region shifts to daylight savings time, dairy farmers need to change their *clock* schedules to maintain their *solar* schedules for milking and feeding livestock. As still another example, we have probably all experienced the shift in meaning, and in levels of attendance and attention, of a class (or even a day of instruction) when it is the last one before a vacation period.

Such conflicting clocks and calendars can pose social psychological issues of some importance. Sometimes the clash of time conceptions involves the very meaning of time and its passage. For example, a long-time employee of a work organization may consider his or her many years of service as an indication of seniority and experience, conditions that should be valued and rewarded with respect and higher pay. The organization, however, may regard such long tenure as evidence of obsolescence, or at least of aging and increased costs, conditions that call for replacement.

Another example of conflict arising from temporal features is the effect on the bodily cycles known as circadian rhythms if an individual is assigned to work swing shift or night shift (e.g., McGrath, Kelly, & Machatka, 1984). Not only is there a potential clash between the bodily rhythms, entrained to the rotation of the planet, and the rhythms imposed by the job, but there is also a potential clash between the requirements of the work shift and the rhythms of the embedding social system. For example, the night shift worker may find it hard to sleep in daytime, in a house in which everyone else is up and active. The problems may be further compounded at weekends, when the night shift worker tries to return abruptly to day shift rhythms to accommodate the surrounding social system, thereby undoing the partial reentrainment of bodily cycles that has gone on during the week, and suffering something akin to jet lag over the weekend and then again on Monday.

Scheduled start times for events offer another example of conflicting temporal conventions. Some start times need to be considered as "no later than" times; for example, you cannot be seated in some theaters after the curtain rises; and you may miss a bus, train, or plane if you arrive after the scheduled departure time. Other start times need to be treated as "no earlier than" times; for example, one may be expected to arrive at a party sometime *after* the stated start time. Dealing with such time indicators requires an intimate knowledge of a given culture or subculture. That is, the *meaning* of these time indicators is social rather than celestial or biological. Furthermore, sometimes such times have different and conflicting meanings for people with different social status—as in the old saying that a college class must wait 10 minutes for a late teacher if he or she is a full professor, but lesser times if the teacher is of lower rank (and, of course, one does not wait at all for those of student rank). Thus, a given period, interval, or time signal has multiple meanings that arise from factors that are social psychological as well as physical and biological.

CONCLUDING COMMENTS

Time as described in this chapter is the time that affects the everyday lives of modern Western humans. It is that kind of time, therefore, that constitutes the temporal aspects of social psychology (or the temporal aspects of any other social or behavioral science discipline) that we explore in this book.

We must keep in mind, however, this reckoning of time is a blend of biological, physical and astronomical processes as well as cultural ones. Certain features of time are fairly tightly tied to human biological processes. Others are tightly tied to celestial processes such as day–night cycles, seasons, and the like. In other words, some, but not all, aspects of time are mutable, through cultural processes, to fit human preferences.

In this chapter we have examined and contrasted conceptions of time, the experience of time, and attempts to measure it. Those human conceptions and measurements—and probably human experience—of time have varied across cultures and over history; social, religious, political, and economic matters, as well as celestial and biological ones, have affected these conceptions, measurements, and experiences. This offers a much more richly elaborated picture of time than one ordinarily makes use of in daily life, where time seems to be "ready to hand" and a natural part of the ongoing flow of everyday events. Such an elaborated view will be useful, we think, as we examine a wide range of "time matters" in relation to social psychological phenomena and inquiry.

In this book we explore, simultaneously, both the social psychology of time and the temporal aspects of social psychological processes. The social psychology of time refers to how people understand time in their own cultural time and place, and how they make use of time in human social endeavors. The temporal aspects of social psychological processes refer to how temporal processes—some obvious, some little noticed—affect the social psychological processes and human actions through which people live out their lives.

AFTERTHOUGHTS

What Is the Nature of Time?

I always know what time is about
At least until someone asks!
But then I find I can't define.
Time wears so many masks!

Sometimes time is simple and plain,
Sometimes it's most complex.
Defining time is a wonderful game
If you don't mind being vexed.

Time is in all, it's everywhere.
It stretches both aft and fore;
It marches, it flies, it's here and it's there,
It's our "now," and our "then," and our "yore"!

Time is so real, yet it's abstract too.
It's reckoned in many ways:
In eons and hours, in minutes and months,
In nanoseconds and days.

Yes, time is a wondrous, magical thing!
Or is it a thing at all?
Is time just a vehicle moving our spring
To summer then to fall?

Is time like matter? One can't add any
Nor delete the time that's there?
Or is time perhaps like beauty,
In your head, not any "where"?

Does time just go forward, an arrow that flies?
Or can we go back in time?
Is time a circle that turns on itself
Like rhythms in a rhyme?

All of these questions indeed perplex
And leave philosophers weary.
Ideas of time are quite complex
They make our thoughts go bleary.

But all of these matters don't matter a bit
For time as we live it each day.
Oh, we wake and we work, and through all of it
Time goes merrily on its way.

We have time to love and time to play,
Time to waste or to spend in our fashion.
We never get more than one day per day
But we never get less than our ration.

There are times we hope for and times we've seen;
Time is writ on a tablet vast.
But every minute is trapped between
Our future and our past.

These verses on time could go on and on
Ere time's glorious story is writ!
But there's one timely thing we can count upon:
There will be an end to it!

Time and Life

Clocks and calendars, tick- and tock-ing,
Mark off Gregory–Newton times.
But human life, enacting, talking,
Flows in rhythms (just like rhymes!).

Real time flows in steady patter
But seems, at times, to oscillate.
But time in life's a different matter
Its rhythmic flow can syncopate.

When time stands still it's really going.
It never speeds and never stops.
But time as lived, in human knowing
Seems to flow in streams or drops.

So you must ever keep in view
That time as lived and time in thought
May often seem as one to you,
But time and life the same are not!

3

TEMPORAL ASPECTS
OF INDIVIDUAL BEHAVIOR

In this chapter we begin our treatment of temporal matters in a variety of substantive areas of social psychological theory and research. The next two chapters (chapters 3 and 4) are about phenomena at the individual level. Chapters 6 and 7 are about phenomena at the level of groups and collectivities. Chapter 5 is about a set of phenomena that bridges those two levels.

This chapter and chapter 4 are devoted to discussion of two quite distinct sets of temporal matters involved in the everyday lives of individuals. The first set, treated in this chapter, is a series of topics that are explicitly temporal. They involve such issues as how people use their time, how they pace their lives, how they perceive time and its passage, and what persistent orientations they have toward time. In this set of issues time functions as a dependent variable: Time is an aspect of the behavior being considered. Unlike many of the topics dealt with in this book, these topics, by and large, have received considerable research attention. Our intent here is to give a broad overview to the reader who is unfamiliar with those areas, and to cite literature that can provide an in-depth treatment of those areas for readers who wish to pursue these topics at greater length.

The second set of individual-level topics, dealt with in chapter 4, has to do with how temporal matters play into a number of more general social psychological processes. These are such matters as how time plays into motivational and action processes, how time affects cognitive and decision processes, and how time-related feelings and emotions affect our thoughts and actions. In this set of issues, time serves as an independent and intervening variable. These involve topics in areas to which social psychologists have given relatively little theoretical and research attention.

SOME TEMPORAL ASPECTS OF EVERYDAY LIFE

In this chapter, we will examine four sets of specifically temporal processes that play a part in human lives, and about which there has been considerable research. These areas can be stated in terms of four "natural" and obvious questions:

1. How do people use their time? How do individuals distribute their time over sets of activities? Much of this has been examined in research using time diaries.
2. How do cultures and contexts differ in the pace of everyday life, and how are those differences related to other aspects of life?
3. How do people perceive time? How accurately do individuals judge the passage of time, and what factors affect those judgments? These questions have a century-long history of research.
4. How do people orient toward time? How extensively do people orient in relation to the past, the present, and the future? There is considerable research in this area, as well, with much of it assuming that such orientations are persistent or trait-like, and with much of it focussed on the importance of a future temporal orientation.

These questions, in a sense, treat time as a dependent variable. In each case, we will try to summarize the main findings from empirical research in that topical area, and emphasize the main factors giving rise to variations in the phenomena. For pace of life, the main differences are cultural and regional. For time use and for time orientations, the substantive findings show systematic variation not only across cultures but also as a function of social class, gender, and ethnicity of the respondents, and over the individual life span. For perceptions of the passage of time, the main factors seem to be how cognitively busy the respondent is at the time the judgment is made, and whether the judgments are retrospective or prospective.

HOW PEOPLE USE TIME

For many years, researchers have been interested in how people use their time on ordinary days. Time budget studies date back as far as 1920 (Andorka, 1987). How people use their time has been regarded as an important social indicator. It tells us something about how productively time is used, how long people travel to and from work, how much time they spend shopping or with their children, and how much time they spend on eating, personal care, household chores, and various other aspects of daily life. In many countries, time-use surveys are conducted regularly on representative samples of people. Much of this research has been done by sociologist and economists rather than psychologists. Time-use studies often are part of larger surveys or panel studies, carried out or sponsored by national bureaus of statistics. Due to international efforts, time-budget data are available for many countries and covering a considerable period of time.

It is interesting to note that, despite many cultural differences among the countries studied, some aspects of time use are similar across the different studies. As an obvious example, people spend about a third of their time sleeping in all the countries studied. There was an average of around 8 hours a night in studies done in 1972 for people in the U.S. and 11 other countries, from the USSR to Peru to France, Belgium, and Germany (Robinson, Converse, & Szalai, 1972). Similar results were found in a later study covering India (Pandey, 2000).

In most countries studied, the average work time is around 50 hours a week (Robinson, Converse, & Szalai, 1972) and has not changed much over time (Bittman & Goodin, 2000). That number includes both paid and unpaid work. Examples of unpaid work in Western countries are most often household duties, but in India, for example, unpaid work includes productive tasks that are not directly paid for such as hunting and fishing for food, horticulture, gardening, and construction work (Hirway, 2000).

In spite of these strong similarities, there are a number of cultural differences. In Belgium, for example, average time spent on paid and unpaid work is somewhat higher than it is in the U.S.; and in the Netherlands it is somewhat lower (Bittman & Goodin, 2000). In the countries of the former Soviet Union, the average hours of work a week was much higher for women and somewhat higher for men than in western Europe and the U.S. (Bittman & Goodin, 2000). One cultural difference is in time spent eating: Several studies have found that people in France used more time for meals than in many other countries (Converse, 1972; Larson & Verma, 1999). Another cultural difference is that in the U.S. both men and women spend almost twice as much time awake and alone as do men and women in any of the eight European countries in the study. The latter occurs partly because people in the U.S. have less contact with colleagues and coworkers during work time (Cseh-Szombathy, 1972).

Time use changes across the life cycle, in ways that fit the different developmental tasks that people undertake at different stages of their lives; but cultural differences persist, too (Singleton, 1999). In a summary of time-use studies of children and adolescents in many countries, Larson and Verma (1999) found, as one would expect, that the biggest differences in time use were between children in postindustrial countries and nonindustrial countries, and the most important influencing factor was whether children can go to school or not. In some nonindustrial countries, children beyond the age of about 9 either do household chores or work for pay, but do not attend school. Even when children do go to school, they often work as well. A recent study in India showed that about a third of children in the age group of 6 to 14 years worked an average of about 14 hours a week. Most of them did unpaid activities, such as crop cultivation or the tending of grazing animals (Hirway, 2000). Cultural differences between children's use of time have also been found in postindustrial countries, in comparisons between the U.S., Europe, and East Asian countries. Although schoolwork takes a substantial amount of time for children in all of these countries, U.S. children spend between 3 and 4.5 hours a day with schoolwork, whereas Eastern Asian children devote 5.5 to 7.5 hours. European children are in between. Eastern Asian children and adolescents thus have only 4 to 5.5 hours free time, which is less than for those in the U.S. (6.5 to 8 hours) or Europe (5.5 to 7.5 hours). These results probably reflect cultural differences in how education is valued. However, a recent University of Michigan study showed that in the U.S. between 1980 and 1997, the amount of unstructured time in children's lives had decreased.

For adults, major influences on time use are employment status, the presence of children in the household, and the level of responsibility for the children. These factors influence the total working time and are similar across cultures (Bittman & Goodin, 2000). Skorzynski (1972) found that unmarried men worked fewer paid hours than married men, whereas the reverse held for women. Employed and married women spent fewer hours at work, but spent about 3 hours more a day for household chores than did men. Men had more leisure time.

Gender differences are very similar across cultures, mainly because the number of children and adults present in the household influence women's time use a lot more than men's time use for unpaid work. On average, controlling for all other related factors, the presence of children increased a women's unpaid work time about 10.5 hours per week, but increased men's unpaid work time by less than 3 hours. Similar results have been found for the presence of other adults in the household: The increase for women is about 8 hours more work a week, for men the increase is less than 1 hour. Although some regional differences were found, these gender differences remained relatively stable across many Western countries (Bittman & Goodin, 2000; Converse, 1972; Singleton, 1999), as well as in India (Hirway, 2000).

In general, people seem to want an appropriate balance between time spent on paid work and on work in the household. A recent study in Canada (Frederick & Fast, 2001) found that women were more satisfied with life if they spent more hours at work and less with household chores, whereas men were more satisfied if they worked at the job less and spent more time with unpaid work, suggesting that a more balanced allocation of paid work and unpaid work increases satisfaction for both men and women.

Besides these large influences regarding work and family, time use has also been found to be dependent on several contextual factors, such as day of the week, shop opening hours, and special times of the year (Singleton, 1999; Webb, 1985). Social class is still another influence on time use. For example, one study found that about 30% of white-collar employed men read before going to work (usually the newspaper), but less than 10% of unskilled workers did so (Stone, 1972).

As people grow older and retire, time use changes somewhat. However, the major influence on elderly people's time use arises from decreased mobility. Only after they have become dependent on others for care do seniors start spending a large proportion of their time in passive activities (Lawton, Moss, & Duhamel, 1995).

Time use has changed somewhat over the years during which it has been studied. Some of those changes are due to general social changes, but some reflect very specific technological developments. As an example of the general factors affecting change, one study that compared time-budgets of the 60s and the 80s showed a general decline in work hours and a small increase of domestic work for full-time employed men, and a small decline of domestic work for full-time employed women. At the same time, time spent for leisure activities increased for both men and women. As an example of specific technological factors, time spent in television watching depends on the availability of television sets in the households (Robinson, Converse, & Szalai, 1972), which is different in different cultures and has increased in all of them over time. These changes may have led to the decline in time spent reading, which was found in a Dutch study to have decreased by 50% from 1955 to 1975 (Knulst & Kraaykamp, 1997). A similar argument may hold for computer use: Computers have been in widespread use only recently, and have only recently been measured with time-budget studies (Suzuki, Hashimoto, & Ishii, 1997). It is likely that future time-budget studies will show substantial increases in average time using a computer, with concomitant decreases in some other categories of time use. Those changes, too, are likely to vary with age, gender, social class, and other within-culture and between-culture differences.

One can regard these findings, overall, as demonstrating that humans' use of time is eminently social and cultural in its variations, as well as being strongly influenced by the biological and environmental conditions of human life.

PACE OF LIFE

In the previous section we examined how much time people spend on different aspects of their life, and cultural differences became obvious. A closely related question is how fast or slowly people perform various activities. Robert Levine and colleagues have done interesting research on the pace of life in different countries and cultures, and also in various locations (e.g., rural vs. urban) within the same country (Levine, 1988, 1997; Levine & Bartlett, 1984; Levine, West, & Reis, 1980; Levine & Wolff, 1985). They defined "pace of life" in terms of a variety of measures, such as the pace of pedestrians walking on city streets, the pace of speech, the average length of time needed to carry out a routine transaction at a post office, and the average accuracy of bank clocks. In their studies (Levine, 1997; Levine & Bartlett, 1985) they compared people in a larger and a smaller city within each of 31 different countries including the U.S., many western and eastern European countries, Asian countries such as Japan and China (including Hong Kong), African countries, and Central and South American countries. They found substantial differences in pace of life among these different countries. Switzerland had the fastest overall pace of life (but this may have been due partly to its extremely high score on the clock accuracy measure). In general, western European countries and Japan had rather fast paces, whereas South American countries and Indonesia tended to have slower paces. The U.S. was in the middle of the 31 countries studied.

They also found a strong association between the pace of life of a locale and the rates of coronary disease and other characteristics associated with stress related disorders, such as scores on type A personality scales. There was one notable exception to those associations: Japan, which had a very fast pace of life on all measures, had the lowest rate of coronary disorders (of the four industrialized countries for which such coronary data were available).

Another study (Levine, West, & Reis, 1980) compared respondents in the U.S. and Brazil in terms of their punctuality and their conceptions of the relation of punctuality to personal success. As expected, they found substantial differences between the two cultures in actual punctuality. They also found that respondents in the two cultures had opposite views of the relation between punctuality and personal success. U.S. respondents thought punctuality to be positively associated with success; Brazilian respondents thought lack of punctuality was more closely associated with success. Apparently, this difference arose because U.S. respondents interpreted lack of punctuality as inefficient organization of time, whereas Brazilian respondents interpreted being late as a prerogative of higher status persons. Work in this program has examined a number of other regional and cultural differences.

Overall, these studies of pace of life make it clear that there are strong cultural and regional differences in these temporal matters, as there are in other aspects of use of time, and that these differences are associated with differences in important outcome variables.

TIME PERCEPTIONS:
HOW HUMANS JUDGE THE PASSAGE OF TIME

How do people perceive and judge the passage of time? When does time appear to stand still? When does time run fast? Work about judgments of duration has a long history and a central place in the psychology of time, and there is a very large body of work on effects of stimulus parameters and judgment conditions on judgments of the passage of time. Time, in these studies, is the dependent variable. Although this area is not always regarded as social psychological, many of the important factors affecting time judgments are interpersonal and social in nature.

In general, studies have examined three sets of questions:

- How do people judge the time elapsed while doing something? We are often surprised at how much (or how little) time something we do has taken. French Psychologist Paul Fraisse (1963, 1984) has made important contributions to that question.
- How fast or slow does time pass in general in people's lives, and what influences the feeling that "time flies" or "time stands still"?
- A third set of questions asked about certain conditions in which time does not seem to be experienced in the usual form of steady, relentless flow. These questions concern the perceived duration of the present, about the experience of timelessness, and about the experience of flow.

These three sets of questions are the focus of the three parts of this section.

Estimates of Duration of Specific Temporal Intervals

Studies about the perception of temporal duration map the objectively measured clock time to the subjective passage of time. There is a long tradition of such studies, and reviews of results have been made by Doob (1971), and Fraisse (1984), as well as Block (1990a, 1990b) and Zakay (1989, 1990). In most of the studies, the duration to be judged was a very short interval, sometimes in the range of milliseconds and often less than a minute.

Results are influenced by whether the person knows that he or she will be asked to judge the duration (i.e., a prospective judgment), or whether, instead, the duration judgment is an unexpected question after the time has passed (i.e., a retrospective judgment). Prospective judgments tend to be less varied, but also longer, than retrospective judgments of duration (Block & Zakay, 1997). Perceptions and judgments of duration are also connected to attentional and memory processes. In prospective judgments, when the person knows in advance that a time judgment will be asked, attentional processes play a bigger role. In retrospective judgments, memory processes play a more important role.

Early studies concerned with time estimation searched for an inner clock: some physiological functions tied to time estimation, such as pulse, breathing rate, alpha waves, or metabolic rate (cf. Gililand, Hofeld, & Eckstrand, 1946; Hancock, 1993). Although the search for a literal clock has had little success, this is not to say that there are no inner timing mechanisms. For example, several researchers have found that body temperature influences time perception; higher temperatures are associated with perceptions of time as passing faster (Hancock, 1993). This association is attributed to the higher general arousal or activation level that accompanies higher body temperatures. Moreover, certain stimulants or drugs can also change the experience of time perception, presumably by changing general arousal levels. Also, lesions in some brain areas have been found to impair the accurate perception of the passage of time.

Over and above these physiological relations, duration perception is heavily influenced by the stimuli to be judged, or by the nature of the actions that are being carried out, or by what is being experienced during the time period that is to be assessed. Long ago, William James suggested that time filled with meaningful tasks passes more rapidly than idle time (cf. Gililand et al., 1946; Shannon, 1976). Empirical results are not conclusive on this point. Often, the reverse has been found (Shannon, 1976). It has therefore been suggested that the type of activity may play a role.

A number of researchers have proposed conceptual models to account for stimulus effects on the perception of duration. Ornstein (1969) proposed that time perception is related to the amount of cognitive activity done or required in a certain interval, and has developed the *storage-size hypothesis*. The more (memory) storage size used during a certain interval, the longer that interval's duration will be perceived to have been. This, of course, applies to retrospective rather than prospective judgments.

The *attentional effort model* attributes the magnitude of duration judgments to the attentional effort needed during the event to be judged. It has been shown that for stimuli of equal complexity, those that required more attentional effort (e.g., because some of the information was masked) were judged to be longer than those requiring less attentional effort. Some have concluded from these studies that attentional effort influences time judgments more than memory load does (cf. Jones & Boltz, 1989).

Block (cf. Jones & Boltz, 1989) hypothesized, further, that the number of contextual changes, either external or internal, influences the perception of duration. External changes are such things as task demands. Internal changes are cognitive processing activities. This line of argument suggests that, in addition to the number of "bits" of information to store, the number of changes (e.g., switching between two types of tasks) also contributes to duration estimates. Block hypothesized that information processing is monitored by a cognitive device that calculates a complexity index based on the actual number of changes.

In prospective duration judgments for which the person knows in advance that the duration has to be judged, the *attentional–gate model* (Block & Zakay, 1997) hypothesizes that some of the attention is devoted to the timing of the task, and that a cognitive counter compares information with a reference memory.

Jones and Boltz (1989) argued that the models previously cited explain duration estimation by nontemporal aspects of the stimuli presented. They argue, further, that in fact many of the stimuli presented in laboratories and most of the stimuli encountered in the real world encompass time markers, such as beginnings, ends, and rhythm. They propose a model that postulates that temporal information contained in the events themselves is used to judge the duration of those events. Stimuli are more or less structured, and more or less predictable, and the person may therefore have clear or ambiguous expectations about their duration. Jones and Boltz propose two different modes of *attending:*

1. If the stimulus is coherent and structured (such as in speech, music, or body gestures) the attending is future oriented, because the stimulus is predictable. In this case, people use their experience to generate expectations about the duration of the event. For example, in listening to music, people may anticipate how the melody will develop, and also have expectations about the rhythmic structure and the duration. Duration estimation in this case is determined by the confirmation or violation of the expected continuation or ending time. If an event terminates sooner than expected, its duration appears shorter (than it actually is in "clock time"). In this example, it is the ending that influences duration perception, but rhythm or velocity also can have similar effects.
2. If the stimulus is not coherent, its duration is not predictable. In such circumstances, Jones and Boltz hypothesize that the duration estimation will be influenced by the attention given to local details, as people try to organize the unstructured information. In this case, they will judge the events that are filled with more items to be longer.

As previously noted, activation levels can influence time perception, and these in turn can be influenced by emotions. Negative emotions seem to increase duration estimation: Thayer and Schiff (1975) showed that negative facial expressions led to overestimation of the durations for which they were presented. Angrilli, Cherubini, Pavese, and Manfredini (1997) found similar effects when pictures were shown with negative and highly arousing content.

McGrath and Kelly (1986) suggested a model that integrates external information processing requirements and internal conditions, taking into account several factors that have an influence on perceptions of duration. The first factor they stress is the actual duration, measured objectively (that is, in "clock time"). The second factor is the ratio of an internal clock to the objective clock. Such a ratio leads to overestimation of the duration if a person is in a state of heightened arousal (because of body temperature, drugs, or for any other reason) and hence has an inner clock that is running at a more rapid than normal rate. The same ratio leads to underestimation of clock time if the person is in a low arousal state, hence has an inner clock that is running slower than normal. An additional factor is the rate of information processing that is required by an event, compared to the person's usual or expected rate of information processing.

So, estimation of duration of specific time intervals is influenced by the state of the person, the stimuli or tasks, and the conditions under which the judgments are made.

Feelings About Passage of Time in General

Besides the studies that have looked at the perception of duration of specific time intervals or sets of events and viewed such perceptions as a set of phenomena general to all persons, other researchers have investigated whether there are consistent and persistent differences in feelings about the speed with which time in general passes. These differences include demographic factors, personality factors, and effects of various kinds of activities. Note that these studies ask people to reflect on their feelings about the passage of time in general rather than to judge the duration of a specific interval of time.

Age is one individual difference factor examined in this regard. For children, time seems to pass more slowly than for adults, and it has been argued that time passes more rapidly for persons of advanced age. Specific life circumstances may also influence feelings about the passage of time. For example, people who are terminally ill perceive time as passing faster, whereas suicidal patients perceive time as passing slower (Neuringer & Harris, 1974).

Ring (cf. as cited in Hinz, 2000) asked people how fast time passes in different circumstances or activities. In general, people responded that time passes faster than they wished it would. They also judged that time passes very fast during leisure time, but also rather fast at work. Attitudes influence these perceptions. Time at work passed faster for people who liked their work than for those who did not. For those who liked leisure very much, leisure time flew even more rapidly.

Estimates of the *Present* and the Experience of *Flow*

Theoretically, the present moment is a durationless slice of time between the past and the future, but some researchers argue that there is a subjective experience of a certain duration of the present moment. William James called it the *sensible present*. Whereas James (1890/1981) thought that the sensible or specious present might reach about 12 seconds, Pöppel (1989) estimated it to be about 3 seconds. Fraisse (1984) argued that the duration of the present has an upper limit of about 5 seconds, but that it is flexible, with its extension depending on the events that fill the present. For example, the whole of a short sentence, or a long word, or a phone number can be perceived as the present.

There are situations in which time may not be experienced as passing at all. Such a sense of *timelessness* is part of a set of experiences that Csikszentmihalyi and colleagues (1997; Csikszentmihalyi & LeFevre, 1989) describe as *flow* experiences. These are very positive states of mind, in which people experience a high degree of focus on an activity, feel highly absorbed and concentrated on that activity, and feel fully in control. In these situations, the sense of time seems to be altered. During flow, people report that they are not aware of time passing at all. Afterwards, many people judge that more time has passed than actual clock time.

Flow experiences are common. They occur more often at work than during leisure time (Schallberger & Pfister, 2001; Csikszentmihalyi & LeFevre, 1989), and are considered to be an important source of happiness. In sport, similar experiences have been labeled as being "in the zone" (Stein, Kimiecik, Daniels, & Jackson, 1995), when athletes report effortless and highly effective performance but also an altered sense of time. Other matters with which flow experiences have been compared are the ecstasy of religious mystics and the aesthetic rapture of artists and musicians (Csikszentmihalyi, 1997). All of these have in common a high concentration, and at the same time a loss of the experience of the passage of time.

Concluding Comments on the Passage of Time

Unlike most temporal phenomena, researchers have devoted considerable attention to factors affecting variations in judgments both of durations of specific time intervals and of feelings about the passage of time in general. Some of the factors affecting these judgments are social psychological in origin. What is not clear, however, are the implications of these findings for other social psychological phenomena. In other words, whereas it is clear that the cognitive, emotional, and behavioral nature of the ongoing situation and activities affects the perception of rate of passage of time, it is not clear whether differences in perceptions of the rate of passage of time have any consequences for other cognitive, emotional, or behavioral activities. To answer the latter question requires a different kind of study than those done thus far in the "judgments of passage of time" genre. This question requires studying how existing differences in time judgments—either naturally occurring or experimentally manipulated (e.g., by studying people engaged in different types of activities or in different states of arousal)—can influence a variety of subsequent activities such as problem solving, decision making, or engaging in interactions of various kinds. Such studies do not seem to have been launched to date.

TEMPORAL ORIENTATIONS

Although we all live in the present, our minds can "wander" in time. We can think about our past experiences and how they shaped and influenced us, and we can think about our future, what we want and expect, where we are going, and what we want to avoid. Lewin (cf. as cited in Zimbardo & Boyd, 1999) considered time perspective as the individual's view of his or her future or past in his or her present, and hypothesized that cognitions and emotions about the past or the future may influence present actions, emotions, and cognitions, as well as future aspirations.

In the ideal case, we can switch between thinking about the past, the present or the future according to the demands of the situation. Remembering our own past experiences is often very useful. For example, it can be very helpful to think about how we liked to spend our weekends as a child, if we are trying to find fun things to do with our nephews or grandchildren. Similarly, our thoughts about what we will achieve in the future may help us to persist on cumbersome tasks that have no immediate positive outcome. So imagining future states may influence what we do in the present, and can help to overcome present difficulties.

However, several researchers have argued that, over and above this ability for functional adaptation of our temporal orientation, there is a relatively stable individual tendency to emphasize a particular temporal frame and, thus, to develop a consistent temporal bias. That is, they argue that different individuals tend to be more future-oriented, more present-oriented, or more past-oriented.

Most of the research on time perspective has focused on future orientation, described as the preoccupation with the future or with future events. Part of this orientation is a tendency to consider more or less strongly the future consequences of one's own or others' behavior (Strathman, Gleicher,

Boniger, & Edwards, 1994; Zimbardo, Keough, & Boyd, 1997). There is, however, no consistent framework for measuring and examining future orientation. Different research groups have emphasized different aspects of how people consider future states or events in their lives, and have used different definitions and measurements of future orientation.

Some researchers have viewed future orientation as a *general time orientation* and contrasted it with present orientation or past orientation (Gonzales & Zimbardo, 1985; Zimbardo & Boyd, 1999). Others have discussed the *duration of time* that is covered by future orientation—for example, how many months or years ahead, into their future, do people think and plan (e.g., Nurmi, 1989; Pulkkinen & Rönkä, 1994). Still other researchers have been interested in the *content of thoughts* about the future (e.g., Nurmi, 1989) or the number of different hopes and fears that get expressed and the *degree of detail* with which future events are imagined (Schmidt, Lamm, & Trommsdorff, 1978). Finally, still other researchers have explored the evaluational component of the thoughts about the future, and distinguished between having an *optimistic versus pessimistic* view of one's future, or the extent to which one expects to have *influence on and control over* one's future (Schmidt et al., 1978). In addition to these variations, all of which are relatively general conceptions, Strathman and colleagues (1994) use a narrow conception, *consideration of future consequences*, which specifically measures the degree to which one considers the future consequences of things done in the present.

Probably the most comprehensive conception of temporal orientation is derived from the Stanford Time Inventory. Gonzales and Zimbardo (1985) developed that measure on the basis of a reader survey in *Psychology Today* in which nearly 12,000 people participated. They initially identified seven factors and later reduced them to five aspects of time orientation (Keough, Zimbardo, & Boyd, 1999). They distinguish two aspects of past orientation: *negative past orientation*, in which the past is predominantly seen as unpleasant and aversive, and *positive thoughts about the past*, in which past experiences or past times are seen in a nostalgic, rosy, and pleasant way. They also identified two aspects of present orientation: The present can be perceived in a *hedonistic* way, as full of pleasure, enjoying the moment without remorse for later consequences of actual behavior. Alternatively one can have a *fatalistic* present orientation. People with this orientation strongly believe in fate, have a resigned attitude toward the present in which they believe it cannot be changed and that they cannot influence either present events or their future. The fifth factor is *future orientation*, characterized by having goals and making plans for the future, and behaving so as to increase the chances of carrying out those plans and realizing those goals.

These various conceptions and measures of time orientation have been used to explore three broad questions:

1. How are past, present, and future temporal orientations distributed in the population?
2. How do such temporal orientations vary over the life span, across situations, and across cultures?
3. What are the effects of having different temporal orientations?

Those three topics will be examined, in turn, in the rest of this section.

Are People Generally More Past-, Present-, or Future-Oriented?

There are differences in the conception and perception of past, present and future in different cultures (Wendorff, 1989). In comparison to many other cultures, most Western industrialized societies can be regarded as future-oriented. There is a strong cultural emphasis on a conceivable and controllable future.

But to what extent is a future orientation characteristic of all of the individuals within those future-oriented Western cultures? The answer to that question, apparently, is that people in Western cultures are largely future-oriented, or else have a balanced future and present orientation. Few are past-oriented (Hill, Block, & Buggie, 2000; Jason, Schade, Furo, Reichler, & Brickman, 1989). Gonzales and Zimbardo (1985) found that a majority had a present and future balanced orientation: that is, they considered both present and future equally. Another third of the respondents were predominantly future-oriented. Less than one percent were predominantly present-oriented. Only one percent was predominantly past-oriented (Gonzales & Zimbardo, 1985).

There are, however, cultural and ethnic differences within the same society. For example, New Zealanders with European heritage have longer future time orientation than do Maoris, (Bray, 1970). Zimbardo and Boyd (1999) also found differences between ethnic groups in the U.S. on some of the time orientation factors. African Americans showed significantly more negative past orientation than other ethnic groups; Asian Americans scored lowest on the positive past scale. Asian Americans also had the highest scores on a fatalistic view of the present, whereas Caucasians and African Americans scored lowest. This study does not report ethnic differences regarding future orientation.

Factors Influencing Time Orientation Over the Life Span

Young children's time span is relatively short, and it is clear that cognitive maturation is important for the development of a future orientation (Piaget, 1927; Trommsdorff, 1983). Nurmi (1989), in a survey of 11 year olds followed up at age 15, showed that the amount and time span of planning, and the expression of hopes concerning the future, all increase with age. At the age of 15 the adolescents felt a higher level of control about their future than they had at the age of 11. They also were more optimistic with regard to their future (Nurmi, 1989). The contents of their thoughts about the future were in accordance with the developmental tasks of their age, and were often about their future family, education, occupation, and material possessions (Nurmi, 1991). Interestingly, it seems that time extension (that is, the time length into the future toward which they oriented) did not necessarily increase with age. Both 5th graders and 8th graders extended their thinking about the future up to about the same age, 20 (Nurmi, 1989). This would make it seem as though 5th graders had a longer future orientation than 8th graders. Similar results have been found in other studies (Webb & Mayers, 1974). However, this could also be interpreted as an effect of "time anchors," with the age of 20 serving as an anchor for both 5th and 8th graders.

Adolescence and young adulthood seems to be the age at which the present is more important than it is at other ages. Gonzales and Zimbardo (1985) found young male adults to be most present-hedonistic oriented, followed by teenagers. At the same time, college students are the most oriented toward long-term future goals.

Future orientation increases with age beyond adolescence up to some point, but then decreases for elderly people. Retired persons have fewer long-term plans (Gonzales & Zimbardo, 1985), and were found to be more present-oriented (Lennings, 2000). Perhaps this is so because they realistically experience a diminished extension in their future perspective. Nevertheless, Lang (1998) found that almost half of a group of elderly people (mean age 84 years) still expressed a positive outlook about their future and held plans for the next year. Their degree of future orientation was influenced by their current social and life situation. As for younger people, elderly who had more extensive future perspectives were also those who were more satisfied with their lives (Wensauer & Grossmann, 1998) and less lonely (Lang, 1998).

Several studies have found that women have a stronger future orientation than men, whereas men have a stronger present orientation (Keough, et al., 1999; Zimbardo et al., 1997). But the content of thoughts about the future also differ for men and women. Men more often mentioned political, occupational, and "public" topics, whereas women noted more topics in the "private" sphere (see also Schmidt et al., 1978).

The perception of time and time orientation not only varies over the life span, but it is also influenced by socialization and life circumstances. For a group of urban African American adolescents, McCabe and Barnett (2000) found that salience of the future, the degree of detail in considerations of the future, and the belief that one has an influence on one's own future, were all related to the amount of involvement of the mother in child rearing, to a family's social support patterns, and to the amount of socialization with regard to future orientation. There is also evidence that future orientation is influenced by socioeconomic factors, with lower socioeconomic strata being less future-orientated (Lamm, Schmidt, & Trommsdorff, 1976; Malmberg & Trempala, 1997; Nurmi, 1991). This may be in part the effect of a realistic perception of relative opportunities. In that same light, for example, more intelligent Finnish children expressed more hopes concerning their future education (Nurmi & Pulliainen, 1991), and Finnish and Polish adolescents attending general secondary schools (a relatively higher education) perceived higher levels of control about their future than adolescents attending vocational schools (Malmberg & Trempala, 1997). Similar results have been found in Germany (Lamm et al., 1976).

Differences in time orientation between social classes have also been found in adult populations: Middle-class adults had a more extended future orientation and were more optimistic about the future than lower-class adults (Gonzales & Zimbardo, 1985; Schmidt et al., 1978).

So in many ways, differences in temporal orientations reflect both differences in experience and circumstances between individuals within a society, and differences in the individual's circumstances over the life span. The question, then, remains: What difference does it make?

Correlates of Differences in Temporal Orientations

Time orientation seems to correlate with many aspects of everyday behavior. In general, people with higher scores on future orientation exhibit more considered behavior, whereas people with higher present orientation scores tend to engage in more risky and unhealthy behaviors. Many studies of children, adolescents, and college students show that higher future orientation is associated with achievement in general, and with school or university performance in particular, as well as with general well-being. Future-oriented college students showed more goal-directed behavior and engaged in a larger number of activities related to achieving these goals (Murrell & Migrone, 1994). At the same time, a strong future orientation can function as a protective factor for children in disadvantaged environments (Chubick, Boland, Witherspoon, Chaffin, & Long, 1999; McCabe & Barnett, 2000).

People who give more consideration to the consequences of future events reported fewer behaviors that would have negative long-term effects on their health, such as drinking alcohol and smoking. They also took fewer risks, and engaged in more HIV-preventive behaviors (Agnew & Loving, 1998; Strathman et al., 1994). In contrast, more present-oriented people engaged in more behaviors such as risky driving, even after controlling for levels of traits such as sensation-seeking and aggression (Zimbardo, Keough, & Boyd, 1997).

People higher in consideration of future consequences not only behave differently, but also show differences in attitudes in ways that seem influenced by concern for long-term consequences. For example, persons with high future orientation scores were less favorable toward offshore drilling, which may have positive short-term consequences for gasoline and heating oil prices, but negative long-term consequences for the environment. They generally held more environmentally conscious attitudes (Strathman et al., 1994).

Many of the measures of time orientation (e.g., Keough et al., 1999; Strathman et al., 1994; Zimbardo & Boyd, 1999) resemble other well-known psychological measures, such as measures of conscientiousness, locus of control, or self-control. This raises the question of the discriminant validity of time orientation measures. Indeed, many studies have found quite high correlations between various other concepts and future orientation. For example, researchers have reported high correlations between present orientation and sensation-seeking or novelty-seeking, and between future orientation and conscientiousness, preference for consistency, self-esteem, and self-confidence (Keough et al., 1999; Nurmi & Pulliainen, 1991; Pulkkinen & Rönkä, 1994; Zimbardo & Boyd, 1999). Strathman and colleagues (1994) also report rather high correlations between their "consequences of future actions" scale and measures of conscientiousness and hope.

One aspect of self-control is control over time. So what researchers have regarded as measures of pure time orientation, namely the preference for past, present, or future, could be a by-product of self-control and action-control processes as these are related to time. However, several studies have established relatively clear discriminant validity of the time orientation measures with respect to self-control measures and show that the time orientation scales account for variance over and above what those other scales account for (Strathman et al., 1994; Zimbardo & Boyd, 1999).

Concluding Comments About Temporal Orientations

So the case for both convergent and discriminant validity of time orientation measures remains problematic, with the time orientation scales of Zimbardo and colleagues and the "consideration of consequences" scale of Strathman and colleagues among the most promising candidates. At the same time, it is clear that whether or not such measures constitute consistent individual differences (or *traits*), the level that any given individual is likely to show on them depends a lot on that individual's life stage, general life circumstances and embedding general and particular cultures, as well as the particulars of the situation. Moreover, there is considerable evidence that having a strong—and long—future orientation, at least within modern industrialized Western cultures, is associated with higher levels of focussed, goal-directed thoughts and actions, and a more thorough consideration of the future consequences of one's own and others' actions. This orientation is also associated with lower levels of risky and potentially harmful behaviors. So regardless of the status of any given measure of it, and regardless of its individual versus situational ontology, the conception of differing temporal orientations is a useful idea for our consideration of the social psychological aspects of temporal issues.

CONCLUDING COMMENTS

In the four areas discussed here, time functions as an aspect of the behavior itself—durations devoted to various activities, pace of actions, experience of time's passage, and the direction of one's orientation with regard to time. These four areas have received considerable research attention in psychology, although they have not all been of central concern in social psychological theory and research. In the areas to be considered in the next chapter, time functions as an aspect of context or situation that affects other social psychological phenomena, either as causal or independent variable or as a factor that mediates or moderates causal relations. These matters have been much less thoroughly treated in social psychological theory and research.

AFTERTHOUGHTS

Where Does the Time Go?

Where does my time go? Let me count the ways.
I spend each average seven days:
With 168 hours each week, I reckon,
That's ten thousand minutes! Half a million seconds!

That seems like tons of time to spare,
Yet I can't find spare time anywhere!
So let's see how I spend each week,
In hopes I find the time I seek!

There must be time for sleep each day.
That's fifty hours gone away!
Then, forty hours of work for sure
(And often it's a whole lot more!).

I also need, say, ten or so
For my commuting, to and fro.
And I must use at least some more
For laundry, cleaning, grocery store.

I need some time to care for me
To bathe, and eat, and reverie.
That leaves, let's see…well golly gee,
I've used more time than time there be!

Yes, I've accounted hours more
Than weeks are apt to hold in store.
My time-use surely does amaze:
I'm living 30-hour days!

4

TEMPORAL FACTORS AFFECTING SOCIAL PSYCHOLOGICAL PHENOMENA

In this chapter, we will examine some ways in which temporal matters affect other social psychological processes, notably human actions, cognitions, and emotions. We will deal with three particular domains, areas in which there has been some research effort:

1. *Goal directed cycles of action.* We will discuss a number of temporal issues that are intertwined with the formation of goals and their attainment via action. Are actions characterized by phases and cycles? How do temporal factors affect planning and predicting? How do humans intertwine multiple simultaneous activities?
2. *Human cognitive processes.* We will focus on temporal aspects of decision making: How do temporal factors, such as deadlines and time until the decision has its impact, affect the decision-making process and its results?

3. *Feelings and emotions*. We will focus on time-related feelings and emotions such as boredom and impatience, that arise in relation to waiting—an inherently temporal matter.

TIME, GOALS, AND
THE ACTION PROCESS

There is a widely shared assumption that people have desired states that they want to attain in the future, known as goals, and that they strive to attain those goals. People develop goals and pursue them via their actions (Gollwitzer & Moskowitz, 1996). A considerable proportion of human behavior is oriented toward the establishment and pursuit of short- and long-term goals (Cranach, Kalbermatten, Indermuehle, & Gugler, 1982).

Goals are intentions and representations about a future state that is not yet realized. Having a goal implies that there is a discrepancy between the actual state of things (the system, the actor) now and an imagined or intended state that lies in the future. One could say that goals span time: They link the imagined future to the present action. Moreover, the process of goal attainment, the action process itself, unfolds over time through several qualitatively different action phases.

Goals and Time

A goal is a cognitive anticipation of a future state. It implies that the actor has an internal conception of what should be achieved in a more or less distant future. This means that the person is able to project himself or herself, and his or her behavior and its effects, into future time.

Many scholars assume that goals are organized in hierarchies (Carver & Scheier, 1999; Cranach et al., 1982; Frese & Zapf, 1994; Oesterreich, 1981). Higher goals are more abstract; they include goals on lower levels, and the higher-level goals can only be realized via the realization of those lower-level goals. The goal of "giving a dinner party," for example, includes lower-level goals such as "decide on the menu," "go shopping," "prepare food," and so forth. Each of these subgoals, in turn, includes goals on an even more micro level: "go shopping" could include establishing a shopping list, planning the sequence in which one wants to drive to the stores, entering a store, choosing items, checking out, and so forth. Each of these subgoals can be divided into still more specific parts, down to single movements (e.g., "start the car," "shift into drive," etc.).

The structure of goals has other features related to time. Because goals on a higher level include subordinate goals, high-level goals are in force for a longer time than low-level goals, many of which can be achieved very quickly. Moreover, for many of the higher-level goals, related subgoals have to be achieved in a more or less strict sequential order. Some of the subgoals have to be accomplished before others can be undertaken, because the fulfillment of one goal may be a prerequisite for working toward another goal. For example, the invitations to a dinner party need to be sent out before the party actually takes place. Some of the sequential requirements may be stricter than others. For example, sending out the invitations must be done some period of time before the party; but if the host plans to give a little speech after the hors d'oeuvres, it does not matter much if he or she does so instead after the main course.

The hierarchical and sequential structure of goals can be even more complicated. There can be several mutually exclusive alternative sequences of subgoals by which to reach a higher-level goal; or there may be rules and detours that apply, depending on rate of progress or difficulties encountered. Methods of hierarchical task analysis attempt to describe such goal structures (Annett & Duncan, 1967; Shepherd, 1998).

Goals can spread over very different time spans, depending on their hierarchical level, but also depending on the tasks their fulfillment requires. Proximal goals relate to the present or the near future, whereas distal goals are further away in time, number of actions, or both. People who stay oriented to proximal goals have been found to have higher levels of goal attainment than those who orient only to distal goals. This happens, most likely, because progress related to *proximal* goals can be monitored and managed easier than progress related to *distal* goals. Bandura and Schunk (1981) found that if a distant goal were divided into several proximal goals (thus making lower levels of the goal hierarchy salient and making the goals concrete), people advanced toward goals more rapidly. In a similar vain, Locke and Latham's (1990) goal setting approach holds that rather short-term, concrete, challenging, but attainable goals elicit the highest rates of performance.

Action Goals and Self-Relevant Goals

The hierarchical and sequential organization of goals described thus far refers implicitly to rather concrete actions, such as "go shopping" or "throw a dinner party." Besides such goals, which are clearly related to action content ("do goals"), there are also more general goals that are related to the person's state or condition ("be goals"). Examples of such goals are "be a nice person," "be socially adept," "be competent," and the like. Motivation researchers assume that such goals are relatively stable over long periods of time and consistently influence a large variety of situations and actions. Such self-relevant goals are normally very abstract goals. Several researchers have proposed that such self-relevant goals are on the top of every person's goal hierarchy (Carver & Scheier, 1999). Self-relevant goals are akin to needs and motives and have also been discussed in relation to persistent personality characteristics. They have also been called personal strivings (Emmons,

King, & Sheldon, 1993), personal projects (Little, 1983), or life tasks (Cantor, Norem, Niedenthal, Langston, & Brower, 1987; Cantor & Sanderson, 1999). Some scholars assume that some of the self-relevant, high-level goals are the same for most people. For example, Ryan and Deci (2000) postulated that goals in the service of autonomy, competence, and social integration are particularly common self-relevant goals and are important for most people in our culture over most of their lifetime. However, some researchers argue that, although most of the self-relevant goals are relatively stable over an extended period of time, they may change within the life span according to different developmental tasks that are salient at different periods of life. "Establish independence" may be a more salient and important self-relevant goal for an adolescent than for an adult, whereas "be a good parent" may become a more important goal only in young adulthood (Cantor & Sanderson, 1999; Havighurst, 1972).

There are two different kinds of goals: promotion and prevention. Attractors, or promotion goals, are goals that people want to attain and strive toward. Avoidance or prevention goals are states or conditions that the person does not want to move toward. For self-relevant goals, an attractor goal could be "have a lot of friends"; an avoidance or prevention goal could be "avoid losing face in discussions." The means by which we regulate behavior may differ for attractor and avoidance goals (Higgins, 1996).

Generally speaking, it seems important for people to be able to pursue valued, self-relevant goals. Both the degree to which goals can be fulfilled and the progress toward attaining goals have been found to be related to well-being. However, forming long-term, self-relevant goals that are not realistic can have serious disadvantages. Goals that are too idealistic and abstract for the person to even come close to achieving can lead to frustration or apathy (Carver & Scheier, 1999; Higgins, 1996).

Goals Imply Action

Goals set up a psychological tension state. Lewin's student Zeignarnik (1927) was the first to show that unfinished tasks, which are related to unaccomplished goals, stayed in memory longer than completed tasks. Goals seem indeed to have a kind of psychological autonomy once the person has committed to them. They stay "active" until actively devalued, either by goal attainment or by being explicitly abandoned (Martin, Tesser, & McIntosh, 1993; Tesser, Martin, & Cornell, 1996).

This persistence of goals is very useful for carrying out actions, because goals are necessary to guide behavior. We can see this in cases where, for example, we leave a room with an intention in mind then find ourselves without knowing what it is we intended to do. We do know that we had an intention, and it is because of this intention that we left the room to start doing something; but the content of the intention got lost, and with it the idea of what behavior we wanted to carry out. Error research describes such instances of "lost goals" and a "what-am-I-doing-here" experience (e.g., Reason, 1990). Reason explains this experience as a failure to periodically refresh goals (or as being distracted from the initial intention) when there is a delay between the formulation of the goal and its expected execution.

However, the goal need not always be represented consciously. Sometimes goals guide behavior automatically, and they can automatically trigger processes that support goal attainment. Martin and colleagues (1993) showed that unfinished goals do not lead to a generally higher activation, but rather increase the accessibility of goal-related information without influencing the ability to process information unrelated to the goal.

In some instances, after failure to attain a goal, some persons seem to repress thoughts related to that goal, because such thoughts painfully remind them of their failures. Martin and Tesser (cf. Martin et al., 1993) tested a time-related model of thinking about goals after failures. They postulated that directly after failing to attain an important goal, people may indeed not access thoughts about this failure. But if the motivation to attain the goal persists, evidence of rumination or goal-related thoughts, as described by Zeigarnik (1927), will reappear later in time. They showed in their experimental studies that people who believed they had failed to demonstrate their intelligence in a task (which is assumed to be an important, high-level goal that will not be abandoned) seemed to repress thoughts about intelligence for a while, but after a certain delay, they became more vulnerable to intelligence-related topics. So there is a temporary inaccessibility of goal-related thoughts after failure to attain an important goal, and then later there is heightened accessibility.

The heightened or directed attention that goals produce is useful not only for keeping the goal itself in mind, but also for directing attention to goal-relevant content. Klinger (1996) called the internal state, after committing to pursue a goal, the "current concern." He postulated and observed that when people were more reactive to cues associated with their concerns (i.e., their action goals or self-relevant goals), this increased the probability that they would continue to process, cognitively and emotionally, stimuli related to the goal. After being committed to the goal, and before goal attainment, the system is temporarily in a latent state of readiness.

Phases of the Action Process

Heckhausen and Gollwitzer have offered a description of different mental states related to different phases of an action (Gollwitzer, 1990; Heckhausen, 1991). They propose a sequential model of general phases in the action process. In the *pre-decisional* state, the actor has not committed to a specific goal, but may be considering several different routes of action. In this phase, motivational processes are important, because they will determine the general direction of action to be chosen. When a goal has been chosen, a first threshold is passed. However, the action to attain the goal may not be carried out immediately. The actor may wait for a better opportunity. The phase in which the goal has been chosen but the action not yet carried out is called the *pre-actional* phase. During this phase, the actor may develop a plan, but action is not yet taken. A second threshold has to be passed for the person to actually start carrying out the action. These authors call that second passage a volitional act of implementation. The actor thereby enters the *actional* phase, in which the action is carried out. In this phase, volitional processes may become important so that the person persists in the action and overcomes difficulties. Upon goal completion, the actor enters a fourth, *post-actional* phase.

The different phases of action are associated with two, qualitatively different mind-sets. The action and pre-actional phases—after having chosen the goal and before ending the action—entail an action-oriented mind-set. The person becomes oriented toward implementing the goal, starts focusing on low-level, short-term subtasks and performance-relevant information. This corresponds somewhat to the low-level action identification described by Vallacher and Wegner (1989).

Before a person has committed himself or herself to a specific goal and course of action, and after the action is finished, (that is, in the pre-decisional and post-actional phases), the mind-set is called *deliberative*: It focuses on a longer time frame, considers several possible action goals, and processes information relevant to each of the different goals. In this mind-set, people are more sensitive to external cues than when in an action-oriented mind-set. In these phases, attention is not directed toward the concrete, behavior-relevant aspects of the situation, but toward more general aspects. These correspond in part to the high-level action identification described by Vallacher and Wegner (1989).

The phases previously described distinguish different sequential parts of an action, and the accompanying general mind-sets. To carry out an action, however, specific steps must be taken. Pursuing a goal (or a task, or an action) can be seen as a sequence of functional steps that the actor has to carry out. People represent the goal cognitively (and thus anticipate a future state), develop plans to reach that goal, undertake actions that are steps toward that goal, monitor their progress toward the goal, adapt their behavior to that progress and to hindering or facilitating circumstances that they may encounter, and, finally, stop acting if (and when) they have attained the goal. This action process unfolds over time. It has been described as a Test–Operate–Test–Exit sequence (Miller, Galanter, & Pribram, 1960).

More recent conceptions have discussed the action process in somewhat more detail. They distinguish steps such as (a) goal specification or goal development, by which the actor chooses or accepts, and maybe redefines, a goal (Hackman, 1969); (b) orientation processes, by which the actor orients him- or herself with regard to the state of the process; (c) planning processes, by which the actor develops plans for behavior; (d) execution of behavior and monitoring of this execution; and (e) stopping the action process once a goal has been reached (e.g., Cranach et al., 1982; Frese & Zapf, 1994; Oesterreich, 1981). These conceptions assume that the different steps of the action process should ideally be carried out in a specific temporal order, which starts with the goal, followed by a plan for how to realize it, then by action and monitoring of that action, and finally stopping the behavior sequence.

Because goal structures are hierarchical, the action process takes place with regard to goals on each of the hierarchical levels. Several authors (Cranach et al., 1982; Frese & Zapf, 1994; Hacker, 1998; Reason, 1990) distinguish different kinds of action regulation on different levels. On the lowest level, action regulation is skill-based. This entails the application of known, often automatic, movements to reach a low level goal such as shifting gears in a car. Skill-based regulation takes place with regard to the immediate activity at hand. On the intermediate level, the regulation of action is rule-based. People have a set of flexible action patterns, applicable in many different situations. Rule-based regulation means that, depending on the situation, an appropriate action pattern is chosen and applied in a flexible way to the problem. An example would be parallel parking, which requires a given set of steps (action rules) that must be adapted to the size of the car and the parking space. Action regulation at the highest level includes knowledge-based reasoning: solving problems cognitively and developing entirely new patterns of action. Regulation on this more cognitive level requires the greatest amount of time and cognitive effort and spans a longer period of time, as, for example, in long-term planning.

Reason (1990) found that people strive to regulate action on the lowest possible level. Regulation on higher levels is only used if lower level regulation is not sufficient. So regulation moves up to higher levels only if necessary, and goes back to a lower level if that will be sufficient to regulate the action. Tschan and colleagues (McGrath & Tschan, in press; Tschan, 1995; Tschan & Cranach, 1996) have described the action process in terms of hierarchically and sequentially organized cycles of action, involving orientation, execution, monitoring, and modification of action. Those cycles are described in more detail in chapter 7, in our discussion of collective action.

Overcoming Difficulties in Action Regulation

We have described goals as anticipations of future states and as powerful guides for human behavior. However, there are often many obstacles to goal attainment. First, there may be several goals that compete for being pursued in a given time period. Second, once engaged in pursuing a goal, the persistence of action often is difficult, and people may be tempted to abandon the action. Both of these are time-related problems.

Atkinson and Birch (1970) proposed a dynamic model of action to explain what happens when more than one goal is competing to be carried out at a given time, and to predict when people will change from one activity to a competing one. Their model includes a crucial time dimension; they assume that the forces that influence the activities increase or decrease in intensity over time. At the onset of each action, there are instigating forces and inhibitory forces. Say, for example, that a student wants to study to pass an exam (instigating force) but fears that he may not fully understand the material (inhibitory force). Instigating and inhibitory forces change in strength over time. Action starts when the instigating forces become stronger than the inhibitory forces. However, instigating forces may be counteracted by antagonistic, consummatory forces that increase while an activity is being carried out, because the actor has the initial motivation partially satisfied. As the consummatory forces increase over time, the probability that the person will continue with the action diminishes, and some other action for which there are strong instigating forces and weak inhibitory forces may be started.

Atkinson and Birch further proposed that there are delays in such activity changes. Even when instigating forces toward a new action are sufficiently great to abandon the current action and trigger a change to another course of action, this change will not take place immediately. There is some *behavioral inertia* that keeps an ongoing behavior going for a certain time. Atkinson and Birch proposed this time lag in the occurrence of changes to explain why continued oscillation between two similarly attractive goals is not very common.

Persisting in an ongoing action that is related to a difficult but desired goal is an important aspect of action regulation. One of the difficulties people have is in continuing over time to do something that may not be fun while doing it. Actors often have to shield an ongoing course of action against tempting actions related to competing motivations.

Volitional Action Control Strategies

Kuhl and colleagues proposed several strategies of volitional action control, strategies that help the actor to maintain a course of action over time, facilitate the enactment of intended actions, and not give in to competing action tendencies prematurely. Some of these strategies are *attention control* (deliberately focusing on aspects of the uncompleted intention rather than thinking about other things to do), *motivation control* (reminding oneself about the attractiveness of attaining the goal), *emotion control* (actively trying to avoid a pessimistic mood if it impairs action completion), and *coping with failure* (processing information quickly about failures related to the action, to obtain correctional feedback, but deliberately not persevering in thinking about the failure, and not linking failure-related thoughts to a general evaluation of oneself; Beckmann & Kuhl, 1984; Kuhl, 1984; Kuhl & Goschke, 1994). Other control mechanisms are *encoding control* (actively trying to avoid processing information not relevant to the ongoing action) and *environment control* (eliminating all distracters from the environment; see Emmons et al., 1993; Kuhl, 1984).

There may be individual differences that help or hinder these processes. Kuhl (1992) proposed two basic modes of orientation toward one's intention: Action-oriented people are adept at maintaining their intentions over time, and are likely to use the previously-mentioned strategies to protect their intentions. State-oriented people tend to ruminate upon non-task-related aspects and unsatisfying present states, and they often process past failures in a way that may discourage them from further actions (Kuhl, 1992). Action orientation and state orientation are similar to the implemental and deliberative mind-sets previously described. However, these mind-sets have been found to be functional for different temporal phases of the action. State orientation (or a deliberative mind-set) may be useful in the preparatory phases of the action, and action orientation (or an implemental mind-set) may be useful during enactment. A stable, trait-like tendency to be state-oriented may hinder the person from engaging in or carrying through many different actions. A stable, trait-like tendency to be action-oriented may minimize the deliberative period before engaging in action, and thus lead to premature goal selection. However, research on these constructs has found that in general, more action-oriented people perform better and have higher well-being than more state-oriented people. The control mechanisms previously described may help people persist in an activity over a longer period, by resisting diminishing motivation and increasing consummatory forces, fatigue, and temptations toward other actions.

Another important mechanism of willpower and self-control is delay of gratification (Mischel, 1974). Individuals often postpone immediate rewards for the sake of delayed but more valuable gratification. To do so, they must resist the frustration created by the pressures and temptations of the moment. Delay of gratification means to engage in volitional self-control. The ability to delay gratification seems to be learned in early childhood. Mischel and colleagues offered small children the choice of either getting a small reward immediately or waiting for a bigger and more attractive one later. To have a reward handy to consume seems to create arousal and the wish to consume it. Children who spontaneously used strategies, or were given strategies, that decreased arousal could more successfully delay gratification (Mischel, 1974). Arousal was lessened in either of two ways: by turning attention away from the available reward or by thinking about the reward in "cool," descriptive terms instead of "hot," emotional terms. Although younger children sometimes spontaneously apply such strategies, it is only when children are 6 or older that they start to understand the self-control mechanisms involved in delay of gratification (Rodriguez, Mischel, & Shoda, 1989). Learning to delay gratification is assumed to be an important aspect of achievement. Indeed, longitudinal studies have shown that children who had learned better strategies for delay of gratification by the age of 4 were, as adolescents, better able to handle stress, able to show greater self-control in frustrating situations, and more able to concentrate (Mischel, Shoda, & Peake, 1988; Shoda, Mischel, & Peake, 1990).

Metcalfe and Mischel (1999) recently suggested the existence of two basic systems that influence delay of gratification and other self-control mechanisms. The hot, emotional system is specialized for an immediate, quick response in the present. It is rather simple and pushes toward action. If the hot system is operational, available rewards are immediately consumed. The cool system is cognitive. It spans a larger time frame, is slow and reflective, and develops later than does the hot system. It helps the person delay gratification. Because the hot system develops earlier than the cool one, smaller children have more difficulties with delay of gratification than do older children. But stress, as well as physiological and dispositional factors, also influence which system guides responses.

The ability to wait for a larger reward instead of immediately consuming a smaller one correlates with personality aspects that are highly regarded in our society, such as being responsible, productive, and interested in intellectual matters, and having high self-control (Funder & Block, 1989). Research suggests that people with certain social difficulties (for example heroin addicts or gamblers) have less ability to delay gratification (Kirby, Petry, & Bickel, 1999; Petry, 2001). The ability to delay gratification, and thus the ability to extend one's control over a longer time span, is such an important predictor of adolescent coping abilities that Mischel and colleagues saw it as one of the key cognitive and social competences (Mischel et al., 1988, p. 695).

Concluding Comments About Goals and Action

As is evident from the material just presented, the processes by which humans establish goals and strive to attain them are complex and eminently temporal. They become even more complex if those goals and actions entail the efforts of multiple actors. We will examine these cycles of action again in some detail in chapter 7, when we consider how people go about carrying out coordinated collective action. We turn now to some of the temporal matters that are a part of human decision-making processes.

TIME AND DECISION MAKING

Time affects decision making in many ways. We consider three clusters of them in this section. First, the decision process itself may be structured and "timed." For example, there may be an inherent length of time that a certain decision is expected to take, and radical departures from that time in either direction appear to be violations of a norm. We consider such inherent time frames and other structural features of decisions in the first part of this section. Second, decisions are made with regard to very different time spans. The time between when the decision is made and when its expected effects will take place can be very short or extremely long, and the size of that interval affects several aspects of decision making. We discuss those effects in the second part of this section. Third, the time effect most frequently considered is probably the influence of time pressure on the decision-making process and outcome. We discuss these effects in the third part of this section.

The Time Structure of Action and Decision Making

The time someone invests while he or she is making a decision is certainly dependent on a number of features of the situation surrounding the decision. The decision-making time is dependent on the nature and complexity of the problem, on the subjective risk involved, on personal habits and experiences, and so forth. Time investment in decisions is also influenced by (implicit) social regulations, or norms—that is, about how long such decisions "ought" to take. For example, people might be puzzled if the choice between two apartments that are available to rent is not made within a couple of weeks at longest. In contrast, if someone decides to marry a person he or she has known only for a few weeks, friends and family may warn about premature decision making and may advise the person to collect more information.

The amount of information processed before making a decision certainly influences the time taken before a decision is reached. However, there is also a norm for making decisions as soon as they can be made. Thus, decision makers often adopt strategies to abbreviate information processing and the decision-making process. One of these is to adopt a strategy labelled *satisficing* (Simon, 1955). That is, for many decisions, we search only until we find a solution that meets our minimal requirements and then adopt that solution without further search. Another strategy for abbreviating the decision process is to consider and eliminate alternatives in a sequential order (Russo & Dosher, 1983). In this strategy, one compares each alternative with the previously considered one, and once an alternative has been eliminated it is not reconsidered again. Another simplifying decision heuristic is to compare all alternatives with regard to the most important attribute, and keep for further examination only those that have passed this first hurdle (Tversky, 1969). All of these heuristics certainly shorten the time until a decision is reached.

Decisions, like action in general, may have different phases, involving different motivational states or mind-sets, as discussed in the previous section. The different motivational states or action phases described by Gollwitzer and Heckhausen may also play a role in determining the time spent for decision making. In the deliberative cognitive state, before having formed an intention or made a decision, people may consider many different alternatives and are open to new information (Gollwitzer, Heckhausen, & Steller, 1990). Heckhausen (1991) suggested that there is an inherent tendency to want to end the pre-decisional state and move into the implemental state. He describes it as a tendency to sum up (*Fazit-Tendenz*), an urge to reach a conclusion and start implementing, and thus to stop searching. This tendency is stronger if the person feels he or she has processed a lot of information, but it is also stronger if the person has the impression that he or she has spent enough time already trying to make up his or her mind. So the amount of time already elapsed in making a decision may speed up the completion of the process independent of the information already processed or the number of alternatives examined.

Kruglanski described the need for closure as "the individual's desire for a firm answer to a question and an aversion to ambiguity" (Kruglanski, 1996, p. 465). People with high need for closure strive to terminate ambiguity as soon as possible. They tend to process less information, and they are more vulnerable to primacy effects.

In summary, then, timing of decision making is dependent on task aspects including task complexity, on expectations about how long a certain decision ought to take, and also on motivational and personality differences that may influence how quickly a person travels through the different motivational states of a decision process.

Time Span of Decisions

Decisions span different time frames in two ways. First, decisions can affect only specific events or actions, or they can have long-term, pervasive, and recurrent effects. Second, there can be different lengths of time between when the decision is made and when its expected outcomes will be realized. For example, there is a difference between deciding which of two actions to take to maximize some desired immediate outcome, such as a profitable sale, and deciding how to plant a forest to minimize avalanches in the Swiss Alps decades into the future.

The time span between the time when the decision is made and the realization of its impacts is an important factor that alters the decision-making process substantially. It influences how we think about a decision and what we treat as most important. Liberman and Trope (1998) showed that for decisions in the near future, practical aspects are more heavily weighted, and for decisions far in the future, desirability aspects are more important.

The time span until the decision has its effects is especially important for risky decisions or decisions with adverse consequences. An aversive decision that is to be realized in the near future evokes more negative emotion than does the same decision if its effects will not take place until later in time. Moreover, many decisions are seen in a different light as the time approaches to put them into practice. People may even revise a decision already made when the moment to implement it arrives (Lowenstein, Weber, Hsee, & Welch, 2001).

Individual time orientations, discussed in an earlier chapter, also may influence decision-making processes. Das (cf. as cited in Bluedorn & Denhard, 1987) found that if the person responsible for strategic decisions in banks had a "near-future" orientation (that is, preferred short-term plans that can be implemented soon), they perceived a higher level of consensus about planning objectives in the organization, compared with people with a long-term orientation. Those with a long-term orientation perceived decision procedures in the organization as less standardized.

Time Pressure and Decision Making

Decisions can be affected, also, if the time to reach a decision is limited by external factors. Time pressure influences decision making in several ways. Time pressure may enhance effort and lead to faster processing of information (Kerstholt, 1994; Maule, Hockey, & Bdzola, 2000; Payne, Bettman, & Johnson, 1993). Most studies have found that with faster processing of information something gets lost. Often, the consideration of alternatives is less careful (Benson & Beach, 1996) and decision strategies become more simplified. Decision makers may use less rigorous decision strategies, may rely more on negative information (cf. Bluedorn & Denhardt, 1987), and may rely more on routine decisions. Payne, Bettman, and Johnson (1993) found that under moderate time pressure, people accelerated their processing and tried to work faster, but without changing their pattern of processing. As time pressure increased, shifts in the pattern of processing could be observed: for example, participants may switch from alternative-based processing, in which they compare two alternatives and discard the losing one, to attribute-based processing, in which they discard any alternative that does not fulfill the most important attribute. Because attribute-based decision making looks at all alternatives, but not at all dimensions of each alternative, it is generally less time-consuming.

Staw, Sandelands, and Dutton (1981) posited that decision makers under time pressure or other threats may have difficulties in adapting their strategies to changing demands. In such situations, they have a tendency to show more rigid behavior, described as the failure to alter and adapt behavior to a new situation. This rigidity is a consequence of two effects of the threat. First, under threat, information processing is altered. Less information is processed because there is a narrowing of the field of attention, and there is a simplification in information processing. Second, there is a constriction in the control system. For individuals, this manifests itself as a tendency toward dominant, well-learned, and habituated behavior, regardless of the needs of the specific situation. Both of these effects of the threat together may lead to a fixation of behavior (see also Betsch, Fiedler, & Brinkmann, 1998; Kerstholt, 1994). However, individuals who succeed in choosing a simplifying strategy that is well adapted for a given task perform better (Payne et al., 1993).

Time pressure may not have uniform effects on all types of decisions and under all circumstances. Kelly and Karau (1999) showed that initial preferences and task characteristics, as well as expertise, may mediate the effects. Time pressure affects novice and expert decision makers in different ways. The latter take time into account more explicitly than novices do. Expert decision makers more often ask explicitly about how much time they have left before they must commit to a decision. More importantly, they estimate the available time more precisely (Cohen, Freeman, & Wolf, 1996).

However, a decision that takes longer is not necessarily always of better quality (Karau & Kelly, 1992). Eisenhardt (1989) analyzed decisions of top management teams and found that decisions made faster were of higher quality. In her study, "fast" decisions of management teams took between one and a half and four months, whereas longer decisions took between twelve and eighteen months. The fast decisions reflected more frequent meetings in the company, more real-time information available, more experienced advisors, and a more integrative way of dealing with disagreements and conflicts. The fast decisions apparently did not suffer from the processes found in experimental research. On the contrary, fast decisions were made on the basis of more information, several alternatives were elaborated simultaneously, and these decisions were more successful. (This latter is an example of the effects of different time scales associated with laboratory versus field strategies, as will be discussed in a later chapter.)

TIME-RELATED FEELINGS
AND EMOTIONAL STATES:
WAITING, BOREDOM, AND IMPATIENCE

In many situations, people cannot directly control the allocation of their own time. Some of these include waiting for some set of conditions to occur or action to be completed. These may engender negative feelings such as boredom and impatience. Such time-related feelings are the focus of this section.

Waiting

Waiting is time one invests to get closer to a goal state, under conditions in which that time cannot be actively used to approach the goal, but must be spent in a more or less passive way that inhibits goal-directed action. Usually, the waiting time cannot be chosen, but is dependent on external variables. Sometimes the wait is because a process takes time and one has to wait until it is done (e.g., one has to wait until a Web site appears on the screen; one has to wait 3 minutes for a 3-minute egg). Sometimes it is because one has to wait for the availability of a scarce resource (e.g., waiting in line to buy a ticket to a football game, or waiting on the phone until an operator becomes available).

Consumer researchers have devoted considerable effort to studying the effects of waiting in line because they have found that it is often associated with negative emotions (Spendlove, Rigdon, Jenson, & Udall, 1987) and may also negatively influence the evaluation of the service being waited for (Houston, Bettencourt, & Wenger, 1998; Tom & Lucey, 1997). But sometimes, waiting time cannot be reduced, so businesses have searched for strategies to reduce customer dissatisfaction caused by waiting. The research from this field allows insights into the dynamics of waiting. It shows that the negative effect of waiting is not only dependent on the amount of time one has to wait or the feeling that time passes slowly while waiting, but is also related to the sense of a "waste of time." This sense is also influenced by uncertainty about the amount of waiting time remaining, by whether one's expectations about waiting time have been met or disconfirmed, and by the perceived reason for the delay (Osuna, 1985).

Consumer researchers have tried to find factors that ease the pain of waiting, mainly via one or the other of two kinds of interventions: (a) by distracting people from the discomfort of waiting by filling their empty time or (b) by making waiting more acceptable or pleasant. The first set of interventions aims at changing the waiting person's feeling about the passage of time directly. The second set of interventions attempts to influence attitudes toward the waiting period in a positive way.

Fraisse (1963) has shown that distractions influence the perception of the passage of time. Waiting-related distractions that have been used include playing music (Kellaris & Kent, 1992; Hui, Dubé, & Chebat, 1997); giving the waiting person something to listen to or read (Taylor, 1995); and using lighting, colors, and special layout in the waiting space (Baker & Cameron, 1996).

In many situations, people have expectations about how long they will have to wait, and if the waiting time does not exceed these expectations, waiting is perceived less negatively (Houston et al., 1998). It therefore seems to be important that people be able to predict with some accuracy the length of a waiting period in order to adjust their waiting expectations. Providing information about the remaining waiting time has been found to increase the acceptance of a waiting period (Hui & Zhou, 1996). But information per se may not be sufficient to alleviate the negative effects of waiting, depending on the content of that information. The importance and legitimacy of the reason why we wait also influences our willingness to "waste" time waiting. Waiting is seen less negatively, for example, if one can attribute delays to technical failures rather than to actions or attitudes of the people providing the service (Taylor, 1994).

Some aspects of waiting are regulated by social norms. For example, norms hold that everyone should have to share in the waiting equally. People are expected to line up at the end of the queue, and intrusions into the queue violate norms of equity and fairness (Milgram, Liberty, Toledo, & Wachenhut, 1986). People often react negatively to such intrusions. One study compared delays of service due either to intruders into the waiting-line or to actions of a service person. Although the amount of additional waiting time was the same, people responded in a much more negative way to waiting-line intruders. The intrusion was seen as illegitimate and a violation of social rules (Schmitt, Dubé, & Leclerc, 1992).

The acceptance of waiting is also dependent on who we are and for whom we wait. Greenberg (1989) found that people who had applied for a high-status job were not willing to wait as long as people applying for a low-status job. Another study found that students were willing to wait longer than professors, and both were willing to wait longer for a high-status person than for a low-status person (Halpern & Isaacs, 1980).

Letting others wait can therefore also be part of a "power game." An observation study found that drivers who were about to leave their parking spaces in malls did so more slowly if someone else was clearly waiting for their spot than if no one were waiting, even though driving away more slowly is contrary to their goal of leaving. When drivers were asked how they would behave in such situations, however, they claimed they would leave faster if someone were waiting, unless the other driver was honking at them (Ruback & Juieng, 1997). A similar phenomenon was found for callers using public telephones who were intruded upon by people waiting to make a phone call. They also occupied the phone longer than those not intruded upon (Ruback, Pape, & Doriot, 1989).

Gasparini (1995) distinguished three types of waiting, differing in the meanings they have for the persons involved. The first is a "blockage of action." The second is an interval filled with meaning and alternative activities. The third is a meaningful experience in and of itself. The first two are reflected in our previous discussions. The third is exemplified in the attitude of people who see the present as prologue to an anticipated major change. For instance, in a religious sense, as in the coming of a messiah; or a political sense, as in the coming of the revolution; or personally, as in being rescued by prince charming and living happily ever after. Gasparini also distinguishes between short-term waiting, such as being in a queue for a matter of minutes, and long-term waiting, such as when waiting for information about results of some evaluation or placement in some new status (getting a job, being promoted, becoming tenured, being diagnosed as having cancer). The latter, often a matter of weeks or months, in some respects foreshadows a new social role. It is the latter kind of waiting that is Gasparini's third type discussed previously (Gasparini, 1995).

Boredom

Boredom is related to the perception that one is not using one's time as one would like to, or not knowing how to use one's time in an enjoyable way. Boredom has been described as (a) the negative feelings one has when trapped in situations in which there is nothing to do, (b) a frustration over the need for novelty, (c) the lack of challenge due to repetitive and unstimulating tasks, (d) the routinization of a job and work underload, and (e) being confined to a situation that is not interesting or lacks personal meaning (Darden & Marks, 1999). It is the lack of sufficient stimulation, or the lack of change of stimuli, that seems responsible for the negative affect. Whether or not one is bored also depends on external factors. Many would experience boredom if the circumstances are such that people are restrained from pursuing personal goals or from leaving the situation, yet there is nothing "interesting" occurring in the situation.

Boredom is not only related to actual situations, but also to long-term plans, so it has a relation to how one plans and organizes one's time. Retirees who had clear purposes in life were less bored than those who did not (Weinstein, Xie, & Cleanthous, 1995). Several studies have found men more prone to boredom than women (Shaw, Caldwell, & Kleiber, 1996; Watt & Blanchard, 1994). The populations of those studies, however, were mostly young adolescents, so this finding may not generalize to all age groups. Moreover, it may be related to the fact that young men do have more "unorganized leisure" time than young women do (a finding derived from time-use studies discussed in chapter 3).

Some researchers have studied proneness to boredom as an individual difference factor or trait. People may be more or less prone to boredom. People high in boredom proneness also feel that time passes more slowly in general than do those low in boredom proneness; but their estimations of actual time intervals do not differ from people low in boredom proneness (Watt, 1991). Moreover, not all people experience boredom in a similar way. There has been some research done on boredom proneness that indicates that people higher in boredom proneness may have less ability for self-control, may show higher "need for cognition" (Watt & Blanchard, 1994), may procrastinate more (Blunt & Pychyl, 1998), and may carry out less career planning and lifestyle planning (Watt & Vodanovic, 1999). High proneness to boredom was also found to be related to lower well-being (Sommer & Vodanovic, 2000).

Impatience and Time Urgency

Impatience describes dissatisfaction because something is happening too slowly. Impatience can also include dislike of something that causes delay, or anxious eagerness to do something or to wait for something that is expected to happen. It often includes feelings of restlessness and irritability. Often situational aspects trigger impatience and the need to hurry events. For example, waiting may make people impatient, as previously discussed. The feeling of being rushed and hurried is higher for students with more exams, papers, and projects than for those with fewer such tasks (Conte, Landy, & Mathieu, 1995). In addition, higher scores of impatience have been found for teachers, managers, and professionals than for students, care workers, and manual workers (Francis-Smythe & Robertson, 1999). However, impatience has mostly been discussed as a trait factor and predominantly in relation to the Type A personality syndrome (Friedman & Rosenman, 1974). Impatience is an aspect of time urgency that has been described as one of the core characteristics of the Type A personality. Measures of time urgency have high test–retest reliability, indicating stability over time and situations (Conte, Ringenbach, Moran, & Landy, 2001).

Time urgency is a concept larger than impatience and is described as frequent concern with the passage of time or heightened awareness of time. Earlier research has treated time urgency as a single construct, but later conceptions distinguish two different, though somewhat correlated, factors (Conte et al., 1995; Conte et al., 2001; Landy, Rastegary, Thayer, & Colvin, 1991). One is the need to have control over deadlines, and the feeling that deadlines are important. People who feel like this often schedule their work ahead of time, make task lists, prioritize tasks, and are more aware of time aspects of the tasks. Such persons have been named "organizers" (Conte, Mathieu, & Landy, 1998). Another aspect of time urgency describes feelings of being driven and "living at a fast pace." In that pattern, time is seen as an opponent. Behaviors described for those hurried "crammers" (Conte et al., 1998) include that they eat fast, talk fast, impatiently finish others' sentences, hurry in doing their tasks, hate to wait and often give the general impression of being in a hurry (Conte et al., 2001).

These two general aspects of time urgency—the heightened awareness of time that translates into including time aspects in planning and scheduling of tasks (the organizers) and the heightened awareness of time that translates into feelings of being pushed, hurried, and driven (the crammers)—are similar to other concepts. For example, Spence, Helmreich, and Pred (1987) distinguished between impatience and irritability, on the one hand, and achievement striving that includes wanting to finish things in time, on the other.

The two aspects of time urgency can also be combined with other time-related concepts. Waller and colleagues have formulated an interesting proposition by combining the distinctions of future orientation versus present orientation and high versus low time urgency (Waller, Conte, Gibson, & Carpenter, 2001). They hypothesized that organizers are time urgent and future-oriented individuals because their planning and scheduling reaches into the future. Crammers are hypothesized to be high time urgent but present-oriented—they are hurried in daily, present behavior. Low time urgent and future-oriented individuals are named "visioners." Although they think into the future, they are not paying attention to the passage of time, nor do they set up time limits or deadlines for themselves. They stay focused on future goals, but without pursuing them with specific deadlines in mind. Low time urgent and present-oriented individuals are hypothesized to act spontaneously out of the moment, enjoy the present, and relate more easily to other people.

Most of the assessments of time urgency rely on questionnaire responses, although some studies have used behavioural measures. Examples of behavioural indicators of time urgency are people who show up early to scheduled meetings, people who wear wrist watches, and people who impatiently finish sentences of a slow and hesitating interviewer (e.g., Warner & Block, 1984). It seems indeed that time urgency can be perceived accurately by others. In one study, there was high agreement between the self-perceptions of college students about their level of time urgency and the view of their parents (Conte et al., 1995).

Both aspects of time urgency are related to other variables. Time urgency has been found to be related to both higher and lower performance (Conte et al., 1998). These contradictory results, however, relate to the two different aspects of time urgency. Organizers, who are called achievement strivers in other conceptions, have been found to show somewhat higher performance; crammers, who are impatient, suffer more health problems (Barling & Boswell, 1995; Conte et al., 1998; Conte et al., 2001; Spence et al., 1987). Barling and Boswell also showed an indirect relation between impatience and performance. Impatience was negatively related to health, health was negatively related to cognitive difficulties (i.e., difficulties in concentrating), and cognitive difficulties showed a negative relation to performance.

Aspects of time urgency can influence quality of cooperation, especially if groups are composed of individuals with different time preferences and orientations. Waller examined teams with or without a high time urgent member. She found that such a person could influence the whole group's behavior. High time urgent individuals tended to impose strict schedules on the group, and pushed the other group members to set priorities for tasks. They also reminded the other group members constantly about the time remaining (Waller, 2000). For teams that have to work for a long time in isolation (such as teams in space), high time urgent subjects may be less able to adapt to time constraints of the situation that delay projects, such as equipment failure, or even delays in communication (Palinkas, 2001). Schriber and Gutek (1987) made a similar argument for organizations. They argued that organizations have different norms about time factors (such as deadlines or pace of work) and that highest performance and highest well-being are obtained when individual preferences and organizational "time culture" converge. (Some of these matters are issues related to collective action and outcomes, as well as to individual level ones, so they will be discussed again in later chapters.)

CONCLUDING COMMENTS

In this chapter, we discussed temporal aspects of goals and actions, temporal factors in decision making, and some emotional states that are closely linked to time. The quality of both decision making and actions may be influenced by how temporal factors are dealt with. For example, the quality of action may suffer if the actor does not shift appropriately from the deliberative mind-set needed for goal choice to the implemental mind-set needed for execution. Moreover, many of these relations are not simple linear ones. For example, decision quality can be impaired both by rushing decisions (e.g., under time pressure) and by delaying them by prolonged procrastination, depending on a constellation of other factors present in the situation.

All of the temporal factors discussed in this chapter and the prior one have been at the level of individual humans. We will discuss temporal matters that operate at group and collective levels in chapters 6 and 7. In the next chapter we turn to a set of issues that spans individual and group level: time in stress and coping processes.

AFTERTHOUGHTS

Decision Time

It's easier, far, to make tough calls
When outcomes come some later day.
It's harder, though, to do what's right
If right now's when you have to pay!

Decisions quick are often praised
As better than the ones delayed.
But sometimes quick deciding leads
To poorer choices, hasty made!

So having ample time to choose
Should better choices generate.
Yet, having lots of time may make
It easy to procrastinate!

Decision time's no simple thing
When hard-nosed choices fill our days.
Heaven knows what time will bring.
Time plays its cards in curious ways!

5

TIME, STRESS, AND
COPING PROCESSES

The study of stress and coping processes entails many temporal aspects at several levels of temporal patterning. Some stress researchers, but by no means all, have recognized the intrinsically temporal nature of stress and coping. For the most part, stress research, like other areas of social psychology, has recognized time's important role in these phenomena, but has focussed theory and research more on its static than on its dynamic aspects.

Stress involves temporal factors that function in all four of the roles discussed in chapter 1: as independent, intervening, dependent, and methodological variables. Stress is also a topical area that bridges the individual and collective levels. Thus, the study of stress and coping processes constitutes a key area in our examination of temporal processes in social psychological phenomena.

Stress has been defined as an imbalance between demands of a situation and response capability of a person or a system. Such an imbalanced situation is viewed as stressful if the failure to meet the demand has important consequences (McGrath, 1976). Depending on the resources they have available, different people will see similar demands as more or less stressful. Individual differences arise also with regard to the importance of meeting any given set of demands. Therefore, whether a person feels stressed also depends on the individual's perception, the individual's motivation, and the individual's assessment of the situation. However, many situations (e.g., short deadlines, work overload, critical life events) have a potential for stress for most people, so in many cases there is clearly an external or objective aspect of stress (Semmer, 1992).

This description uses the term *stress* to characterize the whole situation of imbalance between demands and resources. Following the usage proposed by McGrath and Beehr (Beehr, 1998; McGrath & Beehr, 1990), we will use the term *stressor* (or stress-potential event and condition, *SPEC*) to refer to the situational aspects, and *strain* to describe the consequences of stress for the individual or other social system (Kahn & Byosiere, 1992).

A TIME-RELATED FRAMEWORK
FOR CONSIDERING STRESS AND COPING

Time-related aspects of stress have been discussed by McGrath, Beehr, and Shupe (Beehr, 1998; McGrath & Beehr, 1990; Shupe & McGrath, 1998), and we draw on this work for the present chapter. Many authors have described stress as a transactional process, and taken as a prototypical situation the reaction of individuals faced with a single situation (e.g., Lazarus & Folkman, 1998). On the other hand, one of the main interests in stress research has been the long-term effects of stress. Much of the research on stress is interested in the consequences of enduring chronic stress, both in the form of the accumulation of many stress events over time and in the form of the effects of major life-changing events. Shupe and McGrath (1998) therefore distinguished between a microlevel examination of stress, in which the focus of interest is a single stressor and the reaction to a given event, and a macrolevel examination of what they call "overall stress" which focuses on long-term adaptive and dynamic actions and reactions of a system. Shupe and McGrath are thus concerned with what many call *chronic* stress.

The division of stress research into the two perspectives is far from a straightforward one. How well or poorly a system deals even with a given actual stressor on the microlevel not only influences the system's current and future well-being, but may also have an impact on future resources, and hence on coping strategies available. A growing body of research indicates that earlier experiences of stress, and the system's handling of that experience, will influence the vulnerability of a system faced with new potential stressors (Sapolsky, 1998).

To take account of some of these interdependencies, we will organize our discussion of temporal issues in the stress and coping process in terms of four hierarchically nested temporal levels, which in turn subsume eight temporal patterns, as illustrated in Exhibit 5.1. At the first or *microtemporal level*, we will consider the single stress event or stress and coping episode. Stress episodes unfold over time, and encompass some complex temporal issues that have to do with the relative timing of the stressor, appraisal, coping activity, and short-term consequences.

The second and third levels of our framework are *middle temporal levels*. The second level has to do with the effects of both *multiple reoccurrences* of a given stressor within a short span of time, and the more or less *simultaneous occurrence* of multiple stressor events. The third level has to do with the continuing or delayed consequences of stress episodes. At that level, we will consider (a) how responses to a given stressor may generate additional stressors, (b) how failed coping attempts may hinder later coping efforts, (c) how successful coping with a given stressor may facilitate later coping with other stressors and what the costs of coping are, and (d) how the accrual of an accumulation of not entirely resolved stress episodes can yield continuing long-term strain.

The fourth level of our framework is a *macrotemporal level* (what has often been termed *chronic stress*). This has to do with the overall stress consequences of major life events—such as loss of a loved one, or suffering serious injury, disease, or disability—that have major, continuing, and irreversible impact.

EXHIBIT 5.1
Temporal Levels and Patterns of Stress and Coping

Level A: Single Stress Episodes
  Pattern 1: Stress Events as Stressor–Appraisal–Coping Response–Outcome Cycles.
Level B: Multiple Stressor Events (within a short time period)
  Pattern 2: Recurrence of a specific kind of stressor event (i.e., a given SPEC) within a short period of time.
  Pattern 3: Occurrence of multiple near-simultaneous stressor events (different SPECs) within a short period of time.
Level C: Stress–Coping Cycles with Consequences Extended in Time
  Pattern 4: Coping actions re a given SPEC A give rise to another SPEC B.
  Pattern 5: Failed coping attempts re a given SPEC A make coping with subsequent SPECs B less successful.
  Pattern 6: Successful coping actions re a given SPEC A facilitates coping with subsequent SPECs B.
  Pattern 7: Cumulative effects from multiple, recurrent, and extended SPECs (e.g., Burnout).
Level D: Stress Involving Major Life Events
  Pattern 8: Major life events (e.g., loss of a limb, diagnosis with serious disease, loss of a loved one) can have continuing, irreversible, and major stress consequences (but also can lead to positive growth experiences).

These four temporal levels at which to consider stress and coping processes are, of course, tightly intertwined. But it is possible, and we think useful, to separate them out to examine each of them more closely. The body of theory and research literature regarding stress and coping can be differentiated in terms of these different levels of analysis. Much of the research done in an experimental context has been at the first or microtemporal level. Much of the research done regarding stress in work organizations has to do with the accumulated impact of multiple stressors over an extended period of time, and thus is formulated at the two middle temporal levels. Studies on occupational stress also focus increasingly on long-term consequences (Siegrist, 1998; Sonnentag & Frese, 2003). Still other bodies of research, dealing with the impact of major life traumas (e.g., in health and mental health fields), focus on a still longer temporal interval.

The first two levels, of course, do overlap: Single stress episodes are the stuff of which recurrent and cumulative stress is made. The second and third levels also overlap. Moreover, some aspects of both the third level and fourth or macrolevel have been referred to as chronic stress (and as "burnout"). In spite of these overlaps, given that our focus is on the temporal aspects of the stress and coping processes, and that the four levels we have noted here have distinct temporal patterns, this four way division seems useful here. To give these levels substantive identification, we will label them *single stress episodes*, *multiple stress episodes*, *continuing effects of stress episodes*, and *long-term effects of stress*. We will generally discuss them in the order shown in Exhibit 5.1. But at times, it will be useful to intermix discussions of the different levels.

Level A: The Microtemporal Level—Stress Events as Cycles

In this section we will discuss Pattern 1, which represents stress events as stressor–appraisal–coping response–outcome cycles. Generally, the stress process on any given occasion can be viewed as a discrepancy between the demands of a situation and the possibilities that a given system has for reacting to that situation, given that it is important to the system to meet the demands of the situation. In a more simplified form, stress models state that a given situation is interpreted as a threat or challenge by a person, who then engages in behavior to deal with the threat or challenge of this situation. This formulation implies a logical sequential order of events in time, starting with the occurrence of an external situation, followed by its perception and interpretation by the individual or other system, and ending with the individual's or system's reactions to the situation and the consequences of those actions.

Most process models of stress assume such a sequence of steps, but emphasize different aspects of it. One of the best-known process models of stress was proposed by Lazarus (e.g., 1999), who emphasized the importance of the appraisal process within this sequence. Faced with a potentially stressful situation, the individual engages in two appraisal processes: During the primary appraisal process, a given situation is perceived as either stressful or harmless. In the secondary appraisal process, the person assesses the resources and means available to cope with the situation. The coping response is a result of these two appraisal processes (Lazarus & Folkman, 1998). It is interesting that this model has often mistakenly been interpreted as implying a temporal sequence.

McGrath and Beehr (1990) proposed a more general model of the stress and coping cycle that puts equal emphasis on situational, appraisal, and behavioral processes and sees the stress process as recurring cyclically. In this model, the stress process is described as a cycle consisting of the following elements:

1. Occurrence of an objective situation that includes a potential stressor.
2. An appraisal process that leads to the perception and evaluation of this situation.
3. The actor chooses from a set of possible responses.
4. The actor selects a coping response.
5. The actor executes an immediate or delayed performance process that constitutes the coping response.
6. In time, there is an outcome of that response, which may affect the state of the objective system.

This cycle has a logical sequential order, but only some of the steps in the process necessarily occur in the listed temporal order. For example, ordinarily the outcome of a behavior can only follow the behavior temporally, and the choice to engage in a behavior has to be made beforehand. But sometimes long-term responses (which we will discuss later as preventive coping) are made to stressors that have not yet occurred. In general, some parts of stress event cycles may be carried out simultaneously or they may overlap.

There are temporal aspects important for each of the steps in this stress event cycle. First, there are some general, time-related influences in the stress cycle related to the person (or to the system engaged in the situation), such as experience, knowledge, or other resources acquired over time. Also, the stage of the system's development may affect both its appraisal and its coping processes. Many individual difference variables that influence the stress process can in fact be seen as results of experience, of learning or of developmental processes, and thus as factors influenced by time-related variables.

In addition to these general influences, each of the four steps of the stress cycle is influenced by specific time-related aspects. For example, the objective situation has a variety of temporal facets such as its duration, frequency, regularity of occurrence, and regularity or predictability of onset.

Each of these temporal facets can influence the perception and appraisal of the events, the appropriate coping behaviors, and the effects of execution of those coping behaviors. We turn, next, to a systematic examination of the temporal features of each part of the stress event cycle.

Temporal Aspects of Stress Potential Events and Conditions (SPEC)

The first, situational part of the stress process consists of the occurrence of a state, or condition, or event in the environment of the person or the system potentially experiencing the stress. We will refer to this phase by the term SPEC, which stands for "Stress Potential Events and Conditions" (McGrath & Beehr, 1990; Shupe & McGrath, 1998). SPECs are objective situations that may have the *potential* to induce a stress reaction for a given system; that is, they may be perceived by the system as creating an imbalance between the demands of the situation and the resources available. A given situation may be perceived as stressful by one person, but may not be perceived as stressful by others in the same situation. For example, driving in heavy traffic in Rome may be quite a stressful experience for many when they do it the first time, but it may not be stressful at all for skilled Italian drivers (who may even enjoy it!).

There has been a long-standing and serious controversy as to whether there are actually objective stressor conditions (with objective, time-related features) or whether stress is solely in the perception and appraisal processes of individual systems. The concept of SPECs resolves (or finesses) this problem by describing objective situations as *potential* stressors. One can take a probabilistic approach to this question of the existence of stressful events: Although there are vast individual differences in the appraisal of similar situations, for any given population some events have a high probability of being perceived as stressful by most members of that population. This idea is like the concept of risk factors in epidemiological research. Not everyone sharing the risk factor acquires the disease. Not everyone gets the flu after having been exposed to a certain virus, but being exposed to the virus clearly increases the individual's risk of becoming ill (Semmer, 1992).

McGrath and Beehr (1990) proposed a classification of SPECs with regard to their time-related aspects, which we will present here in a slightly adapted form (see Table 5.1). They distinguish SPECs with regard to (a) their duration, (b) their rate of occurrence (frequent versus not frequent), (c) their periodicity, and (d) the temporal pattern of their onset (regular or irregular, hence predictable or not predictable). In addition, different SPECs may occur in a particular sequence, or simultaneously (or within a given short period of time). These time-related aspects influence not only the timing of the SPECs and their consequences, but also appraisal processes and coping behaviors. We will examine some of those temporal aspects of SPECs next.

TABLE 5.1
Some Temporal Aspects of SPECs

Temporal Form of Event	Persistence of Consequences	Example
Short, 1-time	short term	falling from a bicycle
	persistent	getting a badly done tattoo
Short, recurrent		
aperiodic low rate	short term	cutting self while shaving
	persistent	flare-up for an MS patient
aperiodic high rate	short term	two kids fighting in the back seat of your car
periodic low rate	short term	fill in tax forms each year
periodic high rate	short term	loud chiming of nearby church tower clock
Long-term events		
predictable duration	persistent	raising children
permanent change	persistent	having all your childhood photos stolen

Frequency and Density of SPECs

Frequency and density of SPECs refers not only to the recurrence of similar stressors, but also to the accumulation of different SPECs in a given period of time. Note that we are now overlapping with the second level of the temporal framework (see Exhibit 5.1). All other things being equal, more frequently occurring SPECs may have a higher potential for producing stress than do events that occur more rarely. The frequency and density of SPECs has been emphasized in research dealing with microtemporal levels of stress, for example with so-called daily hassles. Each daily hassle can be regarded as a very minor event, irritating and annoying, but not important enough to elicit a prolonged stress reaction. Examples of daily hassles are missing a bus, being stuck in heavy traffic, having to finish something under time pressure, and the like. Research results suggest that the frequency and density of even such minor events predicts stress reactions (Kanner, Coyne, Schaefer, & Lazarus, 1981). Frequency and density of SPECs within a given time period is therefore an important aspect of the SPEC. Their overall impact also depends on their magnitude, as well as on the combination of different SPECs that might be operating at a given time.

Rate and Duration of SPECs

In their classification of SPECs, McGrath and Beehr (1990) distinguish one-time events from recurrent events. They also distinguish stress events as of short duration (e.g., someone has to get a tooth fixed) or long duration (e.g., someone has to be in a cast for several weeks). Both the fact that the event is unique or is expected to be recurring, and the anticipated duration of the event, can have an influence on appraisal and coping processes. Moreover, events that occur more than once can do so in a regular temporal pattern (i.e., periodic) or irregularly. Such recurrence can be at a low rate or at a high rate. An example of a low-rate, regular SPEC could be the completion of tax forms once a year. A low-rate, irregular event might be a river that floods once in a while. An example of a regular and frequent event might be a daily ride to work on an overcrowded bus.

Sequence and Simultaneity of SPECs

Often not just one but multiple stressful events occur nearly simultaneously or in a more or less predictable temporal sequence. For example, during or after a big storm, there may be flooding, but at the same time, electricity may go out, making pumping the water away more difficult and impeding communication and other aspects of daily life (e.g., gasoline may become scarce, slowing down transportation and preventing the use of generators). Some SPECs may occur sequentially, as a result of earlier stressor conditions that have not been dealt with effectively (Hobfoll, 2001). Note that this touches on level three of the temporal framework.

Temporal Location of SPECs and Their Consequences

Situations that are perceived as stressful can lie in the past, in the present, or in the future. For example, remembering a very shameful or painful situation can elicit stress reactions a long time after the situation has occurred. So, too, can imagining a potential stressful situation in the future. For example, research on job insecurity has shown that the fear of loss of one's job in the future is an important SPEC long before any notice of layoff has been given (Mak & Mueller, 2000). Moreover, a situation might be mild at present but threaten long-term goals that are important for the person. An example would be to be diagnosed with a potentially serious illness; even if the person does not feel that his or her health is impaired at the moment, the potential threat for the future may be highly stressful (Carver, Scheier, & Pozo, 1992). For many SPECs, their possible consequences can be assessed at the time of encountering the SPEC and thereby become an important aspect of the appraisal process. Anticipated consequences of a SPEC can be temporary, if they are tightly coupled in time to the occurrence of the event, or may be persistent if the consequences continue long after the event has occurred. For example, if a person falls off a bicycle and breaks his or her arm, it is immediately clear that the consequences of this one-time, short-term stressor will continue for at least 6 weeks. The direct consequences of having a tooth extracted will most likely be of much shorter duration. McGrath and Beehr (1990) therefore distinguish temporary and persistent consequences of SPECs.

Time Pressure

Another time-related aspect of SPECs is time pressure. Often, an otherwise harmless situation becomes a stressor only because of time pressure: that is, the system could handle the demands of the situation in a qualitative sense, but there is not enough time to do so. Time pressure is an important SPEC at work, and most of the measures of stressors in organizations include items concerning high work demands and time pressure (e.g., Karasek & Theorell, 1990; Semmer, Zapf, & Dunckel, 1995; Spector & Jex, 1998; Vagg & Spielberger, 1998).

Concluding Comments About SPECs

Time-related aspects of SPECs can be of major importance. For example, a regularly occurring SPEC can be anticipated, and in many cases preventive coping can be carried out (see the following section), thereby limiting the negative consequences of future events. On the other hand, anticipating a SPEC may increase anxiety and deplete the resources of the system to handle the event even before the event has occurred.

Time-related aspects are only one set among many factors that influence the stress cycle. We did not discuss here the importance of the nature of the stressor, and many other aspects that are crucial to determining the importance and likely impact of a SPEC. The temporal facets of SPECs, however, certainly have an important influence on the other aspects of the stress cycle: that is, on the appraisal process, the choice of coping behavior, and execution and effects of the coping behavior.

Temporal Aspects of the Appraisal Process

Whether or not a specific condition actually represents a stressor for a particular system depends on how the SPEC is interpreted in the primary and secondary appraisal processes previously described. Lazarus (Lazarus, 1999) mentions three main components of primary appraisal. The fundamental component, *goal relevance*, involves the general assessment of the relevance and importance of the transaction for the individual's well-being. The second component, *goal congruence*, assesses whether the transaction is congruent with the person's goals or is a hindrance to achieving them, and results in a positive (when congruent) or negative (when incongruent) affective tone of the appraisal. Only if the goal is relevant and if there is incongruence with the desired state, will the system be "stressed." The third component influencing the primary appraisal is the *type of ego involvement*. This can be regarded as the implication of a situation for self-relevant goals. If, for example, the protection of self-worth is important in the situation, emotions such as pride or anger are likely to be aroused because of the ego involvement in the situation.

Whereas primary appraisal results in a general assessment of the situation as stressful or not, during secondary appraisal, the person basically asks the question "What can I do in this situation?". That is, the system evaluates coping possibilities for a given situation.

Duration of Appraisal and Conflicting Appraisals

There is an ongoing debate among stress researchers as to whether the appraisal process previously described always has to be a conscious, deliberate, and hence slow cognitive process, or whether it sometimes can be automatized, or whether unconscious appraisal processes can occur. Lazarus (1999) assumes that appraisals can be automatized for situations in which the person has had past experience, and in these cases may be triggered very rapidly by known cues. Researchers who study ego defense goals often assume that unconscious processes can influence the appraisal process. This is especially the case for defensive appraisal processes, because in that situation the person is motivated to not process these appraisals consciously. If unconscious appraisal is possible, this can result in simultaneous appraisal processes that have conflicting appraisal outcomes—one a conscious and cognitively accessible appraisal (e.g., I am not scared), and the other a contradictory, unconscious, negative appraisal (e.g., being scared; Epstein, 1998).

Often, appraisal of a SPEC results in specific emotional states, and some of these emotional states are influenced by time-related features of the situation. For example, very often sadness is related to an event in the past; fright is described as the reaction to an immediate, present, and overwhelming physical danger; and anxiety and hope are directed toward future events—anxiety as dreading a future uncertainty and hope as a somewhat ambivalent, but slightly positive, expectation for the future. Feelings of relief are emotions relating to the evaluation of past experiences that include a goal-congruent change or development over time (Lazarus, 1999).

Predictability and Controllability of a SPEC

Other time-related aspects of the appraisal process have been discussed by McGrath and Beehr (1990). They distinguish two different, but somewhat related, time-specific aspects of the appraisal process, namely the predictability and the controllability of the time-related features of the SPEC. Predictability of a SPEC means that the person has some knowledge about what may happen in the future. One aspect of predictability has to do with the probable time of onset of the SPEC. A student, for example, may know months in advance when an exam will take place. Predictability can also be related to (a) time constraints of a SPEC (e.g., the tax form has to be filed by end of February in Switzerland or mid-April in the U.S.), (b) predictability of the duration of an event (feeding the baby takes at least 15 minutes), (c) the development of an event (if I am not able to immediately stop the fire on the Christmas tree, the house will burn down), or (d) changes in environmental circumstances (we need to finish yardwork before sunset). High predictability of events or circumstances may result in either or both positive and negative appraisals, depending on the situation and the resources available. For example, to know the onset of a stressor can be positive if it can help us to avoid or prepare for the stressor effects (e.g., we cancel a trip because a heavy snowstorm is announced, or students prepare for the exam beforehand). To know how long or how short an uncomfortable situation will last can help us cope with it (e.g., the oral exam will be over after 45 minutes; one can stand the pain at the dentist because she says it will last only 10 more seconds). Predictability may be an advantage if the person can acquire or maintain resources to cope better with the SPEC. On the other hand, if there is no possibility of influencing the onset or intensity of the SPEC, its predictability—or inevitability—may be an additional stressor.

Predictability implies that the time of onset or the duration of the stressor is known, but predictability does not necessarily imply control over these aspects. Control over time-related aspects of the SPEC means that a person can change or influence these aspects. This can include control over the time of *onset* of the SPEC (the student may postpone the exam for one term), control over a *deadline* (plan some extra time for finishing a job) or control over the *duration* of the SPEC (limiting an unpleasant meeting to half an hour).

Appraisal includes assessing the possibilities for coping when faced with a given situation. There may be different coping possibilities depending on the combination of predictability and control over time-related issues. If we can control when an event will occur (predictable and controllable SPEC), we can plan our coping responses to the situation in advance. For example, if a person has control over the deadline for a project, he or she can plan the project in a way that prevents the deadline from becoming too stressful. However, control over the onset or the deadline of an event that is feared to be stressful may also lead to a situation in which people avoid the onset of the SPEC, and may thereby suffer delayed consequences. For example, a person who has high anxiety about going to the dentist may postpone going for too long a time, leading to increased pain and dental damage. If students have control over when to take an exam, they may never face the situation, leading to failure in regard to the whole program.

In many cases, although the time of the onset of the SPEC may not be predictable, people may know that an event has a certain probability of occurring. McGrath and Beehr (1990) mention floods, which are not predictable, but in some areas they are likely to occur at certain times of the year. Such situations allow the system to take long-term preventive actions, either to reduce the probability of the occurrence of a SPEC, or to reduce its likely negative effects. Everyday examples are actions for illness prevention (we may reduce the chances of heart attacks with diet change and exercise) and keeping backups of computer files (we know that computers sometimes crash, but not when ours will, so keeping backups allows us to reduce the negative impact of such crashes if they do occur).

Still other SPECs may be predictable, but their time features are not controllable. McGrath and Beehr cite Christmas, tax deadlines, tides, and the like as predictable events whose onset cannot be controlled. Nonetheless, if the event is predictable, in most cases there is at least a possibility of gaining partial control over outcomes. If Christmas has been a very stressful time, in part because party invitations, gift shopping, and other activities have to be done before a very precise point in time, then starting Christmas shopping and preparations in September can help master the situation. A similar argument may be made for exams, for giving birth, and for other time-predictable potential stressors.

SPECs that are neither predictable in their onset time nor controllable are most likely to become stressful situations: The SPEC comes as a surprise, and prevention is often not possible. McGrath and Beehr (1990) cite accidents, and also new interpersonal encounters, as examples of uncontrollable and unpredictable SPECs.

It is important to note that a SPEC need not have occurred yet to elicit a stress response. Anticipation of a SPEC is sometimes a very powerful response. If a SPEC is predictable, the system may also anticipate the effect of the SPEC. Depending on the control possibilities and other factors, anticipation of a SPEC may have positive effects, if the system can take preventive actions or start controlling the negative effects even before the situation has actually occurred. For example, it has been shown that stress influences the rise of cortisol within 30 minutes after waking up for people who are under considerable (and recurrent) psychological stress, even without being faced yet with any concrete stressful situations that day (McEwen, 1998; Pruessner, Hellhammer, & Kirschbaum, 1999). The feeling of insecurity and loss of control connected with anticipation of future stressors is one of the key processes in several conceptions of stress in work and organizational psychology (Beehr, 1998; McGrath, 1976).

Temporal Aspects of Coping Responses and Behavior in the Stress Cycle

The passage from the objective situation to the perceived situation is mediated by the appraisal process: that is, by the evaluation that the objective situation either is or is not harmful or stressful. Between the perceived situation and the actual response there is a choice process in which one response pattern among several possible response patterns is selected. This choice process is heavily dependent on how the situation is perceived (the system attempts to choose an appropriate response), but also on the availability of responses, or of the resources needed to carry them out.

As a result of the choice process, a coping response gets selected. When the system is an individual, the interpretation of the situation, the choice process, and the selection of an appropriate response are not visible to the outsider, but rather are covert processes internal to the system. For multiperson systems such as a group, however, communication about these matters may make them more overt.

Coping has generally been viewed as a reaction to a SPEC intended to be adaptive, that is, to diminish the negative effects of the stressor. However, coping does not always actually diminish the negative influence of the stressor, and it has therefore been described as an attempt or effort to deal with the stressor, independent of its actual success. Often, coping is overt behavior, but there is also *cognitive coping*, in which the situation is thought through and reinterpreted. In this case, it is often difficult to distinguish the appraisal process from the process of cognitive coping.

Most coping research discusses coping behavior as if it were always an immediate reaction to a specific stressful situation. For example, coping checklists such as the well-known Ways of Coping Checklist (Folkman & Lazarus, 1988) ask individuals to respond to the coping items with respect to how they have reacted to a particular stressful situation in the past. The concept of coping in this research is at least implicitly tied to situations that have already happened. However, there can be different temporal locations of SPECs, as discussed previously. We can sometimes foresee and anticipate stressful situations, and situations that occurred long ago can continue to elicit stressful reactions. So, McGrath and Beehr (1990) distinguished five temporal locations of coping activities:

1. *Preventive coping*: actions taken long before the change event (e.g., building a dam to prevent flooding).
2. *Anticipatory coping*: actions taken just before the event (e.g., evacuating an area that is in the path of an immanent hurricane).
3. *Dynamic coping*: actions taken while the event is happening (e.g., taking appropriate shelter in a tornado).
4. *Reactive coping*: actions taken immediately after the event (e.g., treating wounds).
5. *Residual coping*: actions taken long after the event (e.g., rebuilding a destroyed building).

Preventive and Anticipatory Coping

When a SPEC can be anticipated, or when a SPEC is known or believed to have a high probability of occurring, people can engage in preventive coping a long time before the SPEC occurs or is likely to occur. Preventive actions can sometimes diminish the probability that the SPEC will happen (such as in accident prevention or regular visits to the dentist to prevent painful cavities). In other cases, preventive actions can help prepare for a more efficient coping once the SPEC actually happens, and may attenuate the impact of the SPEC or diminish secondary losses due to a SPEC. Examples are health insurance that covers part of the costs of coping once someone needs medical treatment, and noting one's credit card numbers before travelling abroad to facilitate coping in the event the credit card gets stolen. Insurance bought because of concerns about possible future losses, in itself a stressor, is also a good example of preventive actions for more or less probable SPECs.

Although preventive actions seem to be a good idea because they may help prevent the SPEC from happening or may limit damage and facilitate coping after the event, they are also often costly. Preventive actions are an investment without immediate return, and the system has to balance the risk of the SPEC occurring with the cost and effort of preventive actions. This is sometimes difficult for people to do with precision, because of the known biases in risk perception. People are likely to overestimate small risks if they are framed as losses, or they may be overly optimistic with regard to certain risks (Slovic, Fischhoff, & Lichtenstein, 1982).

Often, the SPEC may only have a certain probability of occurring independent of whether or not the individual engages in preventive coping. Often there may not be feedback available about whether preventive coping actually prevented or attenuated the occurrences of the SPEC, or whether, instead, the situation would also have gone well without preventive coping. So the cause–effect relation between the preventive actions and the nonoccurrence of a stressor often cannot be established. Superstitious behavior is a case in point, in which people engage in behavior rituals akin to preventive coping (such as chasing away the bad ghosts). Psychoneurotic behaviors, such as obsessive–compulsive patterns, may be another example (McGrath & Beehr, 1990).

Whereas preventive coping can be done long before a SPEC is expected to happen, anticipatory coping happens shortly before a specific SPEC is about to occur. For example, if a blizzard has been predicted for that day, it is wise to dress warmly and put sturdy shoes on before going to work, even if the sun is still shining at the moment one leaves the house. Such anticipatory actions can then attenuate the effect of a SPEC. Anticipatory coping shares many features with preventive coping.

Even if a stressful situation such as an exam is foreseeable, and even if anticipatory actions such as studying for the exam seem appropriate to deal with it, not everybody engages in such optimal and well-adapted anticipatory coping. How well anticipatory actions are taken certainly depends on the SPEC that is expected in a given instance, and on the resources available, but also has been found to be dependent on other factors such as self-esteem. Research on self-handicapping tendencies shows that individuals sometimes

take anticipatory actions that do not help and sometimes even hinder effective coping. For example, they do not study for an exam. Such anticipatory
coping behavior seems paradoxical, but actually serves the purpose of providing the individual with the opportunity to externalize failure and internalize
success (Berglas & Jones, 1978). Self-handicapping behavior is more often
found for individuals low in self-esteem. In this respect it can be used as anticipatory coping behavior that provides an excuse in case of failure (Tice,
1991).

Dynamic Coping and Reactive Coping

Once confronted with a SPEC, and once the system appraises the situation as stressful, it may not wait to engage in coping attempts until the SPEC
is over. Dynamic coping is described as coping during the time the SPEC is
occurring. Reactive coping is described as coping attempts immediately after
the SPEC has happened. Many researchers consider reactive and dynamic
coping as the prototypical cases of coping. Most models of coping and most
measures of coping are intended to refer to dynamic and reactive coping.
These models assume that a stressful situation has already occurred and is
dealt with promptly.

Many stress researchers distinguish between emotion-oriented coping
and problem-oriented coping or between avoidance-oriented and approach-
oriented coping (Schwarzer & Schwarzer, 1996). Emotion-oriented coping
aims at mastering the negative emotions that occur during or after the stressful situation, whereas problem-oriented coping focuses on removing or nul-
lifying the cause of the stress. Both forms of coping can be used with regard
to the same stressor, sometimes simultaneously. The two forms of coping
can have any of several temporal patterns. Rothbaum, Weisz, and Snyder
(1982) postulated that problem-oriented and emotion-oriented coping are
often found in a specific temporal sequence. They suggested that people will
engage in problem-oriented coping first, and will only make use of emotion-
focused coping if the stressor cannot be controlled with the problem-solving
efforts. Indeed, Tennen, Affleck, Armeli, and Carney (2000) in their diary
study of stress and coping found that problem-oriented coping was more than
four times more likely than emotion-focused coping to be the only coping
attempt following a stressor. The latter was much more likely observed together with problem-oriented coping, suggesting that some situations can be
resolved after problem-oriented coping, but that emotion-oriented coping
alone is rarely successful in resolving a stressful situation.

However, the opposite temporal sequence may also be plausible under certain circumstances. If the stressor is very strong, a person may have
to apply some emotion-focused coping *before* he or she can go on to apply
the problem-focused coping. In such a case, emotion-focused coping would
be an attempt to regain control over one's own emotional state, thereby to

cool down in order to be able to search for and apply a rational, problem-based strategy. Which of these temporal sequences of coping attempts will be most successful for a given SPEC depends on the situation. This notion led Reicherts and Perrez to formulate their Rules of Adequate Coping. They hypothesize and find different sequences of coping attempts, depending on aspects of the SPEC (Reicherts, 1999; Reicherts & Perrez, 1992; Reicherts & Pihet, 2000; Schwarzer, 1995). For example, one of the rules states that in case of a controllable stressor one should try to influence it and not engage in avoidance behavior, thereby showing environment-directed coping. However, if the situation is high in negative valence, the good thing to do first is to engage in palliative, emotion-focused coping—that is, to try to control one's reaction and to regain one's calm.

Although the evidence is not unambiguous, problem-focused coping has been found to be related to better mental health and well-being, whereas emotion-focused and avoidance coping have been found to be related to poorer health (although this latter finding may be due to the types of measures of emotion-focussed coping). Emotion-focused coping does not change the SPEC, so the source of stress is likely to remain active over time; in contrast, in many cases problem-oriented coping can actually diminish the source of stress.

Residual Coping

There are many situations in which coping cannot take place until long after the SPEC has occurred, for any of several reasons. The system might have to accumulate or replenish resources before coping can be done (Wells, Hobfoll, & Lavin, 1999). It may also be that a SPEC has delayed effects: for example, long-term effects of accidents or diseases. It has often been found that people suffer long-term consequences long after a very traumatic situation. These long-term effects of traumatic situations can occur after periods free of symptoms of distress. Such long-term effects need different kinds of coping actions at different times (Ochberg, 1993).

LEVEL B: MULTIPLE STRESSOR EVENTS WITHIN A SHORT TIME PERIOD

Very often in life, strain is not due to a single, isolated stressor, but to the exposure to several SPECs within a relatively short time—either the recurrence of SPECs of a given kind or the impinging of multiple SPECs. Most measures of strain, particularly studies in work settings, do not measure stress–strain–coping cycles in relation to single SPECs, but rather measure the cumulative effects of all SPECs occurring in a certain period of time. Such multiple stressors can occur in either of two temporal patterns:

- *Pattern 2:* Recurrence of a specific kind of stress event within a short period of time
- *Pattern 3:* Occurrence of multiple, near-simultaneous stressor events (different SPECs) within a short period of time.

Although single intense SPECs may have a major impact on the system, the empirical evidence seems to indicate that the exposure to multiple recurrences of a given SPEC or to the occurrence of multiple SPECs within a short period of time is both a frequent condition in the lives of workers and a crucial factor in stress (cf. Beehr, 1998). In the first part of this chapter, we examined a stress cycle in which a given SPEC is immediately appraised and responded to with specific coping actions. If a person is faced with multiple stressors, additional factors may be important moderators and mediators between SPECs and resulting strain. Beehr (1998) offers a meta-model of occupational stress that emphasizes the interplay among different facets of the stress situation, as well as the influence of time on occupational stress under conditions in which there are multiple and repeated stressors. Although the model was formulated to explain stress at work, it could easily be adapted to fit many other behavior settings.

As in the single-episode models, the process begins with a stressor–response relation. However, the model assumes that several more or less simultaneous SPECs may be present at a given time period. The relations between these stressors and responses to them are mediated by situational characteristics other than the stressor: by the nature of the current task, by personal characteristics such as personality factors, and by the duration of the stressors. Each of these three sets of variables can influence the stress-coping process in many ways, and there are also interactions among them. The result of the interplay of all of these variables—the stressors, the person, the environment, and time—determines the level of strain on the person, but also the level of strain on the embedding systems (e.g., the organization).

Most measures of the *level of strain*, at least in organizational psychology, focus on multiple or recurrent stressors. Among the most often measured forms of stress in organizational stress research are role conflict, role ambiguity, role overload, and time pressure, all of which imply multiple (different or recurrent) SPECs. The level of stress is often measured in terms of the importance of a given family of stressors and the number of different stressors impinging at a given time (e.g., Spector & Jex, 1998).

SPECs are not evenly distributed across jobs. In some circumstances, SPECs tend to accumulate. Dunckel (1985) analyzed combinations of different SPECs at work and found that many workplaces are either high overall or low overall on different SPECs, indicating that workers in some jobs have a multitude of SPECs impinging on them, whereas incumbents of other jobs may have a lot fewer. This has also been found for aspects of private life. For example, a study about economically disadvantaged pregnant women found that SPECs of different types tended to accumulate for these women (Hobfoll, 2001).

Sometimes, simultaneous SPECs are a result of multiple roles. There has been considerable research discussing whether multiple roles (for example being an active parent and homemaker and working for pay at the same time) can be seen as sources of strain. Holding multiple roles means that one is likely to be confronted, within a short period of time, with SPECs connected to each of the roles. Role overload is a likely consequence.

However, most research on multiple roles and strain has shown beneficial effects, rather than detrimental effects, of multiple roles. Most of these findings are for studies involving family versus worker roles (for a recent review, see Barnett & Hyde, 2001), but similar effects have been found for the accumulation of other multiple roles besides homemaker versus participant in the workforce (Thoits, 1994). At the same time, there seems to be an upper limit for beneficial effects to accrue from the accumulation of multiple roles, especially if some of the roles are of lesser importance for the person. In any case, it is clear that simultaneous, recurrent SPECs are more likely to impinge on persons holding multiple different roles than on persons with only one role. So there must be some other factors linked to particular multiple roles that either hinder the full negative impact of the SPECs or somehow generate positive effects. Barnett and Hyde (2001) propose different processes that could contribute to the beneficial effects of multiple roles. Some of them are founded on the idea that multiple roles not only indicate more SPECs, but also more *resources*, such as more social contacts and support, more money, or more self-esteem. Other aspects of multiple roles may influence the appraisal process. Barnett and Hyde (2001) cite an extended frame of reference, similarity of experiences in couples, and gender-role ideology as such factors.

Although it may seem likely that multiple SPECs that impinge at the same time on the system may cause more strain, the actual relation between multiple SPECs and strain may be influenced by many more factors than just the number of SPECs, as the research on multiple roles and strain shows.

LEVEL C: STRESS-COPING CYCLES
WITH CONSEQUENCES EXTENDED IN TIME

If a system is confronted with more than one SPEC, there are multiple and overlapping stress-coping cycles operating over time, and earlier stress-coping cycles may have an influence on later ones. Moreover, at any one time, the system is not only confronted with and responding to a set of stressors, but must deal with an accumulation of residual stress from past stressors that have not been completely resolved. On the other hand, there may also be positive effects (such as increased resources) from having resolved past stressors. Shupe and McGrath (1998) define the overall level of stress of a system at any given time as "the algebraic total of all residual stress and acquired stress-resistance present for that focal system at that time" (p. 89).

There has been little empirical study about how exposure to stress and to repeated stress-coping cycles, over time, influences not only the state of the system but also its subsequent coping abilities, although many have recognized that longitudinal studies to examine those and related issues are of high importance for stress research (Frese & Zapf, 1988). The simplest model of the likely relation between exposure to SPECs, coping attempts, and resulting strain, is certainly a model that postulates that the more stressors a system is exposed to, and the longer that exposure, the more detrimental the effects will be. In that line of reasoning, when the exposure to the SPEC ends then its negative effects should disappear as well. Such a model assumes that coping attempts are at best only partly successful in removing the stress, and that repeated exposure to a given stressor continues to have a negative impact on the system.

However, Frese and Zapf (1988) discuss several other plausible temporal patterns for the relation between number and duration of SPECs and their effects. For example, in organizational psychology there is an *initial impact model* in certain domains such as job transition. In a new job situation, longer exposure leads to higher strain in the beginning. After the person develops proper coping resources the strain diminishes, even though the situation (that is, work conditions) remains the same. This model assumes that the system develops better coping behaviors if it is confronted with the same or similar stressors recurrently over time.

At this temporal level we can identify four different patterns that involve the extended consequences of multiple SPEC-coping cycles:

- *Pattern 4*: Coping actions with regards to a SPEC may give rise to another SPEC, thus increasing the overall level of stress.
- *Pattern 5*: Multiple coping failures may render the system more vulnerable to future stress.
- *Pattern 6*: Successful coping may augment the coping resources for other stressors.
- *Pattern 7*: Continuing strain may accrue as the cumulative effect of multiple, partially unresolved SPECs.

These four patterns are necessarily a simplification of actual processes. Often, coping responses of a system are not single behaviors in reaction to a specific SPEC, but rather a coping response strategy (Shupe & McGrath, 1998). Coping can thus be seen as an "orient, enact, monitor, modify" cycle (as described in chapters 4 and 7). This means that a specific coping attempt will be chosen as a first reaction to the SPECs, and if this is not successful or only partially successful, other coping actions will be taken.

Sommerfield and McCrae (2000) make a similar argument and point out that it is difficult to assess specific coping effects because often there is not a clear and time-limited specific stressor to which there are clear and specific solutions and coping behaviors. If the stressor is multifaceted or of extended duration, a given coping reaction cannot be viewed as a reaction to any specific stressor. Instead, the situation consists of an intermingling of various stress-coping cycles. Coping research therefore must deal with multiple, simultaneous SPECs and multiple coping activities.

Pattern 4: Coping Actions With Regard to SPEC A May Give Rise To SPEC B

Coping activities use resources and may therefore make the system more vulnerable. SPECs that are not potential stressors under normal conditions may become stressors under conditions in which the system is weakened by coping with other stressors. Fletcher and Payne (as cited in Fletcher, 1988) used the term *secondary stressors* for stressors that have been found to be stressful only because the organism was under strain as a result of a primary SPEC. The primary stressor lowered the tolerance threshold for the appraisal of a different SPEC as a threat, and only under such a condition did this additional, normally harmless SPEC become a stressor. In this vein, Hobfoll's (2001) conservation of resources model argues that the loss or threat of loss of resources is in itself an important source of strain, especially if the person is aware of having only limited resources remaining. In that model, the notion of resources covers a wide array of things, such as basic feelings of security, good interpersonal relationships, and material goods.

People often have to invest resources to prevent resource loss. Some resources deplete over time if they are not actively maintained. The need for resource resupply and resource maintenance can be seen as potential sources of SPECs that are generated by dealing with earlier SPECs.

Besides the diminishing of resources from attempts to cope with a given SPEC, some coping activities may themselves generate other stressors. For example, working overtime to deal with a high workload may resolve the problem of the workload, but at the same time may lead to neglect of other areas of life and thereby may generate new SPECs (cf. Schoenpflug & Battmann, 1988). Other examples of coping attempts that generate later SPECs are compromises on quality of task performance that may have to be compensated for with higher effort later. Note that these costs of coping may even occur for coping attempts that are successful with regard to the initial SPEC.

Pattern 5: Failed Coping Attempts With Regard to a Given SPEC A Make Coping With Subsequent SPEC B Less Successful

Even successful coping attempts are costly for the system, and may therefore have negative effects (Schoenpflug & Battmann, 1988) because resources are used. Failed coping attempts do not even have the advantage of resolving problems. They may only be consuming resources. Having fewer resources diminishes the probability of successful coping and increases the system's vulnerability to further strain. Used resources therefore need to be renewed and rebuilt, and available resources need to be maintained. Hobfoll (2001) argues that people with depleted resources from dealing with earlier stress may be so consumed with reactive coping that they cannot afford to apportion resources for proactive coping (Wells, Hobfoll, & Lavin, 1999).

As shown for the distribution of SPECs, resources also are unevenly distributed. Hobfoll found that resources aggregate in what he calls resource caravans. This term suggests that some resources normally come with others, or that the loss of certain resources may trigger losses of others. He cites as an example that self-efficacy is often coupled with optimism. He also found that the level of existing resources influences both the probability of loss of resources and the effort needed to recover from resource loss. If there is still a healthy base of resources, the probability of losing further resources is diminished. Recovery from resource losses is easier if there are more resources left. This implies that initial loss begets future loss. Hobfoll indeed observed spirals of resource loss, but also spiral of resource gains. For example, Lane and Hobfoll (1992) found that lower-income pregnant women had fewer personal resources (such as self-esteem and optimism). For them, fewer resources were related to higher stress, which in turn was related to lower birth weight of their children, which in turn enhances the probability of having children with problems, which uses more resources, and so forth.

Often, the resources used in a SPEC-coping cycle include self-regulational processes, and these resources also can be depleted (Baumeister, Faber, & Wallace, 1999). Many coping activities encompass volitional effort involving self-regulation activities such as self-control, affect regulation, thought control, persistence on a task, maintaining physical stamina, or impulse control. Such self-regulation activities often require the overriding of impulses to do other things or to rest; they therefore use lots of energy and require lots of self-control. This can lead to "fatigue" of the self-regulating system. Baumeister and colleagues (Baumeister, Faber, & Wallace, 1999) found that self-regulation activities on a second task were impaired if a first task required such activities, indicating that the self-regulation capacity is a limited resource. The tasks used in those studies were not connected to each other and needed different self-control behaviors, suggesting that results involved the depletion of a single source of resources for all self-regulation activities.

A special case of a coping activity that sometimes leads to difficulties and negative side effects is the use of social support in stressful situations. Seeking social support has been found to be a very important and often-successful coping response (Beehr, 1995; Buunk, 1990; Wills, 1987). Besides its normally beneficial consequences, however, having to rely on social support may also have long-term negative consequences. On the positive side, social support can enhance motivation to not give up, and thus help sustain coping attempts over time. However, social support also has costs, especially if a person needs social support for a prolonged period of time. Reciprocity rules of relationships state that a favor received has to be "repaid" over time (Argyle & Henderson, 1985; Buunk & Schaufeli, 1999). If a stressful situation is prolonged, the person may not be able to "pay back" in a timely way for the social support received, and this violation of the reciprocity rule may become an additional stressor. Research has found that feeling over-benefited from social support is related to negative affect (Buunk, de Jonge, Ybema, & de Wolff, 1998). Whereas paying back favors often has to be done rather fast with colleagues in the workplace (Argyle & Henderson, 1985), the time span for reciprocity can be wider with close friends or family, making those sources of social support less apt to generate additional stressors because of delayed pay back.

Asking for social support also means that other people are aware that one cannot deal well with the prevailing stressful situation, and this may be a threat to self-esteem (Buunk et al., 1998). Peeters, Buunk, and Schaufeli (1995) showed, for example, that instrumental social support triggered feelings of inferiority and was accompanied by more negative feelings. Finally, the content of the supportive communication may be such that it enhances stress because it convinces the recipient even more strongly that things are really bad. For all these reasons, social support is sometimes found to increase rather than ameliorate the consequences of stress (Beehr, 1995; Elfering, Semmer, Schade, Grund, & Boos, 2002).

If failures accumulate, feelings of not being able to cope can generalize and lead to loss of self-efficacy and self-esteem, and this can lead to what has been called *learned helplessness* (Seligman, 1975). In this case, the individual may lose faith in his or her coping attempts and stop undertaking them altogether. Research on learned helplessness has shown that reactions to multiple failures depend on task difficulty. For example, in some instances, people may increase their coping efforts on a simple task (Ford & Brehm, 1987), yet they may also continue to depend on habitual styles for explaining or accounting for events (Peterson & Park, 1998).

Sometimes, after the failure of coping attempts, individuals reduce their expectations or readjust their goals. Although readjustment of goals seems an adaptive reaction to multiple failed coping attempts, in many situations it may also have negative effects on self-esteem, at least in the long run (Carver et al., 1992; Semmer, in press). This is especially the case if the readjustment of goals involves feelings of resignation. As another way of exploring the impact of shifts in expectations as a reaction to SPECs, Carstenson and colleagues (e.g., Kennedy, Fung, & Carstensen, 2001) have done work on people's emotional regulation in the face of altered temporal perspectives (e.g., as with elderly people or people with terminal illnesses).

Pattern 6: Successful Coping Actions With Regard to SPEC A Facilitates Coping With Subsequent SPEC B

Successful coping often leads to the re-creation of resources that will help cope even more effectively with similar or different SPECs in the future. Experiences with successfully handled situations may lead to better strategies and increased knowledge, which in turn help to cope with future situations (Shupe & McGrath, 1998). Having been able to cope with difficult situations may also increase self-efficacy and self-esteem, valuable resources for facing other SPECs in the future.

This argument is supported by a study by Thoits (1994). She compared work and relationship problems that were resolved successfully with problems that were not dealt with well with regard to their impact on subsequent mastery levels, self-esteem, and strain. The majority of work-related problems were reported to have been resolved, whereas the majority of relationship-related problems were reported as persisting and not being resolved. Thoits found indications that successful problem solving is a good resource for subsequent coping. Successful problem-solvers at work showed increased mastery levels and had increased self-esteem, as compared with people who failed to solve the problem and with those who did not even try to solve the problem. Marriage problems showed a different pattern: For relationship problems, people who engaged in problem solving showed increases in mastery levels, higher self-worth, and higher levels of control independent of the success of the problem-solving attempt, as compared with people that did not try to solve the problems. Similar results are reported by Turner and Avison (1992), who found that people who felt that they could grow as a consequence of past life events showed less strain (Holahan, Moos, Holahan, & Cronkite 1999).

Successful coping with SPECs can give the system the experience of being able to do so also in the future, and therefore may change the appraisal of a similar SPEC. Successful coping can also enhance resources by learning and adaptation processes, and can influence, in a positive way, self-efficacy and self-esteem, which are both very important resources.

Pattern 7: An Accumulation of Residual Effects of Not Entirely Resolved Multiple, Recurrent, and Extended Specs May Produce Long-Term Major Strain (e.g., Burnout)

Frese and Zapf (1988) suggest that long-term reactions to prolonged stress may show different effects over time, even after exposure to the SPEC has ended. They distinguish five different possible curves for how generalized long-term reactions to extended exposure to stress may play out:

1. Their *stress reaction model* assumes that the strain on the system increases the longer the system is exposed to stress, but that if

the SPEC is removed, the system recovers. They cite research on unemployment that shows such a course.

2. Alternatively, strain can increase with longer exposure, but if the SPEC ends, the level of strain stays stable, indicating that the long-term exposure has done some irreversible damage to the system. Examples are long-term effects of shift work (Frese & Semmer, 1986).

3. A third possible reaction curve is called the *dynamic accumulation model*, which states that even after the SPECs are removed, there can be a further increase in strain. This can happen if the exposure to stress has led to a general weakening of the system and to increased vulnerability to other SPECs. It can also be the case for certain psychosomatic illnesses such as depression, in which the reaction pattern to the initial stressor may trigger a vicious cycle that leads to a further deterioration of the system.

4. The *adjustment model* states that an adjustment to the SPEC exposure takes place even before the SPEC has ended. In this case, the level of strain decreases before the offset of the SPEC, perhaps because better coping skills have been developed.

5. In the *sleeper effect model* the negative effect of the exposure to the SPEC is delayed in time, sometimes until long after the SPEC has disappeared. Frese and Zapf cite exposure to radioactivity or other toxic substances as having such delayed effects (see also, Barak, Achiron, Rotstein, Elizur, & Noy, 1998, for an example).

Each of these longitudinal patterns may be related to different types of SPECs, but there also may be different curves within a particular type of SPEC. An additional complication is that different long-term effects may have specific, different time frames within which they appear (Dormann & Zapf, 1999; Garst, Frese, & Molenaar, 2000).

The SPEC-coping cycle implies specific physiological reactions. In general, the stress-related physiology is highly adapted for short-term flight or fight behavior. The effects of those physiological reactions, however, become dysfunctional for the system if the stress is cumulative or long term (Sapolsky, 1998). McEwen (1998) discusses the long-term effects of stress as allostatic load. He uses the term *allostatic response*, in contrast to homoeostatic response, to describe the ability of the organism to actively adapt to new situations. Allostatic responses allow the system to react to challenges and changes, and the normal physiological changes in a stressful situation are such a highly functional allostatic response.

After the stressor has disappeared, however, the organism should return to normal or baseline. The healthy response to physiological changes after stress is a gradual return to the normal state. Continued and recurrent stress, however, can lead to difficulties in shutting off the allostatic response in a proper way.

Allostatic load describes the effects of suboptimal rates of return to normal. McEwen distinguishes several types of allostatic load:

1. In case of "repeated hits" of stress, the physiological response goes up, and there is no time for recovery.
2. The failure to unwind sets the system under a prolonged response of stress. There are some negative effects for the cardiovascular system, and for other aspects of health (Sapolsky, 1998).
3. There are situations that elicit a high stress response the first time a SPEC is encountered, but then the person becomes habituated. If the system does not habituate its physiological response, the system's stress response is prolonged.
4. Another pattern of responses is described as *hyporeactive*. In this pattern, a system does not show an adaptive reaction to a stressor in some respects, and this inadequate response leads to compensatory hyperactivity of other aspects of the physiological response.

For physiological reactions, not only is the intensity of the reaction important, but also its change over time. Physiological changes under stress are highly functional if the "unwinding" occurs very fast after the stressor disappears. Delayed unwinding, however, can indicate a lack of coping.

Long-term exposure to multiple, recurrent, and extended SPECs can have detrimental effects on the whole system. *Burnout* is such a syndrome. It sometimes arises, for example, in response to chronic interpersonal stress on the job in human service settings. Schaufeli and Enzmann (1998) describe the development of burnout as starting with tensions resulting from a discrepancy between expectations, ideals, or intentions of an individual and what they encounter in the workplace, followed by a gradually developing strain due to this imbalance, followed by specific forms of coping attempts by the individual. The burnout response usually has three aspects: (a) exhaustion and a depletion of emotional and physical resources; (b) an impression of being ineffective on the job; and (c) increased cynicism, depersonalisation, and detachment from the job (Maslach, Schaufeli, & Leitner, 2001).

Burnout has time-relevant aspects. The burnout syndrome occurs only after a long-term exposure to multiple SPECs. The physical exhaustion, typical for burnout, can be attributed to the extension of a stressful situation in time. A similar argument can be made for emotional exhaustion, an effect of depletion of emotional resources over time. The third aspect, the development of more negative attitudes toward others (especially clients), may in fact be a nonadaptive reappraisal process in which the person changes his or her perception of the SPEC over time.

Although it is hypothesized that burnout develops over time, there are few longitudinal studies of burnout, and they show unclear and conflicting results with regard to the longitudinal link among causes and the stability of burnout levels (cf. Schaufeli & Enzmann, 1998). Several longitudinal studies have indeed found burnout levels to be relatively stable over time (Greenglass, Fiksenbaum, & Burke, 1995). According to Schaufeli and Enzmann (1998) who provide an overview of those studies, methodological shortcomings may be one of the most important causes for the lack of coherent results.

A second time-related question regarding burnout concerns the sequential or simultaneous development of the three facets of the burnout syndrome. If a specific sequence of burnout phases could be found, this could be important for prevention and interventions by allowing early detection of signs of burnout. Several sequences have been proposed (Maslach et al., 2001). One proposition sees depersonalisation and cynicism as occurring first in the development of burnout, followed by feelings of inefficacy and finally exhaustion (Golembiewski & Munzenrieder, 1988). The initial sequential model of burnout advocated by Maslach posited emotional exhaustion as the first and one of the most important reactions to interpersonal demands, leading to a distancing from the client or patient, which leads to depersonalisation. As a result of this, the quality of the interpersonal relationship with the client deteriorates, which in turn leads to the feeling of impaired accomplishment.

However, later research showed that in addition to interpersonal demands, workload and other work-related stressors also contributed to emotional exhaustion. Although the link between exhaustion and depersonalisation has been rather well established (Maslach et al., 2001), it also has been shown that other factors, specifically the lack of resources, have an influence on level of depersonalisation (Leitner, 1991). The link between cynicism and feelings of inefficacy is much less clearly established. Researchers have found that the sense of a lack of personal accomplishment is influenced by many factors besides depersonalisation, and reduced feelings of accomplishment may develop independently of depersonalisation and emotional exhaustion (Lee & Ashford, 1996; Maslach et al., 2001). Furthermore, most of the empirical evidence about the proposed sequences of burnout stems from cross-sectional studies, and therefore may not encompass developments and sequences over a sufficiently long period of time (Leitner, 1991). A notable exception is the work of Greenblatt (2001) on the temporal patterning of depleting and restorative activities in a study of burnout among staff at Club Med. So these questions of the sequence of development of burnout remain very much in doubt.

LEVEL D: STRESS INVOLVING MAJOR LIFE EVENTS

In this section, we will discuss the one pattern of Level D stress, which is Pattern 8: Major life events can have continuing, irreversible, and major stress consequences. Some SPECs have a major impact on the system not because they are chronic or repeated, but because they change, irreversibly, the future of the system. Examples are major life events such as diagnosis of chronic and incurable diseases, accidents with high impact, and social and psychological events such as the loss of a loved one. In such cases, the exposure time to a SPEC (or the actual event) may be very short, yet the impact of the event may be irreversible. An individual often needs to adapt to a whole new situation, change behavioral habits in a major way, and readjust his or her life (Folkman, 1993).

Extreme stressors with irreversible effects elicit immediate stress responses, but then also have long-term effects. Such life events also often entail further stressors beyond the event itself. For example, victims of crimes may have to undergo stressful police investigations or medical procedures, or medical rehabilitation may be additional stressors beyond the initial injuries after an accident (Pynoos, Sorenson, & Steinberg, 1993).

Such a major life event can be seen as a crisis that challenges the normal course of life. If such an event can be integrated into a person's biography, the crisis can be perceived as resolved. Turner and Avison (1992) therefore distinguish between resolved and unresolved life events. A life event is regarded as resolved if an individual can derive positive meaning from it, or if people generate more confidence, new skills, or positive attitudes as a result of efforts to deal with the life event. Unresolved life events are those that continue to be emotionally distressing, because the person cannot integrate those events into their ongoing lives.

Life events that are very disruptive—that is, that need major changes and adaptations of lifestyle—often require a major cognitive reorganization of the person's self-concept, integrating the new facts (Pynoos et al., 1993), and adapting his or her lifestyle to the new and changed situation. The reorganization of one's beliefs and life after a traumatic event depends partly on the event. We will discuss several classes of such events: (a) coping with chronic illness, which often implies a deterioration of health over time despite coping efforts; (b) injuries that lead to the loss of bodily functions, which often are the result of an event that implies a sudden, drastic change with, at most, limited recovery; and (c) loss of a loved one, which implies irreversible changes.

When an individual is confronted with a chronic illness, he or she needs to make multiple adaptations. Many chronic diseases have different stages: uncertainty and first symptoms; the realization that one has the disease and the accompanying disruption of normal life; the recovery of the self and restoration of well-being, if possible; or, if the disease is incurable, passage to a final stage. Each of the stages of chronic illness requires multiple adaptations, and may need different coping strategies. Chronic diseases are not only a health problem, but also influence other aspects of life so that the patient not only has to cope with impaired health, or chronic pain, but also with career and relationship changes. In addition, the patient may need to construct a complex revision of the self.

Additional stress can arise because of medical treatment. Surprisingly, it has been shown that most outpatients with chronic diseases such as diabetes, cancer, or rheumatic diseases do not suffer higher levels of general stress and have comparably high levels of personal well-being in comparison to healthy subjects. Two exceptions are during the first stages of diagnosis, which requires a higher level of adaptation and entails the highest amount of strain, and during the final stage of a terminal disease (Maes, Leventhal, & de Ridder, 1996).

A personal loss of a bodily function can be seen as a special case of a chronic condition. The loss of a limb, for example, is not life-threatening, but needs a major readaptation of the system as does a chronic disease. Often, such losses are the result of accidents, and represent immediate and major changes in the life of those concerned. Mikulincer and Florian (1996) distinguish coping and succumbing processes as two general reactions to such events. Successful coping adjustment emphasizes positive strivings, recognizes one's assets in life, and finds sources of satisfaction. Such copers adjust to the disability by viewing themselves as people with a disability rather than as a disabled person, thus making an attempt to integrate the loss within an existing concept of themselves rather than adopting an identity in which the concept of being disabled is dominant. Succumbing, on the other hand, contains wishful thinking, disengagement, increased negative views of oneself and the world, and an increasing concentration on difficulties.

Adaptation to the loss of a beloved one is one of the most challenging tasks in a person's life. Some psychological theories suggest that a grief process may be beneficial for later well-being. However, other studies do not support the grief-work hypothesis (Mikulincer & Florian, 1996). The distress about the loss of a close person seems to diminish with time, even without specific interventions (Stroebe, Stroebe, Schut, Zech, & van den Bout, 2002). The use of written discussion techniques, which have been found to have beneficial effects for other traumatic experiences (Smyth & Pennebaker, 1999), seemed not to be beneficial for the bereavement process. A recent study (Stroebe et al., 2002) showed that distress, intrusive thoughts, and visits to the doctors decreased over time for all people faced with a loss. A group that had been asked to write a diary containing their emotions and thoughts about the loved one did not profit from this intervention; it did not facilitate adjustment. For bereavement processes, it seems that this otherwise helpful coping method may not show additional beneficial effects. One interpretation by the authors of the study is that after the loss of a loved one, a process of mourning and readjustment is expected for the recently bereaved, which includes a fair amount of emotional disclosure, so additional disclosure may not be beneficial.

CONCLUDING COMMENTS

In this chapter, we presented several time-related features of the stress process, including temporal aspects of single stress episodes as well as multiple and recurrent stressors; temporal consequences of successful and failed coping; and the effects of long-term, chronic stress. Although the framework presented distinguished different temporal patterns of the stress process, these patterns overlap, and it is very clear that short-term and long-term aspects of stressors, strain, and coping processes have a strong mutual influence.

Considerable research has been done on each of the temporal patterns of stress discussed here. However, most of that work has been limited to only one or two of the temporal patterns of stress in any one study. Also, most of that work has been cross-sectional. Longitudinal studies of stress and coping are rare. Thus we know little about which time frames and which conditions and combinations of SPECs are likely to lead to what type of strain and what patterns of coping actions (Frese & Zapf, 1988; Garst et al., 2000).

AFTERTHOUGHTS

Stress Episodes

Stress episodes of many kinds
Beset our lives, bemuse our minds.
    With each we must somehow decide
    To take it on, or run and hide,
Give in to it, or draw the line!

Stress episodes, they come and go.
Appraisal processes, we know,
    Determine just what stresses us
    What threatens or depresses us
What bodes to lay us low!

Stress episodes, we surely hope
Are things with which we learn to cope.
    Our coping actions, we expect,
    Will keep those stressors off our neck,
But sometimes they have broader scope.

Stress episodes oft persevere,
They just don't fade away, I fear.
    Their consequences carry o'er
    A second day—or three or four.
We never make them disappear.

And stress events, we sometimes find
Can yield results of happy kind.
    Can make us better, it would seem,
    And even gain in self-esteem.
Some stress events are in the mind!

6

GROUP DEVELOPMENT
AND CHANGE

Much of the world's activity takes place when humans are acting together in groups or other collectivities. Groups are ubiquitous, and they form
for many reasons. A group that has formed, or is in the process of forming, is
subject to four sets of temporal forces.

First, there are *developmental forces*. A group, like all human systems,
is subject to forces for change that have to do with its own life course, its
growth, development, and perhaps decay as an intact system. Developmental
forces are internal, so to speak, and reflect a kind of Aristotelian formal causality. That is, they are inherent in the system, and partly determine the form
or design the group may have at different times in its development.

There also are *adaptational forces*. Groups, like all human systems, are
embedded in several partially nested dynamic contexts—physical, technological, organizational, social, and cultural—and thus are subject to forces
that derive from changes (and anticipated changes) in those contexts and
the group's explicit and tacit reactions to those changes. Adaptational forces

arise externally, but their meaning and the group's responses to them are also affected by the group's internal states and actions.

In addition, there are *experiential forces*. A group, like all human systems, is subject to forces for change that derive from its own experience. In individuals we call those experienced-based changes *learning*. Here, we will adopt that term for experienced-based changes in groups as well. The experiential forces are *historical*; the group's state today is a function of its state and actions yesterday and before, as well as of the conditions under which those actions took place.

These three sets of forces all have to do with the status and functioning of the group as an existing system or entity. In addition to the three sets of forces which have to do with the group as an intact system, a fourth set of temporal processes has to do with the operation of the group as an acting system, as it carries out its projects and tasks in pursuit of its purposes. These *operational forces* are temporal processes that come into play for the group regarded as an acting system: that is, for the processes involved when a group is carrying out some tasks or projects.

All four sets of forces are intrinsically temporal. All four sets of forces operate continually and simultaneously, and are of course interdependent; but it is useful to distinguish them for analytic purposes. We will go into more detail about the first three sets of processes in this chapter. We will devote the next chapter to the fourth of these sets of processes when we describe groups as acting systems.

In this chapter we first discuss the temporal aspects of group formation and developmental processes. We also introduce an alternative theoretical conception of groups that helps highlight the temporal issues of development and of other temporal processes. Then we will deal with adaptational processes by which groups react to and anticipate changes in their relations to embedding contexts, and with experiential processes by which groups change as a function of their own experience: that is, by which they learn as they carry out efforts to fulfill their intrinsic functions (of attaining group goals, fulfilling member needs, and maintaining system integrity). Chapter 7 deals with temporal processes involved in collective action.

Note that we are focusing on *temporal* issues, and we recognize that there are many nontemporal factors that are also of consequence in each of those domains. We have dealt with several of these temporal issues in our earlier publications (e.g., Arrow, McGrath, & Berdahl, 2000; McGrath & Argote, 2000; McGrath & Berdahl, 1998; McGrath & Kelly, 1986; McGrath & O'Connor, 1996; McGrath & Rotchford, 1983; McGrath & Tschan, in press; Tschan & Cranach, 1996), and we will draw on those sources here. In particular, we will draw on our formulation of a theory that presents groups as complex acting systems (Arrow, McGrath, & Berdahl, 2000; McGrath & Tschan, in press).

GROUP DEVELOPMENT AS TEMPORAL PATTERNING

Most work on group development has attempted to identify a series of regular and predictable stages through which a group must go, or through which groups usually do go, or through which groups should go to become mature and well-functioning groups. Such stages are often based on analogies to the developmental paths of individual humans from infants to mature and older adults. Such stages usually are assumed to reflect a prespecified order of development, and it is usually assumed that groups will go through each of them in turn within a reasonably specific time period. Such stages are seen as relatively independent of the nature of the group or its tasks, and of the basic characteristics of its members.

We need to make a distinction, here, between stages of development of the group as an *intact system* or *entity*, which is part of the topic of this chapter, and phases of group *task performance* as a group goes about carrying out its projects, which will be part of the focus of the next chapter. Some of the theories to be discussed in chapter 7 (e.g., those of Bales & Strodtbeck, 1951; Poole & Roth, 1989a, 1989b; Fisher, 1970) have often been labeled as theories of group development, even though that work concentrates on the phases of a group's performance of a certain type of task (thus, on the group as an *acting* system), rather than on the longer-run development of the group as an entity. Their generalizability to groups doing other tasks, or even to the same groups on the same tasks but over a longer life course, is unclear. In this section, we therefore concentrate on conceptions that are meant to apply to a wide variety of groups, independent of specific tasks, and that have reference to the development of the group itself, rather than just its performance of a particular set of tasks.

The history of theory and research on group development can be regarded as a progressive consideration of more and more complex temporal issues. The temporal issues in this domain start with the question of whether group development can be described as a sequence of stages. They move on to consideration of the number of stages, their order, the temporal pattern for the duration of each stage, and the question of whether groups do, or can, or should cycle back and forth through some of the stages more than once. All of these issues are then confounded further by asking whether whatever pattern of stages is hypothesized might differ for different kinds of groups, or groups doing different kinds of tasks, or groups under different kinds of operating conditions.

Thus, it is clear that the idea of patterns of group development subsumes many temporal aspects, and several of these temporal issues remain controversial in regard to group development. McGrath and O'Connor (1996, p. 28) view these group development issues as a cascading series of progressively more complex temporal issues. They start with the question of whether all groups change over time, and if so, whether all groups change in the same way, or if a given pattern of changes over time is unique to some groups or certain types of groups. If all groups do not change, or do not change in the same way, there is a further question as to whether different types of groups can be distinguished in terms of patterns of development.

Such different developmental types could be understood on the basis of distinctions at different levels. There could be group developmental patterns founded on differences in the overall purposes of the group (e.g., therapy groups versus work groups versus social groups), differences in their specific purposes (e.g., steel puddling crews versus basketball teams versus software development teams), differences in their formative paths or structural forms (e.g., task forces versus teams versus crews), or differences in even more specific features (e.g., size, diversity of group membership on any of a variety of attributes, types of technology available and in use, and the like).

On the other hand, if indeed all groups or all types of groups change in the same way, then one can ask whether such temporal patterns in groups are in fact developmental stages with the changes patterned so that the same kinds of structures and processes occur in the same fixed sequences for all groups. If there is a fixed sequence of stages of development, it would be important to know if the stages are of equal or differential durations, and if all groups go through the stages at the same rate. It would also be useful to know whether that pattern of stages is immutable or subject to alteration by unique circumstances or external events in the group's embedding system. Finally, if a given group does not follow a fixed sequence of stages, is a variation in the sequence indicative of malfunction in a group's development or maturation, or does it merely express normal variations arising because of differences in initial features of the group and contextual conditions.

We will now examine some of the established theories of group development against the background of this array of temporal issues.

THEORIES OF GROUP DEVELOPMENT

Tuckman (1965) has the most widely and solidly established stage theory (see also the later Tuckman & Jenson, 1977, revision), which he induced from a considerable body of empirical studies, mostly of therapy and training groups. His stages have been summarized as *forming, storming, norming, performing,* and *adjourning*. In the forming stage, the group members engage in orienting and testing each other, the situation, and the task requirements. They then move on to a stage with more emotional potential (storming), in which the group members negotiate the group structure and the acceptance and definition of the task. The next stage (norming) includes the development of group cohesion, which allows the group to approach the task in a coherent but open manner. Then the group moves to the performing stage, in which members cooperate and focus on the task, without much emotion. The last stage (adjourning) describes the dissolution or the ending of the group. This model is very widely known, but its empirical basis is rather limited.

Tuckman's model is a successive-stage model. Such a model implies that a group will do essentially all of its forming before it does much or any of its storming or norming, and that it will be done with all of these before it begins performing. This succession describes the usual, normal order of the stages.

Wheelan and colleagues (e.g., Verdi & Wheelan, 1992; Wheelan & McKeage, 1993) have done work that draws on the theoretical perspective of psychoanalyst Bion (Bion, 1961). Wheelan (1994) describes group development as a process of groups achieving maturity rather than as a strictly sequential process. Her first stage is called *dependency and inclusion*, when group members like to please, to get integrated, and to explore the norms. The second stage is *counterdependency and fight*, characterized by conflict but also by establishing role clarity. If the conflict at stage two can be resolved, the group members develop *trust*, and more mature interaction is possible at stage three. The fourth stage, *work*, is when the group is optimally prepared for effective task performance, because norms, roles, and rules are developed. The fifth stage is *termination*, which marks the ending of that group as a distinct social entity. Although Wheelan's stages include some sequential patterning, they are seen as "stages of group maturity": A group can attain a certain stage but then fall back to another stage.

Theorists such as Hill and Poole and their colleagues (e.g., Hill & Gruner, 1973; Poole & Baldwin, 1996) have questioned the temporal implications of these stage models, including the idea of a single sequence of phases that applies to all groups, the idea that a group goes through a set of phases in a particular order, and the idea that a group goes through some set of phases only once. Moreover they reject the normative idea that any deviation from that fixed order of the set of phases is evidence of some flaw in that group or some extraordinary circumstance in that group's development. Poole and Baldwin (1996) argue that, while specific stages may be identifiable, all groups do not necessarily go through the same stages, nor in the same order, nor only a single time. Which stages a given group will go through is contingent on multiple factors.

Other authors see group development as a result of critical events or milestones that are turning points in the group's process. These can occur at a specific time period. Gersick (1988, 1989) found, for example, that both laboratory groups and groups in real-world settings went through a transition phase at the midpoint of their lifetime that changed their behavior patterns profoundly. Fisher and Stutman (1987) analyzed the impact of routing statements (their term for process and procedural statements) as breakpoints of group phases. They found that phases are typically introduced by prospective routing statements and typically are brought to a close by retrospective routing statements.

Group Development in Relation to Individual Members and External Contexts

Whereas early work on this topic concentrated on the development of the group as a whole, some more recent work has begun to recognize that development involves an interplay between the group and its members, on the one hand, and between the group and its embedding contexts on the other. Recently, for example, Worchel and colleagues (Worchel, 1996; Worchel, Coutant-Sassic, & Grossman, 1992; Worchel & Coutant, 2001) have offered a six-stage developmental schema that reckons stages by taking into account both the state of the group and the state of the individual members. It considers the importance of the group for its members' needs and interests, but also considers the group's intragroup behavior and intergroup perceptions. Groups may repeatedly recycle through different stages.

Worchel's six stages consist of the following:

1. *Discontent* is characterized by an alienation of the individual from the group because it has become of low importance for that individual. At the group level, groups may suffer from low and irregular attendance or group member departures.
2. A *precipitating event* may "wake up" the group and lead to identification of which members want to remain in the group and comply with the group's norms and goals.
3. Groups then begin to establish *identity* and *independence*. In this stage, group membership, member positions, and group boundaries are established. Group members develop a sense of cohesiveness and belonging, but also exert pressure on deviants to conform to group norms. The in-group is perceived as homogenous and superior to out-groups, and group members may even seek out conflict and competition with the out-groups.
4. After identification is established, the group can turn its attention to group *productivity* and set and achieve goals, which often involves seeking out and using relevant individual skills to reach the common goal. Because goal achievement is so important, some cautious cooperation and alliances may be sought with relevant out-groups, as long as this cooperation does not threaten group identity.
5. A well-functioning group needs less attention, and thus members can turn their concerns to *individual needs* and be preoccupied with their own individual relations with the group (e.g., by seeking personal recognition or equity). The relationship

to out-groups becomes more cooperative as group members evaluate the individual benefits that can be achieved from out-groups.

6. *Decay* is the stage at which the individual's needs are predominant and the group becomes less salient. This can lead to more open conflict. Failures are attributed to the in-group rather than to the out-group. Thus, out-groups can become attractive alternatives for some group members.

Using this conception of development, Worchel and colleagues (1992) predicted and found that many group phenomena, such as groupthink, stereotyping, and social loafing, are more likely to occur in some stages of group development than in others.

Moreland and Levine (1982; Levine & Moreland, 1991) have addressed the socialization process, an aspect of development that is very much concentrated on the relationship between the group and individual members. The underlying model states that groups and their members evaluate the instrumentality and attractiveness of each other for fulfilling their needs. Depending on the fit between group and member needs, adjustment processes or role transitions may take place that alter the relation between member and group. One such transition is group entry; another is the acceptance of a person as a full member; a third is group exit. Such role transitions are a result of the basic two-way evaluation process between member and group, both initially and in subsequent negotiations between the member and the group, to maximize mutual gains. Depending on the outcome of those negotiation processes, a group member goes through different stages, from a *prospective member* before acceptance into the group, to a *new member*, to a *full member*, if the person has negotiated his or her role in the group. If the role negotiation fails, or if needs or circumstances change, the group member may become *marginal* and a resocialization process begins. Resocialization has two possible outcomes: either the member regains status as a full member or group membership terminates, which makes the person an *exmember*.

The transition between different statuses of group membership depends on meeting the respective evaluation criteria of both parties. For group entrance, the entry criteria have to be met; the transition from new to full membership is done if the *acceptance* criteria are met. If the mutual commitment falls below the *divergence* criteria, transition from full to marginal member occurs.

There is a logical sequence of the different socialization steps, but there can be recycling between full and marginal member status. The pace of role transitions, however, is dependent on many factors, and may occur at different paces for different members. Moreland and Levine see a mutual influence of group member socialization and group development. Acceptance of new members, socialization, resocialization, and even the remembrance of exmembers may affect group development. Depending on the developmental stage of the group, the different socialization stages may be omitted or altered. The Moreland and Levine model puts emphasis on the interplay between the individual group members and group development. As with Worchel's model, Moreland and Levine recognize that the group's development and the members' socialization both may differ as a function of what the group is experiencing in its own operations and in relation to its embedding systems (i.e., its own "learning" and adaptation processes).

Concluding Comment About Stages of Group Development

The more fully developed of these formulations—in particular, those of Wheelan, Worchel, and Moreland and Levine—begin to address many of the more complex temporal issues posed earlier in this chapter. They all embrace the idea that groups do change over time and in many respects. They offer some formulations about different kinds of stages or phases of group activity. They generally do not posit that a given set of phases occurs in a fixed order and temporal pattern for all groups. Rather, they recognize a set of phases that is more or less inherent in the formation and development of social systems and propose that the particular phases exhibited, and their specific sequence, depends on several factors: (a) what the group is doing (i.e., its tasks or projects), (b) its initial conditions (including the pattern of characteristics of members), (c) its own past history (including early successes and failures), (d) its anticipated future (including whether or not its actions now will have important consequences for its members in later situations), and (e) actual and anticipated events in the group's embedding system.

It is clear from the preceding section that the theoretical ideas about developmental processes in groups have become much more sophisticated with regard to how they deal with the array of temporal issues listed earlier. The empirical evidence assessing these more complex notions about group development, on the other hand, has been scarce. There are good reasons for this. These temporal issues are difficult and costly to examine. That is especially so given social psychology's strong preference for a research paradigm that gives privileged status to experimental studies that generate quantitative data and analyze it using inferential statistics. That paradigm encourages researchers to work with short-term designs that treat the systems under study as static entities; tend to emphasize only directional, linear, and efficient causal forms; and isolate the systems under study from their embedding contexts. Some of these methodological issues are discussed in chapter 8. If these temporal issues are important to our understanding of group development as well as many other social psychological phenomena, as we have been arguing throughout this book, then it seems clear that we need to think anew about how we can go about examining empirically what happens in groups over time. Some ideas toward this end are discussed in chapter 9.

GROUP DEVELOPMENT IN
COMPLEX ACTION SYSTEM THEORY

In some recent publications, we have attempted to offer an alternative view that treats groups as complex, adaptive, dynamic systems. Arrow, McGrath, and Berdahl, (2000) have offered a complex systems view of small groups (see also McGrath & Argote, 2000). McGrath and Tschan (in press) have extended that theoretical view by combining it with some elements from Action Theory as applied to groups (Cranach, 1996; Tschan & Cranach, 1996). McGrath and Tschan (in press) refer to their extended conceptualization as Complex Action Systems Theory (CAST), and we will use that acronym here. Those formulations offer a different perspective on some of these temporal issues regarding group development. To articulate that perspective, though, requires that we present an overview of the fundamental ideas of CAST. That is the focus of the present section of the chapter (see Arrow et al., 2000, for a more detailed presentation).

In CAST, groups are regarded as complex, adaptive, dynamic systems. They are open systems that are interdependent both with the smaller systems that are contained within them (e.g., individual members) and the larger systems within which they are embedded (e.g., organizations, communities). They attempt to fulfill several intrinsic functions: achieving group goals (expressed in the form of completing group projects), fulfilling member needs, and functioning so as to maintain and enhance the integrity of the group as a system.

Groups reflect three levels of causal processes that operate continuously and simultaneously throughout the group's life. Those causal processes are referred to as local, global, and contextual dynamics. *Local dynamics* refer to the complex interdependencies among members, projects, technology, and features of the embedding contexts, as they play out over time. *Global dynamics* refer to system-level processes that emerge from, and subsequently shape and constrain, the operation of local dynamics. *Contextual dynamics* refer to the complex interplay between events in the group's embedding contexts and the system's responses to those events.

In CAST, the developmental history of a group is to be reckoned in terms of a matrix of three modes of a group's life course and the three levels of causal dynamics discussed previously. The three time-ordered modes of a group's life course are formation, operations, and metamorphosis. That is, groups form, they do what they do, and at some point they may cease to exist or get transformed into a recognizably different system.

Groups encompass three kinds of elements: (a) *people*, who become the group's *members*; (b) *intentions*, which get transformed into group *projects* (with tasks and subtasks) and member *needs*; and (c) *resources*, which get transformed into *technology* or a set of *tools* (which include both tangible physical objects and "software" such as norms, procedures, and rules) by which the members can do the tasks involved in the group's projects. Group members differ in myriad ways, both in what they bring to the group (their task, process, and interpersonal skills; attitudes and values; and their personality, cognitive, and behavioral styles), and in what they want from the group (i.e., member needs for achievement, affiliation, power, and material resources). Projects differ in terms of the extent to which they require task, process, and interpersonal skills for their accomplishment, and the extent to which they involve different instrumental functions (such as information processing, conflict management, or coordinated action). Tools differ in terms of the extent to which they afford or constrain the execution of task, process, and interpersonal activities and the pursuit of various instrumental functions.

As a group forms, it develops a rudimentary pattern of relations among those elements: a *coordination network* that is a pattern of member–task–tool relations. This pattern becomes more richly articulated in the operations mode when the group undertakes the execution of particular projects. The pattern becomes specified as a member–task–tool–time process structure. That structure gets modified as action unfolds. This facet of the theory is talked about in much more detail in chapter 7. From the point of view of complex action system theory, a group's structure is a complex set of relations that derives from, or emerges out of, its action. These structures, in turn, guide and constrain subsequent action. In this view, group development—both potential and actual—depends on what kinds of projects that group is going to do, as well as on which members are a part of it and what technologies are in use. From the point of view of CAST, there is no such thing as a generic and ordered set of developmental stages except for the quite abstract three modes: formation, operations, and metamorphosis.

Different groups are formed with more or less emphasis on the different constituent parts: members, projects, and technology. One type of group that is very prevalent in organizations and in studies of groups in organizations is what complex systems theory calls *task forces*. Here, the main emphasis is on a single project that is the central purpose for which the group was created, and on the member–task relations or labor network by which that project will be done. Another type of group is one that complex systems theory calls *teams*. Here the emphasis is on membership and on the member–tool relations or role network. A third type is a *crew*. Here, the technology and the task–tool relations or job network are most important. All three types are very prevalent in work organizations, although many groupings that are called teams are actually task forces or crews.

Because of their different developmental histories (i.e., which constituent elements and subnetworks are developed earliest and given most emphasis), these different types of work groups are differentially vulnerable to different kinds of change. Task forces are most vulnerable to a change in project. Teams are most vulnerable to a change in membership. Crews are most vulnerable to a change in technology.

As we noted in the preceding section, there has been little empirical study of these temporal issues in part because it is difficult to do so in terms of our dominant research paradigm. The complex systems formulation shifts researchers' attention to an alternative logic of inquiry. The essential logic of inquiry of our dominant research paradigm is to attempt to predict (average) levels of particular process or outcome variables from knowledge of levels of one or more input conditions or from imposed experimental treatments. In CAST theory terms, these amount to predictions of interdependencies among local variables.

Instead, complex systems theory invites the researcher to trace the trajectory or pattern of evolution of important global (i.e., system level) variables over time. Within that logic of inquiry, the idea of stages of development takes on a new meaning. CAST would not regard different kinds of system activity (e.g., Tuckman's forming, norming, etc.; or Wheelan's dependency, pairing, trust, and so on) as successive stages of the group's development. Rather, complex systems theory would suggest that each of those kinds of activity—pairing, trust, work, or whatever—be regarded as a global variable reflecting a feature of the system, and that we should trace the pattern of each of those global variables over time. Following that view, we would likely find that each of those global variables waxes and wanes at different times, that some of them are likely to wax and wane and wax again (that is, they are cyclical, or at least not "single-peaked"). Moreover, we would likely find that, in any given group, some of them may not wax at all during a given period of observation. In this view, we would regard each kind of activity as a meaningful process in itself, not as a phase or stage. We could distinguish groups with different temporal patterns for the waxing and waning of different kinds of activity—that is, different processes. We could then ask what conditions distinguish groups with different temporal patterns from one another, without positing a single fixed set of stages for all groups, much less imposing a normative idea of the "correct" sequence of development. That is, we could regard such different kinds of activities as reflecting multiple, continuous, parallel processes, each with a cyclical temporal pattern that may have different time courses and cadences. This potential revision of our logic of inquiry will be discussed in more detail in chapter 9.

The CAST interpretation of groups offers a different picture of the idea of group development, as well as a different conceptual paradigm for inquiry into those temporal processes. We will use that CAST viewpoint in the rest of this chapter and the next. The sections to follow examine temporal aspects of change processes that arise from forces other than the group's own development. Then, chapter 7 examines temporal processes involved when people attempt to engage in collective action, including group task performance.

ADAPTATION TO CHANGE IN EMBEDDING CONTEXTS

Both adaptational processes and learning processes are also eminently temporal. The relation between developmental and adaptational processes is like the relation between inside and outside forces for change. Group development, as commonly conceived, is driven by intrinsic or internal forces that derive from the particular group's constituent parts and their patterning (i.e., their local dynamics). Development results in and is the product of the group's own structure and processes. In contrast, adaptation is driven by actions and events in the group's various embedding contexts. Adaptation refers to changes both in the group as a system and in parts of its embedding contexts, that arise in response to various actual and anticipated actions and events in the embedding systems that will or may affect the group. Adaptation carries the implication of "response to change." It does not necessarily carry the implication of "effective response." Adaptation is the topic of this section of this chapter. Experiential processes, which we will discuss in a subsequent section, are a combination of the two. They arise out of the group's own experience, which includes both its own activities and events and conditions that impinge on it.

Though most social and organizational psychologists would probably accept the assertion that groups carry on continuous, multifaceted interchanges with aspects of their embedding contexts, nevertheless relatively little theory or empirical research explores how embedding environments affect groups as systems and how those groups respond. Notable exceptions include work by Ancona and colleagues (e.g., Ancona & Caldwell, 1988, 1990) and by Hackman and colleagues (e.g., Allmendinger & Hackman, 1996; Gersick & Hackman, 1990; Hackman, 1990, 1999, 2002). There is also a recent volume on groups in context (Wageman, 1999), many chapters of which deal with temporal features of adaptational processes in groups. There is also an extensive theoretical treatment of these issues in Arrow, McGrath, and Berdahl (2000), McGrath and Argote (2000), and McGrath and Tschan (in press), all reflecting the complex systems theory orientation offered here. We will draw heavily on those presentations.

Complex systems theory proposes that groups operate in a *fitness landscape*. Some "locations" (i.e., states) of the group in relation to its external contexts are better for the group than others—they have better payoffs for the group and its members or they have lower costs. For example, a work group or organization is in a better location in its fitness landscape if it makes a product for which there is a high demand but few or no competitors, than if it deals in a product for which there is either low demand or an oversupply. Any event in the external contexts, or in the group, has the potential for altering the group's location in that fitness landscape. Changes in the group's relation to its external contexts are sometimes advantageous to the group and sometimes detrimental.

Types of Change Events

Change events come in various forms. First of all, changes may be intrusive or nonintrusive. Nonintrusive changes simply change the environment, with no direct impact on the group—they change the fitness landscape that the group is operating in. An example would be that another group introduces a competing product. Intrusive changes are ones that have a direct impact on the group itself; for example, a manager might reassign a key group member to another group.

Change events also differ in their magnitude and valence. Some changes are large, some small. Some changes pose threats to the group, some offer potential opportunities, and some do both. Embedding contexts vary in richness (potential resources) and volatility (that is, in their rate and temporal patterning of change). Change events themselves have several temporal properties (a number of these were discussed in chapter 5, in the context of stress and coping processes). They vary in abruptness and predictability of onset and in rate and frequency. They also vary in temporal patterning of various kinds (see definitions of temporal parameters in Appendix A). A series of changes all of the same kind and in the same direction represents a trend, and its course is relatively predictable. Alternatively, a set of changes may collectively constitute a cycle. It begins at some state, changes to other states, and eventually returns to its original state. As still another possibility, a set of changes can vary in an apparently random way, constituting "fluctuation" in no discernable pattern.

As previously noted, change events vary in predictability, and they may also vary in controllability. Events that are both predictable and controllable can be prevented or, if they are favorable, can be induced to occur at the time and circumstances of the group's choosing. On the other hand, changes that are unpredictable or uncontrollable may pose potential problems for the group.

Time-Shifting of Responses to Change

Groups often can anticipate how the context is likely to change and *time-shift* their response to those anticipated change events, placing the response *before* the actual event to which it is a reaction. In contrast, groups sometimes do not respond to environmental changes until some time after the changes have occurred, either because it takes time for the effects to be recognized or because it takes time for the group to muster the resources needed to produce a useful response. Such time-shifts thus may place the responses to the events either well before or long after the change events themselves.

The five temporal zones for coping responses to potentially stressful events described in chapter 5 also apply for coping responses of groups (McGrath & Beehr, 1990). Whereas for negative events these responses are reasonably called "forms of coping," the temporal zones can also be applied for positive events. Here, they would reflect different timing in the pursuit of opportunities.

Coping or opportunity responses can take place before or after the change event occurs:

1. Preventive responses describe actions taken long before the change event (e.g., building a dam to prevent flooding).
2. Anticipatory responses are actions taken just before an event occurs (e.g., putting sandbags to reinforce existing dams before the rising water has actually reached the region).
3. Dynamic responses are simultaneous with the ongoing event (e.g., while the water is rising, adding more layers of sandbags in front of the doors to minimize flooding of the basement).
4. Reactive responses are actions taken immediately after the event (e.g., pumping out water from basements).
5. Residual responses are actions taken long after the event is over (e.g., rebuilding and repairing buildings that have been damaged by the flood).

Preventive and anticipatory timing of response may try to prevent the event, but more often they are attempts to minimize its consequences. The building of a levee along a riverbank does not prevent some later rise in the level of the water in the river, but rather prevents or attenuates the negative consequences of that high water for land beside the river. Reactive and residual coping often occur as reaction to multiple occurrences of a given kind of event, or to occurrences of multiple events; hence it is often difficult to assign specific antecedent events to specific responses with precision. Some of the methodological implications of such time-shifted responses are discussed in chapter 8.

Types of Adaptation to Change Events

Relations between external events and the system's responses to them can be very complex. There is a range of potential patterns of response to external events and actions, including accommodation to them, attempts to assimilate the changes or attenuate their effects, and doing nothing, which is sometimes both a deliberate and a wise strategy (Heckhausen, 1991). Moreover, there is often a nonproportional relation between amount and type of change event and the size and direction of subsequent change in the group. Sometimes big events yield small changes or none at all; sometimes small events yield big changes. Furthermore, changes lead to unintended consequences as well as to (or instead of) intended ones.

The adaptation process can be *directed* or *undirected*. Undirected adaptation is like species evolution; it is a cycle of *variation* (in system structure, in system behavior, or in conditions in the environment), *selection* (of a particular pattern of response), and *stabilization* (retention). Directed adaptation is intentional action on the part of the system; it is a cycle of *information processing* (about the system, its environment, and their relations), *planning*, *choice*, and *self-regulation*. We will discuss these processes in detail in the next chapter, in the context of groups carrying out collective action.

There are some barriers to both kinds of adaptation. For example, a fluctuating and unpredictable environment is not conducive to either directed or undirected adaptation. Nor are conflicting motive situations in which there is a disparity between what is good for individuals or parts of a system and what is good for the system as a whole. Undirected adaptation is also hindered by conditions in which there is too little variation in the environment, or if the environment is too forgiving. Undirected adaptations may fail to take hold under conditions in which it is difficult to maintain or stabilize the new form. Directed adaptation will be hindered if there is a misunderstanding or erroneous prediction of the state of the environment (that is, if the group's mental model of the fitness landscape is inaccurate). It will also work poorly if the group fails to achieve a coordination of interest or of understandings, hence fails to agree on a strategy, or if they cannot effectively coordinate actions needed to produce the intended changes. The group also may be unable to keep on track after setbacks, and there may be explicit or tacit resistance to the changes by entrenched routines or factions.

The last several examples suggest that factors internal to the group also affect the group's ability to adapt. In addition to the nature and patterning of the contextual changes, adaptation also depends on what type of group it is, on the state of the system at the time of the event (i.e., the group's current structure and functioning), on its "legacy of the past" (its history, including its entrenched routines and its record of past actions and effects), and on its envisioned future.

As noted earlier in this chapter, different types of groups (such as teams, task forces, and crews) are differentially vulnerable to different types of changes. Moreover, different types of groups may show different *change models*. For example, crews may fit a crisis adaptation model in which one pattern holds for all normal operations, and a different structure and process "kicks in" when there is an emergency (e.g., the crew staffing a hospital emergency room when a major disaster occurs nearby). Task forces often may fit a punctuated equilibrium model, as did Gersick's (1988, 1989) groups: that is, groups begin work with a pattern of structure and process and, when they reach a point at which they conclude that the group is not working effectively, revamp their patterns of action drastically. Only certain types of teams, which are organized with the expectation of persisting for considerable time and of carrying out multiple projects, may fit the kind of developmental stage model that is the most prevalent one used in research on group development (see earlier discussion).

From a systems-process point of view, there are three general forms of responses to such external contextual actions or events:

1. *Negative feedback loops.* These are system responses that attempt to attenuate or eliminate the impact of the change on the system, restoring the system to its preevent status.
2. *Positive feedback loops.* These are system responses that magnify the impact of the change on the system. This can be in the form of (a) switching (before, during, or after the event) to alternative structures or functions; (b) increased disorder beyond what is directly produced by the change event itself; and (c) if the increased disorder is extreme enough, either creative innovation or collapse.
3. *No response.* The system may give no apparent response to a given event. This may occur because (a) the group failed to note the event, or assumed it would not alter the group's fitness landscape; (b) some feature of the group's history, its self-regulatory processes, or its routines prevented or impeded an effective coping response; or (c) an apparent "no response" may be an artifact of the observation process because the response was time-shifted. An observer may, erroneously, assume the system made no response to a given event because the system's response to the event was time-shifted to a point in time either before or after that observer looked at the group.

Negative feedback dampens the impact of events. Positive feedback magnifies the impact. Time-shifting obscures the impact. Hence, we should not expect to find the impact of events on the system to be isomorphic, in either valence or magnitude, with the valence and magnitude of the event.

This discussion implies several "principles" of adaptation that are worth noting:

1. There is no reason to expect strong proportionality between magnitude of change events and of responses to them.

2. Temporal displacement can obscure the fact of, and the nature of, adaptive changes.
3. Responses to change events often have unintended consequences, both desirable and undesirable.

Moreover, we need to keep in mind that all changes are not adaptations. Some are spontaneous innovations by the group. In human systems, new patterns of action may occur that are not traceable to any particular event in the system's embedding contexts, but rather reflect the intentionality of the system, or of its embedded members.

EXPERIENCE AND CHANGE IN GROUPS

It is clear that groups change as a function of many kinds of forces. We have talked about two sets of these: developmental forces internal to the group and adaptational forces in response to external events. A group's own experience encompasses both of these and more. A group's experience encompasses its own initial and subsequent states, the oft-changing states of its embedding contexts, and its own activities and their consequences. A group changes as a function of all of these forces. In this section we will discuss some additional temporal aspects, arising from the group's own history and from its own experience (i.e., its "learning").

Group History and Anticipated Future

At any given point in time, a group's current structure and actions are partly shaped and constrained by the particulars of its own past history and by its anticipated future as a group. Each group has its own particular history. This includes what complexity theory might refer to as *initial conditions*: for example, the background and attributes of its charter members, key events early in its existence that had important effects on the group's structure and subsequent actions, past additions and losses of members, critical member–member interactions in its early stages, and so on. Sometimes the group's early successes or failures have enormous effects in shaping both the group member's own perceptions of the group and the reputation that group gains in the eyes of persons external to it (e.g., see Cohen & Denison, 1990).

Each group also has, often from its inception, some anticipated life span. The relation of the group to its own past and future varies for groups of different types. For the type of group we call the *task force*, its life span consists of the duration of the project that is its main reason for being. Often task force assignments carry with them a deadline as well. Therefore task forces know in advance how long they will continue to exist and function as a group. Such groups are always working in the context of "time passed so far" or "time remaining" for their mission. Gersick (1988, 1989) found that every one of the task force type work groups in her studies—some lab groups and some in field settings—underwent a dramatic shift in its structures and procedures at a time corresponding to the midpoint of its expected life course, even though for some of those groups this "half-life" was only a few hours and for others it was weeks or months.

For another type of group that we call *teams*, members can reasonably anticipate that the group will continue in operation for an extended period of time with the same membership and with recurrent projects of the same type. With such an extended time horizon, such groups can afford to invest time and effort in training members in their tasks and roles, and in cross-training members in each others' tasks and roles. Over time, teams develop an extended and richly articulated group history, which provides the group structure and part of the context within which their current actions take place. Their emphasis on having continuing membership makes such groups especially vulnerable to loss of a member, but the cross-training of members provides them with a basis for overcoming the effects of such loss.

A third type of group, which CAST calls crews, has yet another type of temporal history and expectation. A crew consists of a job setting in which there is a tight coupling between tasks and technology, such that each member is assigned to a job or position (i.e., a task–technology "slot"). Members may or may not have worked together before, and may or may not know each other. Each is drawn from a pool of persons qualified for that job slot (e.g., operating room nurses, surgeons, and anesthesiologists for an operating room crew; or pilot, copilot, flight engineer for a commercial airline flight). That crew will exist for a particular shift (e.g., a flight from New York to Los Angeles and return). So it has little history as a group and a very prescribed anticipated future. Usually, all members have undergone extensive training to prepare for carrying out the particular job to which they are assigned, with that job consisting of a tightly coupled set of tasks and tools. As a consequence, for example, even an experienced pilot has to retrain to be eligible to fly a different type of aircraft. Thus, individual crew members often have an extensive history and an extended anticipated future (a career path) with regard to their jobs, although the group itself has no history and a sharply delimited anticipated future. This lack of common history can hinder crew performance (Hackman, 1993, 2002).

Thus, different types of groups have different relations to their own pasts and futures, and these affect how group members perceive one another and the group and how they carry out group projects and fulfill their own and fellow member's needs. It also affects the extent to which they attend to—and the very meaning of—continued functioning of the group as an intact system.

Although there has been some study of the effects of a group's past and anticipated future, as indicated in some of the works cited in the preceding paragraphs, this area, too, is also one within which we could gain much in our understanding of groups from further study of temporal patterning and its effects.

Group Learning

As groups continue their lives, while changing as a function of their own developmental processes and of changes in the embedding contexts, they also undergo change as a function of their own experience. Like individuals, groups learn from their own experience. Argote and colleagues (Argote, Gruenfeld, & Naquin, 1996) define group learning as the process through which members acquire, share, and combine knowledge into a collective product through experience working together. Group learning manifests itself through changes in group knowledge or performance.

Groups learn what actions work and which ones don't work to accomplish group purposes. They learn which members have what skills and thus what tasks should be assigned to them. They learn what tools will effectively do what tasks, and which members have the skills to use those tools. They learn which members can work together most effectively, and which cannot, and hence what patterns of member–task assignments will be most productive. Learning implies a relatively permanent change in some aspects of group structure or functioning. That is, the change that results from group learning must be retained somewhere, in some repository.

CAST theory, which we discussed earlier, refers to the group's structure and functioning in terms of a coordination network. That coordination network consists of the patterned sets of relations among the group's constituent parts: its members, the tasks by which it will carry out group projects, and the tools (both hardware and software) that make up the group's technology, by which it will do those tasks. That coordination network encompasses six subnetworks, namely a network of member–member relations; a network of task–task relations; a network of tool–tool relations; a network of member–task relations, often referred to as a division of labor; a network of member–tool relations that CAST refers to as a role network; and a network of task–tool relations that CAST refers to as a job network.

Viewed in these terms, we can propose that there are six "locations" that can serve as repositories for group learning: (a) some or all of the members themselves and the pattern of member–member relations; (b) some or all of the tasks that make up the group's projects, and the task–task relations; (c) some or all of the tools that make up the group's technology, and the tool–tool relations; (d) some parts of the network of member–task relations; (e) some parts of the network of member–tool relations; and (f) some parts of the network of task–tool relations. Those six locations differ considerably in terms of their feasibility and limitations as repositories of group learning (see McGrath & Argote, 2000, for a review of these issues).

Group learning can be triggered and supported by internal processes, but groups also learn from information outside of the group; that is, there is transfer of learning between groups (Argote, 1999; Levitt & March, 1988). However, how much groups learn from the outside depends on the relationships they have with those outside sources of knowledge. Darr, Argote, and Epple (1995) analyzed the progress of learning in pizza stores franchised from the same corporation but owned by different franchise managers. Learning over time could be found in all stores. Often a new procedure was suggested by an individual and then established in a group. Thus, knowledge transfer from the individual to the group level occurred. Groups also learned from each other: Pizza stores often adopted new techniques from other stores that had already established them. However, knowledge transfer was more apt to occur between stores owned by the same franchisees than across stores with different owners, indicating that better information exchange and a relational network facilitates such learning.

Groups learn at different rates, even if they work at similar tasks under similar conditions. Pisano, Bohmer, and Edmondson (2001) analyzed how well and how fast groups in hospitals learned a new operation procedure and found large differences between the groups studied.

Group learning is eminently temporal in several senses. First, it takes place over time. Second, the state of the group at a given time is partly dependent on its own actions at earlier times. Third, learning is cumulative. Fourth, part of the learning process involves aspects of its imagined future as well as of the experienced past. Learning is enhanced by expected future rewards as well as by obtained past reinforcements. That is, the group attempts to retain changes that it *expects* to be beneficial to its future actions.

Groups learn, but groups can also forget. Darr and colleagues (1995) showed depreciation of knowledge in groups. The rate of depreciation in the pizza stores was very fast, so the groups had to work continually to replenish the stock of knowledge. The rate of forgetting in groups seems to be dependent on how much of the knowledge is embedded in the technology as compared to knowledge that is held by people. Groups in production work settings seem to forget less than groups in service settings.

Assuming that groups do in fact make use of all six of the repositories noted earlier to retain beneficial changes, then over time all aspects of a group's basic structure—its coordination network—will change. There will be changes in members, in tasks, in tools, in division of labor, role network, and job network, as a function of the group's own experience. Such changes are conceptually distinguishable from—although they are operationally intertwined with—changes that arise from developmental forces and changes that arise from changing contextual conditions, both discussed earlier. Changes due to learning are also related to, but distinguishable from, the dynamics involved in group action itself (i.e., operational processes), which will be the topic of the next chapter.

CONCLUDING COMMENTS REGARDING
TIME, GROUPS, AND CHANGE

This chapter has discussed some of the temporal factors in group formation and development and change arising from adaptation and experience. Each of those kinds of processes in groups encompasses several temporal issues. We have presented this material mostly within a theoretical frame that treats groups as complex, dynamic, contextually embedded systems. We did so because it is a framework that highlights the importance of temporal issues.

We have been concerned with temporal features of groups as a particular—and ubiquitous—kind of intact system or entity. In the next chapter, we turn to a discussion of some additional temporal issues that arise when groups attempt to take collective action.

AFTERTHOUGHTS

As Time Goes By

We must remember this:
Groups live, not just exist,
    Their needs must satisfy!
And groups will always
    seem to change
As time goes by!

New projects they will face,
Some learning will take place:
    On that we can rely.
And groups will always
    welcome change
As time goes by!

Process and structure
    never stay the same;
Each member learns to
    play a different game;
And all the while
    They one another tame
And habits routinize!

It makes our task demanding
Our quest for understanding
    Of how groups run and why!
Cause groups will always
    seem to change
As time goes by!

Group Types

Groups that were, and will be later,
Behave, alas, group goals to fit.
But groups that have no past or future
Hardly ever give a whit!

Task force groups with single mission
Never really play the game,
Each guy thinking how to profit
Other groups from whence he came.

Crews can use their well-trained skills
To do the job when things go smooth.
But if they've never worked together,
When hell breaks loose they're apt to lose.

Teams are often quite effective,
Synchronized, can work quite nice.
But training teamwork's damned expensive:
Not everyone will pay that price!

Groups who have envisioned futures
Behave much more with goals in view.
But ad hoc groups, no future pending,
Care less, by far, 'bout what they do.

7

TIME AND
COLLECTIVE ACTION

In the previous chapter we dealt with temporal matters as they play out in formation, development, and change in groups regarded as complex, intact systems. In this chapter, we will examine temporal issues in the operation of groups as they carry out their projects. We will first lay out some temporal issues that are inherent in all collective action, and then use those issues to structure a discussion of task performance in groups. This discussion deals with three levels of group action, which derive both from the inherent temporal issues and from our conceptualization of groups as complex action systems. These three levels are strategic planning, operational planning, and execution. They are the topics of the three main sections of this chapter. These sections are followed by a discussion of synchronization and entrainment. The chapter closes with a discussion of an issue parallel to the stages of development issue discussed earlier: Do groups have a characteristic sequence of phases in their task performance activities?

THREE TEMPORAL ISSUES
INHERENT IN COLLECTIVE ACTION

If people set out to carry out some actions collectively, they need to somehow reckon with several inherent problems, each of which has a key temporal aspect:

1. The inherent scarcity of resources, including temporal resources.
2. The inherent ambiguity or uncertainty about future actions and events, including uncertainly about the *when*, *if*, and *what* of them.
3. The potential for multiple conflicting interests on the part of different individuals and of the collective, including temporally conflicting interests.

From the point of view of both the collective and its individual members, these three inherent problems bring with them particular kinds of requirements for resolving them. The first of these, the inherent scarcity of time and other resources, brings the need for setting priorities. This in turn brings the need for strategic planning, including the selection and acceptance of collective goals or purposes and the allocation of resources to their attainment. The second problem, the inherent uncertainty about future events and actions, brings the need for predictability, and thus for operational planning, including the scheduling of the *who*, *what*, *how*, and *when* of various activities required for attainment of those goals. The third problem, the potential for conflicting demands, brings the need for *coordination*, hence for the *synchronization* both of multiple actions by a given individual and of actions by multiple members of the collectivity.

Note also that although allocation, scheduling, and synchronization are all temporal matters, they make use of different time-reckoning systems. Allocation is typically done in terms of amounts of "staff time" that will be devoted to the particular projects under consideration. This represents time in terms of a portion of the temporal resources available to the collectivity within some larger chunk of time. Scheduling, on the other hand, is usually done with respect to a clock and calendar system, a time-reckoning system whose reference is external to the collectivity. Synchronization and coordination of action have to do with when specific actions will take place with respect to each other, reckoned in terms of an internal or collectivity-defined time. That is not to say that one cannot use the terms of a general clock and calendar time-reckoning system—days, hours, and minutes—to represent allocated time and synchronization signals. Rather, it is that those times—the durations involved in allocation, and the sequences and timing intervals involved in synchronization—refer to time parameters of system operation, not to time as located in relation to Greenwich Mean Time or the Gregorian calendar.

Those three inherent problems thus are dealt with in three interrelated arenas: strategic planning and allocation, operational planning and scheduling, and coordination and execution. In earlier publications (McGrath &Tschan, in press) we have used a similar set of three domains, regarded as three hierarchical levels involved in group task performance. We will elaborate that conceptualization here, and then discuss each of the arenas, or levels, in more detail.

A COMPLEX ACTION SYSTEM THEORY
INTERPRETATION OF THE DYNAMICS
OF COORDINATION AND TASK PERFORMANCE

Complex Action System Theory (CAST; McGrath & Tschan, in press) argues that group action on complex projects is hierarchically and sequentially organized. It posits that group action entails three levels of hierarchy that we call *purpose*, *planning*, and *performance* levels.

The most macro level is the purpose or project level. It consists of the selection, acceptance, and modification of the group's projects and the allocation of resources, including a general period of time and a complement of members and tools that will be devoted to its fulfillment. The purpose level is knowledge- and intention-based: that is, it is driven by members' intentions, preferences, and information. In the present context, we will call it a *strategic planning* level.

The middle level is the level of *operational planning*. It is the structuring of the process by which the group will carry out its projects. It involves a hierarchical, sequential, referential, and technical structuring. That is, it specifies *what* will be done, *when*, by *whom*, and *how* (i.e., with what tools and procedures). In complex system theory terms (Arrow et al., 2000), it involves the establishment of a member–task–tool–time network of relations. Action Theory (Frese & Zapf, 1994; Tschan & Cranach, 1996) calls this level "rule-based," but CAST (McGrath & Tschan, in press) expands that notion to say that it is "lore- and logic-based." It is founded on logic in the sense that planning draws on rules, reasoning, and well-formulated procedures. It is founded on lore in the sense that the structuring of action often has a basis in the traditions (how we have always done it!) either of that group or of groups to which its members have previously belonged.

The third level is the level of *performance* or action. This consists of a series of interrelated orient–enact–monitor–modify cycles (see discussion in chapter 4). This third, microlevel is action-based, but that includes cognitive and verbal actions as well as motoric action.

If the monitoring shows that specific actions had the desired results for a particular task or subtask, then no modification is needed. If monitoring shows that the action did not get the desired results for that task or subtask, then a modification is called for in the enacting part of that recurrent cycle. The modifing part of each cycle looks first of all to the action itself: that is, at the lowest level of the hierarchy. If modifying the action does not correct the problem, then the modification process is directed at the planning level—a change in the structuring of the process. If that is also insufficient to deliver the intended results, then the modification process may be directed at the project or purpose level. Thus, these recurrent orient–enact–monitor–modify cycles at the micro or action level potentially can cascade upward to the higher levels of this hierarchical array (i.e., to operational planning or strategic planning levels).

As noted in the previous discussion, those three arenas are both hierarchical and partially nested. Each sets the boundaries of and guidelines for the next one downward in the hierarchy. Strategic planning and allocation sets the boundaries and guidelines for operational planning and scheduling, which in turn provides the boundaries and guidelines for execution and coordination of action. Moreover, if the recurring orient–enact–monitor–modify cycles of execution indicate that the enacted action did not attain its intended result, modifications are made in the reverse order: First is a modification in the action; if that fails, then a modification may be made in the operational plan; and if that fails, then a modification may be made in the strategic plan (i.e., in goals, projects, or overall allocation of resources). We will discuss each of those three levels of action in the next three sections. Then we will discuss the idea of entrainment, and the issues involved in the idea of a specific or ideal problem-solving phase sequence, and present a CAST interpretation of those issues.

Time and Strategic Planning: Choosing Goals and Allocating Resources

At the purpose or strategic planning level, the group translates its intentions into the formulation of a group project, and an overall allocation of its resources (tools, member time, and effort) to carry out that project. In effect, the group selects, accepts, generates, and modifies one or more potential projects that it intends to undertake within a given time frame. The group also needs to select, acquire, and modify members and tools that will be allocated to various parts of its projects.

The choice of projects and the allocation of resources depend heavily on how the group is initially formed. In complex systems theory terms (Arrow et al., 2000), some groups form primarily on the basis of "top down" or directive forces, either internal to or external to that group. Other groups form mainly on the basis of "bottom up" emergent forces (self-organizing groups) or on external conditions (circumstantial groups).

For the most part, *work groups* in organizations are deliberately formed, top down, by someone sufficiently powerful to reallocate people, time, and other resources to form the new group for specific purposes (Argote & McGrath, 1993). Those purposes are translated into projects that provide the rationale for that group's formation and existence. The group itself thus may have its major projects imposed upon it. Such groups are likely to spend little or no time choosing a project, and time limits for project fulfillment may also be externally imposed. The group may, however, redefine imposed projects and adapt them to its capabilities and needs (Hackman, 1986). The group will still need to give attention to acquiring (or modifying) the members and resources necessary for carrying out any given project, as well as to the coordination it will need for interweaving the execution of multiple projects that it might want to pursue simultaneously.

Self-organizing groups, on the other hand, face a wide array of potential purposes and projects that they might pursue. Their purposes and projects emerge during the course of group formation, and selection and modification of those projects will likely command a lot of explicit attention.

Circumstantial groups are groups that emerge out of unexpected circumstances: for example, a group of tourist speleologists surprised in a cave by rising waters. In this case, specific circumstances impose the project and sometimes also the time resources available.

Whether group projects are assigned or emergent, the allocation and often the very acquisition of appropriate resources for project fulfillment is almost always a crucial problem that requires time and attention by the group. They must get an appropriate number of group members with appropriate attributes (knowledge, skills, and abilities; values, beliefs, and attitudes; and personality, cognitive, and behavioral styles). They also must get an appropriate set of tools (both hardware and software) that are adequate for project accomplishment and that are within the capabilities of members, and must allocate a sufficient portion of members' time to the project.

Strategic planning, allocation, and resource acquisition activities of groups often involve interactions between the group and various agents in the group's embedding systems. Little research is available on these issues (for exceptions, see work by Ancona & Caldwell, 1988, 1990; Ancona & Chong, 1996; Lacey & Gruenfeld, 1999). Past research in social and organizational psychology, even when dealing with extant work groups in organizational settings, has generally neglected the investigation of transactions across that group-organizational boundary, including those involving resource acquisition. Moreover, laboratory-experimental research on groups has, for the most part, tacitly assumed that available resources, as well as assigned projects and members, are "givens" for any particular group. Consequently, the processes by which groups choose or refine projects—when they do—and the processes by which they acquire and allocate resources of various kinds, are areas requiring focussed research attention in the future.

The timing of such acquisitions and refinements of resources may be crucial to the group's ability to launch its projects effectively and in a timely fashion.

Time and Operational Planning:
Structuring and Scheduling the Work Process

Structuring the Work Process

When the group has fixed on a project, and a general allocation of resources for its accomplishment, it then needs to integrate available information into a plan for collective action. That plan must adapt the group's existing coordination network, established during group formation or in pursuit of earlier projects, into one organized for execution of this particular project. That is, the group must somehow distribute tasks, tools, and other resources among group members; pool relevant information; plan timing, sequencing, and coordination of actions; and so forth. This includes operational plans regarding how the group will proceed as well as plans regarding the content of the group's task products (Fisher & Stutman, 1987; Putnam, 1981).

An ideal time for such planning would seem to be at the start of a group's work on a given project. In practice, however, the group may or may not begin by engaging in an explicit discussion about how to proceed and how to establish or modify the role network, division of labor, and job assignments for a given project. Groups often fail to discuss their task-performance plans spontaneously (Hackman & Morris, 1975), and do not often do so at the beginning of their work. Hackman, Brousseau, and Weiss (1977) showed that groups did not plan ahead and organize their work unless they were told to do so. Weingart (1992) found that preplanning rather seldom occurs. If groups are forced to plan at the outset, however, their task performance improves (Larson & Schaumann, 1993; Shure, Rogers, Larsen, & Tassone, 1962), at least if the task is sufficiently complex to require preplanning (Hackman et al., 1977). Indeed, in recent work Hackman (2002) has argued for and presented evidence that the critical time for effective planning in regard to performance strategies is at or near the midpoint of the group's projected work time on a project. And Argote (1999) has argued that the effectiveness of planning at early stages depends on the nature of the embedding contexts. Early planning may be helpful in environments that are stable and foreseeable, but not in fast environments. For example, in an analysis of the speed of innovation of new products in the field of computers, Eisenhardt and Tabrizi (1995) found that a longer phase of advance project planning did make the innovation process slower, contrary to their initial hypothesis. It was more frequent testing using iterative processes that led to faster product development. The so-called simple rules approach in which strategic steps at the beginning of the process are replaced by seizing opportunities, and by jumping into confusion and then learning-by-doing, seems to work best in ambiguous, rapidly changing environments (Eisenhardt & Sull, 2001).

Not all planning is explicit. Whether or not a group deliberately and explicitly plans how it will do its projects, it must somehow structure its patterns of action. When groups do not engage in explicit planning at the outset of project activity, it is often because they are adopting, tacitly, a structure of action already in place from previous group activity or a default structure common to group activity within a given culture. Groups that arise from bottom up or emergent forces often develop structures of activities in an emergent fashion: Structure emerges from actions and then subsequently guides them.

Whether or not groups engage in explicit project planning may be influenced by task characteristics, by the existing member attributes and division of labor and status networks, by the group's experience as it works on the project, or by externally imposed procedures. More *complex projects*, with tasks requiring greater interdependence, need more planning behavior than simpler and less interdependent projects. Lord and Rowzee (1979) showed that interdependence requirements of tasks led to an increase in problem definition, planning, and coordinating or directing behavior by group members. However, groups may not always realize that investments in early planning, which are costly in the short term, will in the long run pay off. Weingart (1992) found a decrease in preplanning activities by groups with a complex versus a simple task. She interprets this as group members wanting to start work immediately rather than "waste time" on planning discussions.

The *existing role network*, division of labor, and other aspects of the group's structure also influence the occurrence of planning behavior. For example, whether or not there is a clear formal leader should make a difference in whether the group engages in planning behavior, because a leader's role is in part to be responsible for planning-level aspects of the group's work. This appears to be the case, even when leaders are assigned by a random procedure, as in Tschan and colleagues' study of computer-supported air-traffic controller groups. Those leaders did indeed assume responsibility for most of the planning discussion of the group (Tschan, Semmer, Nägele, & Gurtner, 2000). Boos and Meier (1993) found that groups working on a very complex decision-making task who had assigned leaders showed a higher density of procedural acts aimed at organizing the group than did groups that had less hierarchic organization.

Planning is also affected by the group's *previously established coordination network*: both what got established through early adoption of routines and what got modified through experience. Groups quickly adopt common task patterns (Bettenhausen & Murnigham, 1985; Gersick, 1988), often tacitly (Wittenbaum & Stasser, 1996). Once a task plan is adopted, there is less need for explicit planning, thus freeing the group's time and efforts for direct task action. This can enhance group efficiency in the short run. However, Gersick and Hackman (1990) point out some potentially dysfunctional consequences of rapid development of such habitual routines, especially if they are not revised or adapted under conditions of either major changes in the task environment, ineffectiveness in progress on the task, or dysfunctions of the group as an intact system.

Some organizations *impose uniform task procedures* on all their groups, and train members to carry out those procedures, even for complex tasks, thus providing detailed operational plans externally. This is especially the case for contexts in which consequences of a mistake are drastic. For example, the members of cockpit crews of commercial airlines are trained to function in very prescribed ways. As a consequence, pilots can minimize the time it takes for mutual adjustment in new crews (Hackman, 1993). Rapid mutual adjustment in crews whose members have not previously worked together, however, is no guarantee of *effective* working together. Hackman (2002) notes that more than 70% of the accidents in the National Transportation Safety Board's database occur in a crew's first day of flying together, with more than 40% of them in the crew's first flight. Kanki and Foushee (1989) found indeed that crews that have flown together made fewer errors than newly composed crews.

Not all planning statements make a difference in group action. They only have an effect if they are properly timed and relevant to the issues with which the group is currently dealing. Premature and irrelevant planning statements are often ignored by the other group members (Fisher & Stutman, 1987). Research on how experts work suggests that they revise their plans periodically, pay attention to and adapt to new knowledge, and engage in deliberate practice efforts (Ericsson & Lehmann, 1996; Sonnentag & Schmidt-Brasse, 1998). West's work on reflexivity suggests that those same tactics should help groups (West, 1996). Even groups composed of highly trained members seem to profit from explicit planning discussions. More successful cockpit crews, studied in simulators by Orasanu (1993, 1994), used low-workload periods for planning discussion. For example, they planned alternate routes or studied landing procedures for alternate airports. In emergency situations, successful crews explicitly discussed plans for problem solution and for team coordination. This indicates that it may be useful for groups to plan even if the task at hand does not, at the very moment, require operational planning. Groups may develop plans to have on hand for later and faster use.

Scheduling as a Match of Times, Activities, and Social Units

Scheduling involves the matching of (a) specific sets of activities to (b) specific periods of time when they are to be done and (c) specific social units (individuals or groups) who are to perform those activities. It is by no means a simple matter to build a feasible schedule for a complex project that involves multiple sets of tasks that must be done in some particular temporal relation to one another, with many of them involving multiple actors in their accomplishment.

Time, as experienced, is epochal rather than homogeneous (see chapter 2, this volume). Therefore, periods of time of the same objective size are not always interchangeable in terms of human activities (McGrath, Kelly, & Machatka, 1984). Some activities are inflexible with respect to time: If they cannot be done at a particular time, they cannot be done at all, or can be done only at a high cost. Similarly, some periods of time are not very versatile in terms of what kinds of activities can be efficiently done in them. Starting a project one hour before closing time compared with starting it an hour after opening time may have quite different consequences for effective project performance. Carrying out a project at nighttime rather than during daytime is not always feasible (e.g., if it requires auxiliary services that will not be available at night); but for some projects such nighttime completion is desirable (e.g., if it ties up facilities that need to be running during the daytime). For instance, some cities have begun doing repairs of major traffic arteries at night, so as to minimize their impact on rush hour traffic.

Moreover, there are differences among sets of activities in how *modular* they are. That is, some kinds of activities, but not all, can be subdivided into smaller parts, and done in short periods of time distributed over a longer time period. Conversely, some but not all activities can be aggregated into larger sets and done efficiently all in one block of time. For example, a parent cannot aggregate all of his or her childcare activities into one big chunk and do them all on Saturday; they must be done, one activity at a time, as circumstances dictate. Conversely, it is really not efficient to launder each pair of socks as it becomes soiled; it makes more sense to accumulate laundry for a week to be done all in one period of time. Thus, time–activity matches are particularistic, with regard both to time and to activities.

Furthermore, the "size" of both activities and time periods does not remain constant over all conditions. There is a certain amount of *elasticity* regarding the amount of time it takes a certain individual or group to do a certain set of activities. There is evidence, for example, that stringent time limits often lead to faster rates of performance of the same task on later trials (Kelly, Futoran, & McGrath, 1990; Waller, 2000), perhaps with some loss in quality. We will deal with some of these elasticity issues later in this chapter in the section discussing deadlines and entrainment.

One feature of groups that plays a key role in the effective matching of time, activities, and social units is the nature of the technology available for performance of the activities. In recent years there has been considerable research on one particular aspect of technology, namely, the use of electronic technology for communication in groups. (See McGrath & Hollingshead, 1994, for a review of that work.) It is clear that electronic communication technology has some starkly different temporal features than does the more familiar technology for within-group communication that we call face-to-face conversation. Some of those features make communication within a group easier; some make it more difficult. These temporal differences for electronic communication include (a) different rates at which various communication activities can be carried out (e.g., people can talk faster than they can type; but they also can read faster than they can listen); (b) therefore, different lags in both transmission and feedback; (c) separable time intervals for different components of the communication process (e.g., composition, editing, transmission, and reception are all separate and distinguishable times for computer communication, whereas they are all a single inseparable time period for face-to-face communication); and (d) a more turbulent flow of communication for electronic communication when there are many interacting members, each able to generate messages at the same time and to read incoming messages at any time. These complex temporal features of a group's technology must be taken into account in operational planning, as part of the scheduling of the time–activity–social unit match.

Time and Task Performance: Execution of the Group's Projects

The two levels discussed previously, strategic and operational planning, prepare for the execution of concrete acts. On the microlevel, an act consists of effort toward a subordinate goal, and regulation and execution activities associated with attaining it. At this action level, performance consists of a series of recurrent sequences: Groups and group members plan or *orient* with regard to the intended action, *enact* it, *monitor* that action with regard to its effects, and if needed, *modify* the action, the plan, or the goal.

There has been some past research on the temporal sequencing of such performance functions. Besides his more prominent work on overall phases of group problem solving (which is discussed in a later section of this chapter), Bales also did some early work on microlevel sequences of actions in problem-solving groups (Bales, 1950). He found two distinct patterns. One was a tendency for sequences to involve "more of the same." That is, an act of a certain kind (e.g., a task solution proposal) tended to trigger more acts of the same type. The other pattern was a conversational tendency. For example, a question tended to elicit an answer.

Other researchers have postulated different expected structures of sequences of action. For example, Stech (1975) proposed a "generalized sequence of the discussion process." It starts with (a) a question or problem statement, followed by (b) an answer, a proposal, or a clarification of substance, followed by (c) either a positive or negative evaluation. Stech claims that a high percentage of all sequences of interactions of different categories fits this structure.

Gundlach and Schultz (1987) did a sequential analysis of group communication for groups doing a "Tower of Hanoi" task. They distinguished between proposals for the next move and evaluations of proposals, and predicted and found a relation between the complexity of proposal-evaluation cycles and effectiveness of problem-solving performance. Better-performing groups showed longer sequences of discussion before making a move. The sequences included both proposals for moves and multiple evaluations of those proposals.

Implicit in these approaches is the idea that group productivity should be higher if the communication process follows an "ideal" sequence in the microstructure. Stech (1975) found that groups whose communication patterns followed the proposed sequential structure tended to perform better. Tschan (1995, 2002) identified a microlevel sequence for motoric actions: plan and orient, execute, and evaluate. She found that high performing groups had a larger percentage of their cycles as ideal cycles—cycles that included all three elements and in an ideal sequential order (i.e., starting with orient and ending with evaluate).

This research on ideal sequences suggests that a well-ordered sequential structure not only reflects a better understanding of the requirements of the task (in that all the necessary acts are done), but also represents a relatively efficient task performance process (hence fewer "process losses") because it minimizes redundant and fragmented activities. Note that the sequence considered here is a process sequence of communications; it does not imply any particular sequence in the content of the task acts. Thus, these findings do not suggest that there is "one right way" to do projects in a content sense; rather it leaves open the idea that many group projects have multiple paths to the solution. Nor does such an ideal process sequence suggest that one already has to know how to do the task in advance to get it done. Thus, the communication process sequence—in CAST theory terms, the orient, enact, monitor, and modify cycle—holds for difficult and uncertain tasks as well as for familiar and well-structured ones.

SYNCHRONIZATION AND ENTRAINMENT

But sequence is not the only temporal aspect of operational processes. Activities within the group's task performance processes also entail complex patterning of pace and timing. That is, they involve *synchronization*, or the temporal coordination of multiple activities.

Synchronization is a complicated concept involving ideas of simultaneity, succession, and coordination, which are themselves quite complicated ideas. Synchronization can be defined as the coordination of two or more actions in time. The actions may be similar or complementary. They may be simultaneous or in a fixed sequence with predetermined temporal relations among them. They may be done by a single individual or group or by different social units. Synchronization means ensuring that the appropriate person or group carries out each intended action at the appropriate time.

Synchronization can be considered at each of several levels. Intra-individual synchronization involves time-sharing across tasks by a single individual. Interindividual (or intragroup) synchronization means coordination of the actions of two or more members. External synchronization means coordinating the actions of a group (or of its members) with actions or events external to that group (e.g., an externally imposed deadline).

Doing More Than One Thing at a Time

A strong cultural prescription says one should only do one thing at a time (and do it well!). Yet, people violate that prescription all the time, often seeking out tasks that can readily be done while in the course of accomplishing some other, low-demand task. For example, many people read, or make lists, while waiting for or riding on busses, trains, or planes.

Beyond those mundane examples, individuals or groups are often faced with the need to do more than one activity within the same block of time. When that is the case, they can take any of three courses. First, they can *time-shift*: that is, they can do one task, and put the others off until later. But, of course, that is not always feasible. Second, they can resort to a *division of labor*: that is, one individual can do one task and others can do the other tasks. But that, too, is not always feasible, certainly not for the case of an individual working alone. Third, they can *time-share*: that is, they can attempt to do multiple tasks at the same time. The question is under what conditions can humans do more than one task at the same time (or in the same small block of time) and do all of them well (or well enough)?

There has been considerable human engineering work on time-sharing for motor tasks, and some cognitive science work on parallel processing for cognitive–verbal tasks. Mary Riess Jones (1985, 1986; Jones & Boltz, 1989) has done especially interesting work on what she calls the "interleaving" of multiple simultaneous tasks.

In general, doing more than one thing in the same block of time (e.g., having a "business lunch," or reading while riding on a train) works well to the extent that the following conditions hold:

1. The activities do not require the same input and output modalities; for example, one requires talking and the other requires a motor activity such as driving a car.
2. The activities have temporally intermittent attention requirements (e.g., reading while waiting for a bus works because the latter needs only intermittent attention), or one of the activities is automatized (for example driving a car and talking at the

same time).

3. All activities are helped, or at least not hindered, by ambient conditions (e.g., talking business at lunch requires that the restaurant not be too noisy).

Mutual Entrainment and Coordinated Action

One way to state the key question considered here is to ask: How is the flow of interaction in a group patterned over time? Temporal patterning has to do with the frequency, duration, periodicity, sequencing, and temporal locations of various interaction events. Under some conditions, the behaviors of individuals who are interacting with one another become mutually entrained to one another. Entrainment means the synchronization, in phase and periodicity (and sometimes in magnitude), of some particular behaviors or patterns of action by two or more interacting individuals. Such entrainment need not be either deliberate or noticed by the participants. For example, Warner and colleagues (Warner, Waggener, & Kronauer, 1983) found that interacting dyads entrained (that is, synchronized the timing of) both their conversation and their respiration. Chapple (1970) found that smoothly entrained cycles provide more pleasant interpersonal relationships for the participants. Considerable research is yet needed to determine what behaviors can be entrained, the conditions under which that does and does not occur, and the consequences of such entrainment for individuals and groups.

External Synchronization:
Entrainment to Deadlines and Other External Temporal Markers

People use deadlines to regulate their own and other's actions. Deadlines function as *time markers* to help structure behavioral fields just as place markers do. The temporal structuring of behavior so that it reckons with deadlines and other external time markers is a form of entrainment as well. Several researchers (e.g., Ancona & Chong, 1996; Kelly & McGrath, 1985; McGrath & Kelly, 1986) have shown that various aspects of individual task performance and communication activities tend to become entrained both to the activities of other individuals with whom they are interacting and to the occurrence of pacing signals external to the group. For example, Kelly and colleagues (1990) have shown that deadlines on early trials of a task lead to entrainment not only of the rate of productivity but also the patterns of interaction on later trials. Such entrainment can involve either slowing down or speeding up of productivity rates, depending on the combination of task and time conditions. Waller (2000) shifted the deadlines of teams after they had already started work, either extending the time they could use or advancing the deadline. Both of the interventions led to an increase in performance, apparently because there were higher activity levels in groups who were attentive to time. Mann (2001) did a study to explore whether the midpoint transitions reported by Gersick (1988, 1989) were paced by internal or external "time." He used an external clock rigged to run fast, or slow, or accurately. He found that groups with an accurate external clock showed a single, midpoint transition, but that groups with an inaccurate external clock showed *two* transition points. One of those transition points corresponded to the midpoint for the external clock they had available (either fast or slow), and the other corresponded to the midpoint for "accurate" (hence, internally sensed) time.

Entrainment facilitates within-group coordination of overt action, and also has an impact on the group's adaptation to features of its embedding contexts. In these and other ways, member and group activity at the microlevel yields patterns of member–task–tool relations involving complex temporal patterning.

IS THERE A CHARACTERISTIC SEQUENCE OF TASK PERFORMANCE PHASES?

In this section we return to the idea of stages of group development discussed earlier. There is a long history of conceptualizations of groups as having a characteristic set of phases of group task performance. The overall question of whether there is a problem-solving phase sequence for group task performance encompasses a series of related issues. First is the question of whether groups, confronted with a project (for example a decision to make or a problem to solve) characteristically follow a particular sequence of phases of task fulfillment. If there is such a predictable sequence of different types of task activity, there is the further question of whether that sequence is instrumentally related to task accomplishment. Assuming that there is a most-effective phase sequence, some researchers have pursued a further question of whether various potential process interventions could be used to improve group performance by increasing the extent to which groups adhered to that ideal sequence. In this section, we will examine research on those questions historically, and then reinterpret these issues in the light of our theoretical framework about time and collective action (i.e., CAST).

A Brief History of the Problem-Solving Phase Sequence Issue

Past theory and research on a fixed sequence of well-defined phases of group activity has dealt mainly with problem-solving tasks. Some of the proposed sets of phases have been derived from Dewey's (1933) propositions about how we think (Fisher, 1970). Of the several normative models that have been proposed (e.g., Bales & Strodtbeck, 1951; Fisher, 1970; Hirokawa, 1983), the best known is Bales and Strodtbeck's three phase sequence: orientation–evaluation–control. They proposed that sequence, and found evidence for it using laboratory groups engaged in what they referred to as "full-fledged problem solving." That phrase meant that, for the sequence to apply, the group had to deal with the whole problem from beginning to end: from problem analysis, to proposing criteria and solutions, to evaluating alternatives and implementing solutions (and presumably doing so within a single work session). Talland (1955) and Psathas (1960) found mixed support for this phase sequence in some kinds of extant groups (e.g., therapy groups).

Both the normative aspect and the fixed-sequence aspect of phase models of group problem-solving behavior have been questioned by several researchers. Regarding the fixed-sequence aspect, critics argue that even if phases can be distinguished in a group's problem-solving activity, there is often a recycling of some of the phases, especially for difficult problems (e.g., Burnstein & Berbaum, 1983; McGrath, 1991). Regarding the normative aspect, Hirokawa (1983) tested a sequence model of problem-solving phases and did not find the theoretically proposed sequence, nor any other specific sequence, as being superior for group productivity. However, he did find that successful groups engaged in problem analysis early on, whereas less-successful groups tended to skip problem analysis altogether. (We discussed this idea in the section "Time and Operational Planning" earlier in this chapter.) This is in line with research on more and less successful individual problem-solvers (Janis & Mann, 1977). On the basis of these findings, Hirokawa proposed a task-contingent model that holds that no single fixed sequence of phases leads to high performance, but rather that groups do show certain phases contingent on task requirements, but not necessarily in a fixed order.

Poole and colleagues (1981, 1983; Poole & Roth, 1989a, 1989b), working from an adaptive structuration theory, present an even more complex model, reflecting results from detailed analysis of interaction of problem-solving and decision-making groups. They distinguished three kinds of acts: task content, task process, and relational activity. For task content, they found different phases recycling several times as the group continued to work on the task. They did not find support for any single best phase sequence. How many phases, and their pattern of recycling, depends on an interaction among task process activities, relational activities, and task-content activities. Poole and Roth found, for example, that the level of conflict combined with the power structure of the group predicts the amount of solution-searching activity that will occur (Poole & Roth, 1989a, 1989b).

Hackman (2002) argues that there are different focal performance processes at the beginning, midpoint, and the end of a team life cycle. At the beginning, effort is the process that fosters performance, and motivation therefore is important. At the midpoint of the cycle, groups have been found to rethink their strategies, so the choice of a good performance strategy becomes important. At the end of the cycle, teams can evaluate their performance without being preoccupied by ongoing work, and the evaluation of experiences and acquisition of new knowledge and skills for performance on subsequent tasks becomes important. On the basis of these general phases and their focal processes, Hackman (2002) suggests that coaching interventions focused on motivation are appropriate at the beginning of the team life cycle; consultative, strategy-focused intervention at the midpoint; and educational, knowledge-focused, and skill-focused coaching can be done most effectively toward the end of the cycle.

Some other conceptualizations about this issue are compatible with the hierarchical, sequential perspective formulated in CAST (e.g., Gollwitzer, 1990; McGrath, 1991). For example, McGrath postulated four modes of activity in groups. The first, goal choice or the acceptance of a project, and the fourth, execution of project or goal attainment, are a necessary part of each completed group project. Moreover, they usually are done in this temporal sequence; that is, goal choice precedes goal attainment. The other two modes—means choice (that is, planning procedures) and policy choice (that is, the resolution of differing views about desired outcomes)—may or may not occur depending on task requirements, past experience of the group, group member characteristics, context conditions, and the like. Duration and sequence of the four modes is variable and depends on requirements of the actual coordination network. Moreover, these two, three, or four mode sequences may recur. The two essential modes of this classification—goal choice and execution—are akin to the macro- and microlevels of the hierarchical schema discussed earlier. The middle two—means choice and policy choice—are related to the meso or operational planning level.

As discussed in chapter 4 of this volume, Gollwitzer (1990) proposed a somewhat different kind of phase sequence. It contains four different phases of an action, or task fulfillment, and those phases are akin to the three hierarchical levels dealt with in CAST. It starts with a pre-decisional phase of an action, in which preferences are created. Here, action tendencies (wishes) are considered in a rather unstructured, open-minded fashion that Gollwitzer calls deliberative mind-set. Conclusion of this phase leads to the building of an intention, a decision to pursue a specific goal. This is like the purpose or strategic planning level in CAST. After having adopted the goal, the actor makes a transition to a much more focused implemental mind-set, and prepares for implementation of the actions required to attain this goal. That is, he or she plans the "when, where, how, and how long" (Gollwitzer, 1990, p. 290) of task fulfillment. This phase, between the decision on the goal and the initiation of the action, is named the pre-actional phase. This is like CAST's operational planning level. Only after this phase is the action initiated, in an implemental mind-set, focusing on the goal and the necessary steps to fulfill it. After goal completion, the actor enters the post-actional phase in which he or she evaluates whether further goal attainment actions are worthwhile.

This is, again, a more open and less structured deliberative mode. These last two phases reflect the orient–enact–monitor–modify cycles of the execution or performance level.

In groups these different phases may be reflected in different communication patterns: less focused and structured communication before concrete implementation plans have been worked out, and more focussed communication during planning and once the action is initiated. Some of Gersick's (1989) data seem to fit this theory quite well. Gersick states that, after the transition phase that occurred in most of her groups at about the temporal midpoint, the groups showed a "shift of attention." She describes the transition as when a system turns from confusion toward clarity. Gollwitzer's action phase model also fits a model proposed by Silver, Cohen, and Rainwater (1988). And, as previously suggested, it is also quite compatible with the hierarchical, sequential CAST model proposed here.

There has also been a failure to find single sequences of decision-making phases in work organizations. Instead, most studies seem to find iterative processes and recurrent cycles of different sets of phases (Mintzberg, Raisinghani, & Théorêt, 1976), with the phases and cycles influenced by problem type and problem complexity (Nutt, 1984).

As noted, there has been some research designed to provide process interventions that will produce a best phase sequence and thereby improve group task performance. That research seems to suggest the following general conclusions: Any given, reasonable, deliberate intervention that forces or induces groups to adopt a fixed structuring of their task process is likely to lead to better performance than for groups with no intervention at all. But any such process intervention is not likely to lead to better group performance, compared with any other reasonable alternative intervention (Brilhart & Jochem, 1964; Hirokawa, 1985; Jarboe, 1988, 1996; Sambamurthy, Poole, & Kelly, 1993). This could be for any of several reasons: (a) because all reasonable interventions work, but are more or less equivalent; (b) because all interventions that have been tried have common properties (such as that they all structure the group's task performance) which is the key to their success; or (c) because the fact of intervention produces a kind of placebo or "Hawthorne effect."

Concluding Comments About Phases of Group Task Performance

As implied in our earlier discussion, for complex action system theory (CAST) group task performance is highly patterned but not in a form reflecting a single, fixed sequence of phases or even different sequences of phases for tasks of different types. In this conception, group task performance reflects a hierarchical, sequential patterning of project, tasks, subtasks, and so on. At the highest or strategic planning level, project choice and resource allocation must to some degree get done early on, albeit sometimes tacitly, and need not be addressed again unless the group encounters major difficulties or unusual circumstances. At the middle or operational planning level, the process can be structured once, explicitly or tacitly (a planning phase, early in the period of group work and often again at the midpoint of the group's work), and that too does not need to be addressed again unless its implementation proves to be unfeasible. At the micro or action level, work unfolds in recurrent cycles (orienting–enacting–monitoring–modifying) on a sequence of tasks and subtasks that reflects the operational plan. If the monitoring part of the cycle indicates that a correction is needed, and the modifying part of the cycle indicates that a change in action will not suffice, this can lead to a cascading modification of the higher-order plan, or even of the goal choice. Such a complex patterning—hierarchical, sequential, and differentiated with respect to technology and enactors—is not likely to be "discovered" by data analysis that simply slices up a group's work session (or lifetime) into a certain number of equal temporal segments (which, in fact, is how much of the analysis of empirical data on problem-solving phases has been done). Although it is intricately temporally patterned, group task performance does not reflect a single sequence of task performance phases.

The temporal structure of group task process thus seems to be flexible, and it is influenced by the state of the entire coordination network: members, tasks, tools, and their interrelations. Groups show fixed sequences of phases only if the projects they carry out have clear sequential requirements. The different hierarchical levels of project activity influence each other.

Thus group performance, like group development, adaptation, and learning, is intricately temporal in its patterning, but those temporal patterns cannot be described adequately in terms of some single sequence of stages or phases. Rather, there is a complex patterning of action at different hierarchical levels, each with its own time line or cadence, and group task performance consists of an intermeshing of all of them.

AFTERTHOUGHTS

Synchronize!

Synchronize, synchronize, or we'll never win the prize!
We must work in close accord, strife and conflict can't afford.
When you say jump, I'll have to hop; and when I spill you'll have to
    mop.
When e'er I bungle, you jump in; and when you're stuck, then I'll
    begin.
Oh we must function smooth as silk. Don't drop the ball or spill the
    milk.
It will all turn out just fine. You do your job, I'll do mine!
We'll be fine, I surely think, if we can just behave in synch!

Working Cycles

Allocate resources scarce, plan the schedule, carry through,
If the acts aren't up to muster, modify and act anew.
If no actions meet objectives, change the plans, or goals review.
Yes, groups do work in cyclic patterns: These temporal matters matter,
    too!

8

TIME AND
THE RESEARCH PROCESS

In the preceding chapters we have examined conceptual issues regarding the nature of time and substantive issues regarding time in relation to individual behavior, stress, group development, and collective action. In this chapter we will consider temporal issues in regard to the methodology of our field. We will consider several methodological issues that arise if one begins to take temporal factors seriously as aspects of the conceptual and substantive phenomena of social psychology. Then, in the final chapter, we will offer a limited attempt to suggest some ways in which we can deal with those temporal issues, in conceptual, substantive, and methodological domains, in future social psychological research.

Temporal processes are heavily implicated in all aspects of our research methodology. They are part and parcel of the logic of causality that underlies the positivistic paradigm. They are heavily interconnected with—if not indeed confounded with—our ideas of validity and reliability. Furthermore, the various research strategies available to us (e.g., field studies and laboratory experiments) are characterized by different time frames, and those time frame differences are part of the reason why it is difficult to compare findings on the basis of those different strategies.

Some of these temporal and methodological issues are treated in detail in several sources (Kelly & McGrath, 1988; Mitchell & James, 2001; Slife, 1993). We will draw on those sources here. These temporal and methodological issues are also related to our discussion of conceptions of time in chapter 2. This chapter focuses on four sets of these temporal and methodological issues: (a) temporal factors in our logic of causality, (b) temporal factors in our conceptions of validity, (c) temporal aspects of our theory of measurement and error, and (d) the differing temporal scales of different research strategies.

TIME AND CAUSALITY

The methodological paradigm underlying most of modern social psychology—positivism or logical positivism—supports a very narrow interpretation of causality. Of the four kinds of causality discussed by Aristotle, the positivist paradigm honors only one—efficient or mechanical causality—and treats that form of causality rather narrowly. In positivism, the idea of efficient causality has been tightly coupled, both historically and logically, with the idea that cause–effect relations contain both a logical and a chronological-order relation. Cause must come before effect; or at least, effect cannot come before cause. Some have argued that, in principle, this chronological order relation is not necessary to the logical order relation, and that cause and effect could be simultaneous in time (cf. Slife, 1993, chapters 9 and 10). But in practice, because simultaneity is relative to the measurement units being used, empirical studies done in the positivist tradition have almost always insisted on a cause-then-effect sequence to be willing to talk about causation.

That principle of chronological causal order shapes our research strategies and is part of the definition of a "true experiment": The cause must be known to have preceded the effect, else the direction of causation, if any, could be the reverse. It is worth noting, as Hume did, that even a logical and chronological order of putative cause and observed effect, though a necessary condition for the imputation of causality, is not a *sufficient* condition for doing so.

Forms of Causality

The Humean line of reasoning makes several additional presumptions. First, it presumes a unidirectional causal process. Mutually reciprocal causal processes are by and large ruled out of our reasoning. When we do suspect potential bidirectional cause–effect relations between two variables, we are likely to construe them as A affects B and then B affects A and then A affects B again, and so on. That is, we are liable to construe them as, and analyze for them as, a series of unidirectional relations.

Second, the principle of a chronological order of cause and effect assumes that mechanical or efficient causality is the only form of causality. If we permit any of the other Aristotelian forms of causality—formal, final, material—then entirely different time relations may be involved. The time relations for final causality are equivocal. In one way of looking at it, the intended state is the "end state," so in a sense the cause occurs after the process by which the effect takes place. But more to the point, human systems are characterized by intentionality, which is the equivalent of final cause in the Aristotelian sense. Intentionality may precede the effect, or be concurrent with the effect process. But it need not stand in any particular fixed temporal relation to it.

Aristotalean formal causality can also be viewed in two ways with respect to the temporal relations of cause and effect. One way is to presume that the cause has been inherent in the system from the beginning; it exists before, but usually long before, the particular effect. Another way to view it is to say that the formal causal process is contemporaneous with the effect process, and perhaps inseparable from it. That same kind of dual temporal interpretation holds for Aristotalean material causality as well: The cause is inherent in the properties of the system either from the beginning or while the effect is occurring.

Cause–Effect Intervals

None of these other forms of causality offer the clear and unequivocal cause-then-effect time order of efficient cause. Moreover, there are still additional assumptions underlying the positivist use of efficient cause. These additional assumptions have to do with the nature of causal agents or forces, and the nature of effects. One of these assumptions is that the causal processes and the processes that constitute the effects are distinctive entities or forces, not aspects of the same systemic processes. In a sense, the formal cause idea involves precisely the latter, namely that the cause and effect are integral parts of the same formative processes.

The positivistic use of efficient cause makes two additional assumptions: (a) that the cause involves a process that takes some finite amount of time to produce the postulated effects, and (b) that there can be no action at either spatial or temporal distance. These two assumptions open up a whole additional set of concerns. If there can be no action at a temporal distance, then the causal process must "fill" the interval between the onset of the cause and the occurrence (and observation) of the effect. If the causal processes take a finite amount of time, then (a) if we look for the effect before that time, we will not find it, or we will not find it in "full" form; and (b) if we wait too long to look for the effect, we may not see it in "pure" form. If we wait too long, we may instead see the effect in partially "decayed" form, some second stage or further effects produced by the original effect, or some effects produced by systemic "counterforces" brought into play by the original effects.

How are we to know for any given cause–effect relation the proper length of time to presume it takes for the full effect to occur and other effects not yet occurring? We have totally ignored this issue in social psychology. Virtually no theories in social psychology or related behavioral science disciplines specify the "proper" temporal interval needed for their postulated causal processes to have their postulated effects (see Kelly & McGrath, 1988, and Mitchell & James, 2001, for extended treatments of this issue).

If we cannot specify theoretically the proper time interval between cause and effect, then we are faced with two additional requirements for our empirical studies. First, we need to postulate what we should expect to observe if an empirical study does not wait long enough for the causal processes to have occurred. Second, we need to postulate what we would expect to observe if an empirical study waited much longer than the long enough interval for the causal processes. This includes several further questions: Will the impact of the causal process wane, or the effect "wear off"? Will artifacts enter into the picture to confound things (e.g., maturation, history; see the later discussion of validity)? Will the impact of the causal process trigger off other system forces? If the latter answer is yes, then would those system forces tend to mute or nullify or even reverse the expected effects (as in negative feedback loops) or tend to amplify such effects (as in positive feedback loops)?

All of this is stated as if both cause and effect were specific and time-bound events. Actually, both causal processes and effect processes have many different "temporal shapes" (cf. Kelly & McGrath, 1988; McGrath & Kelly, 1986). Sometimes a cause is a single time-bound event: for example, the touchdown of a tornado in a specific location. Sometimes, however, the causal process is more like a repetition of a class of events: for example, dropping sales for three successive months. In such a case, the effect process could be a separate response to each event, or it could be a response of accumulating magnitude as the causal event is repeated. Or it could be a response that only occurs after the causal process has accumulated to a certain frequency or magnitude.

Time-Shifted Responses

The translation of cause–effect relations into empirical observations sometimes takes on an even more complicated temporal tangle. McGrath and Beehr (1990), in the area of stress and coping, offer a good example of why time intervals between cause and effect matter and of how a lack of consideration of them can lead to empirical results that misinform us (see discussion in chapter 5). They point out that many system reactions to environmental stressors are time-shifted, either to long before the stressor event (preventive coping or anticipatory coping), or to long after the stressor event (reactive coping). As a consequence, researchers sometimes identify a stressor and observe that the system made no response to it within their observation interval, when in fact the system had anticipated the event and carried out preventive or ameliorative measures beforehand, or the system did not manage to respond to the stressor overtly until long after the research observation period had ended.

The idea of time-shifted responses further complicates the "cause must precede effect" axiom with which we started this section. Humans are capable of taking anticipatory action. If they anticipate that some event will occur, they sometimes make appropriate responses before the event. So, *effect precedes cause*, a violation of the basic Humean premise. To preserve the idea of a fixed temporal order (cause then effect), we must redefine the cause in such cases as the anticipation of X, not the occurrence of X. Indeed, instrumental learning is built on the idea that the organism makes the appropriate learned response in the *expectation* of reward.

One can reasonably argue, in such a case, that the "real" cause is the anticipation of the causal event rather than the occurrence of the event itself, and that anticipation does indeed come before the response. But even if we accept that rationale, it remains a difficult empirical problem for the researcher to demonstrate empirically a cause-then-effect sequence to make a causal claim within the positivistic paradigm.

Thus, a full consideration of the temporal relations involved in causal patterns raises several issues that together suggest that our simple, unidirectional, time-ordered cause–effect idea of efficient cause may not be adequate to cover all human behavior.

TIME AND VALIDITY

In recent decades, social psychologists' ideas about validity of study findings have been guided by the work of Campbell and colleagues (Campbell & Stanley, 1966; Cook & Campbell, 1979). Those ideas involve some very interesting temporal features, which we will discuss in this section.

Cook and Campbell (1979) identified four types of validity: *internal validity*, regarding the validity of conclusions drawn from study findings; *external validity*, regarding the degree to which those findings could be generalized to other participants, conditions, and times; *construct validity*, regarding the degree to which the variables as operationalized map to the concepts that are intended to be examined; and *statistical conclusion validity*, regarding the degree to which the quantitative findings might have occurred by chance or due to statistical artifacts. They also identified several factors that, if present in a study design (or in events that occurred during a study), would represent plausible rival hypotheses (rival to the hypotheses the researcher is examining). The plausibility of such rival hypotheses would call into question the validity of interpretations of findings in relation to the hypotheses being investigated. The first two of these four types, internal and external validity, are eminently temporal matters. We will discuss them in some detail below.

Internal Validity

Cook and Campbell (1979) specified seven threats to the internal validity of a study's findings:

1. *History:* Events that happened to the participants in the experimental conditions, other than the intended experimental manipulations, and that did not happen to those in the comparison conditions.
2. *Maturation:* Changes in the participants in the experimental condition during the course of the study.
3. *Testing, or reactivity:* Reactive effects of the experimental operations per se—either the experimental treatment or prestudy measurements—on the dependent variable measures.
4. *Attrition, or mortality:* Differential rates or patterns of participants' dropping out of the study from the experimental versus the comparison conditions.
5. *Instrument effects:* Changes in the measuring instruments during the course of a study, such as wear on a physical instrument, or boredom, fatigue, or learning on the part of an observer.
6. *Selection:* Effects of unmeasured differences among cases in different study conditions when cases were assigned to conditions on the basis of selection on prestudy measures of some independent variable (rather than being randomly assigned).
7. *Regression to the mean:* The effects on poststudy measures of having cases assigned to conditions on the basis of extreme values of those measures at the start of the study.

The first five of these effects involve crucial temporal intervals. Time is important for history because the longer the interval between onset of the causal process and measurement of the effect process, the more opportunity there is for differential conditions to occur for experimental and comparison cases. Time is important for maturation because the longer the interval between onset of the causal process and final measurements of the effect processes, the longer the time during which participants can "mature," and hence change their levels or patterns on particular variables. Time is important for attrition because the longer the time between the initial experimental operations and the conclusion of the study's measurements, the more opportunity there is for participants to withdraw from the study or to otherwise be unavailable for inclusion in later sets of measurements. Time is important for instrument effects because the longer the time during which the measurement process is extended, the more opportunity there is for changes to occur in the measurement instruments. Finally, time is important for reactivity because the *shorter* the time interval between initial experimental treatment condition, or initial measurements, and subsequent measurements of dependent variables, the more likely it is that the latter reflect testing or reactivity effects.

Note that for the first four effects, the longer the time interval between "experimental conditions" or prestudy measures (Xs) and dependent variable measures (Ys), the more likely it is that the confounding condition will occur. For the fifth, the confounding condition of reactivity is more likely to occur the shorter the time interval between initial events and later measurements (i.e., between X and Y).

Campbell and colleagues (Campbell & Stanley, 1966; Cook & Campbell, 1979) discuss several ways in which features of study designs can help eliminate or attenuate the various threats to internal validity. For example, if the independent variable conditions are implemented by experimental treatment, under the experimenter's control, and participants are assigned to conditions by a random procedure, rather than having cases assigned to experimental conditions by selection on prestudy measures (that is, if it is a "true experiment"), that will effectively reduce the threat from selection and from regression to the mean.

However, some of these threats to validity cannot be entirely controlled by the experimenter or by experimental procedures. For example, attrition from the study, instrument changes, and reactivity can occur against the wishes of the experimenter. To avoid those confounding conditions, the experimenter needs both (a) to make the X-to-Y interval as short as feasible, to avoid or minimize the effects of history, maturation, instrument changes, and attrition; and (b) to make the X-to-Y interval sufficiently long so as to avoid or minimize testing or reactivity effects. Thus, the researcher is caught in a temporal dilemma.

To make matters worse, not only do we have no basis in substantive theory for specifying the "right" length of time between X and Y for full and pure causal effects, as discussed in the previous section of this chapter; we also do not have any "methodological theory" to guide us in regard to time intervals to avoid or minimize these artifactual threats to validity.

But the researcher's problems with these temporal matters are even more complicated. Several of these time-related threats to internal validity—notably history and maturation—are not necessarily artifacts at all. History, after all, refers to the system's past and events in that past. For human systems, not only their present state but also their present actions are fundamentally affected by their own past history. And maturation is another word for "development"; the system's current state and actions are in part a function of its own past development as well. Far from being merely unwanted artifacts that are to be "gotten rid of" by experimental or statistical means, history and maturation are important aspects of the substantive systems being studied.

Some proponents of complex systems theory approaches to the study of human systems (e.g., Arrow, McGrath, & Berdahl, 2000; Baron, Amazeen, & Beek, 1994; Vallacher & Nowak, 1994) have argued that we need to shift the form of our typical logic of inquiry, or at least to extend our methodology to incorporate some distinctly different approaches. The positivistic approach, especially in its experimental form, focuses on comparing experimental with comparison cases as to their aggregate or average values on some variables at a given point in time. Alternatively, these authors argue, our analyses could also focus on tracing the pattern in which specific system variables evolve over time for each case. In this way, we could assess the relations of history and maturation (and any other time-related changes) to any given system variable of interest, for each case considered separately. We could then examine these patterns for similarities and differences among multiple cases, with or without experimental treatments. Such an additional logic of inquiry could permit us to attend to temporal patterning much more effectively than we have done, while essentially setting aside for these analyses much of the logic underlying the positivistic-quantitative-experimental paradigm that has dominated our field for some time.

Structural equations modeling is another approach that provides an alternative logic of inquiry, one that effectively encompasses some of the complex temporal features of causal relations. Although structural modeling is formulated within the directional, efficient-causal formulations of logical positivism, it nevertheless allows both for simultaneous and sequential cause–effect relations. Moreover, it allows for multiple sequential causal patterns and, in principle, for reciprocal causal processes. It might also permit taking history and maturation effects into account, as well as differences in other initial conditions, perhaps by adding them into the model as "dummy variables" at appropriate early locations in the logical sequence of the model. It does not, however, account for temporal intervals or durations, nor does it provide any conceptual tools for specifying, anticipating, or predicting the durations of cause–effect intervals.

As to the future, whether or not the complex systems approach, the structural equations modeling approach, or some other yet-unformulated approach is the most effective means for doing so, we clearly need some way to take into account the natural effects of the histories and development of human systems, without letting those factors operate as experimental confounds that bias our study findings.

External Validity

The issue of external validity also has temporal aspects. The aim of external validity, or generalizability, is to try to assess the likelihood that a given set of findings—obtained in a given study with specific operationalizations of experimental treatments and measures of effects, and with particular populations of participating systems and contextual conditions—would hold more generally. The question here is whether those same findings (or their conceptual equivalents) would occur if a study were done (a) using different operationalizations of independent and dependent variables, (b) under different contextual conditions, (c) with different populations, or (d) at different times. It is probably more appropriate to put the question in the following way: Over what range of operationalizations, contextual conditions, populations, and occasions would those findings hold?

Note that external validity of a given set of findings can never be determined definitively. The researcher can only use his or her intuition, and general base of knowledge about conditions, populations, and so on, to make a highly speculative estimate as to how broadly findings from a given study are likely to hold. Just as we have no substantive theory about the effects of passage of time on the variables involved, and we have no methodological theory about the appropriateness of time intervals for effectively dealing with the time-related artifacts of history, attrition, and so on, we also have no theoretical or empirical basis for estimating how contextual conditions might change over time or how given effects might or might not hold up over changing populations, times, and conditions.

Concluding Comments About Validity

We will not discuss the other two Campbellian forms of validity here. Construct validity has to do with the relation of operational measures of the study and the intended conceptual variables—an exceedingly difficult problem, but not a particularly temporal one. Statistical conclusion validity has to do with the *reliability* of the statistical findings, and that is somewhat related to the topic of the next section of this chapter. So we will turn now to the temporal issues involved in our theory of measurement and error.

TIME, MEASUREMENT, AND ERROR

Social psychology has adopted psychology's classical theory of measurement. That theory holds that one is always attempting to capture the *essence* of a construct in one's measure, and that any given measure does so fallibly. One can have a measure that captures part but not all of a construct, or one that captures all of the construct but also encompasses surplus information not a part of the construct, or one that overlaps with the construct and captures part but not all of it, with some surplus information. Various strategies can be used to purify or at least narrow down the imperfections of a measure. Most of those strategies involve the convergence among multiple measures of the same construct. By and large, that theory of measurement tends to assume that the essence (sometimes referred to as the "true score") is a timeless value that remains the same across situations and occasions.

The question of consistency of a measure—that is, whether it in fact delivers the same information every time it is used to measure a given variable on a given system—is addressed in the concept of reliability. The strict definition of reliability is the agreement of two measures of the same property of a system, under the same conditions, with the same measuring instrument, at the same time, but independent of one another. Of course that definition contains a logical contradiction. The two measurements cannot be the same in all those respects and still be independent of one another. Hence the strict form of reliability is never actually assessed. Instead, researchers relax one or another of those "sameness" constraints. They use two different measures that are judged to be of the same construct (e.g., split half or alternate forms reliability); or they use different samples of a given population of systems (i.e., split sample assessments); or they use the same instrument but at different times (i.e., test–retest reliability). The last assumes that the system does not change from one measurement occasion to another, and that relevant conditions that might affect the measurement do not change either. Those are strong assumptions.

The idea of using repeated measurements raises temporal issues in another context as well. Sometimes researchers measure a variable repeatedly over an extended period of time and then combine those measurements (adding and averaging, for example) to obtain a single value that is regarded as a more reliable estimate. For example, one might count the number of units produced by a work team over an hour, or a day, or a week, and use that total measure as a basis for an average production rate. That, too, assumes that there is no change in the system or surrounding conditions that affects the variable in question during that extended period of time. Whether or not that is a reasonable assumption depends on several things: (a) the volatility of the construct being measured, (b) the volatility of the contextual conditions that affect the construct, (c) the duration of the time period in question, relative to the rates of change of the system, the context, and the construct in question.

For example, if there are seasonal factors at work, averaging over a whole year would not be as informative as would averaging over some shorter period of time. It there are variations in rate within a day (e.g., morning and evening production peaks), a single measure of daily rate would lose that information, as would any time period longer than a day. If there are short-term rhythms at work, time intervals in minutes or even seconds might be needed to accurately reflect them.

For most purposes, for example, it would really not be very helpful to measure ambient temperature or the level of the tide averaged over the whole day. It is the variations within such time intervals that are of most interest. That social psychological research tends to add and average over multiple measurements of many variables, in the interests of "more reliable estimates," is evidence that researchers in that field do not take seriously the idea of systematic changes over time, much less the idea of complex temporal patterning of those changes as we have discussed throughout this book.

But if we do not have conceptual theories that deal with changes over time in the systems we are studying, we have no way to anticipate which time intervals are safe to average within for a given variable in a given system. Hence, we are likely to average away meaningful differences in our efforts to get "more reliable" estimates of our variables.

At the same time, if we measure only once (as is most frequently done) or if we average over multiple measurements, we will not discover, empirically, any systematic changes over time in our variables that need to be taken into account in our theories. Hence, we will not generate an empirical basis for building those time factors into our theories. This produces a "cycle of neglect" of temporal patterns affecting both theory and empirical studies (Kelly & McGrath, 1988). This is another temporal dilemma that social psychology needs somehow to transcend.

TIME FRAMES OF DIFFERENT RESEARCH STRATEGIES

The questions discussed earlier about the precise temporal patterning of cause-and-effect processes and of the intervals between them opens up another whole set of temporal aspects of our methodology, namely: Our different research strategies have different time frames within which events occur. In field studies, events happen in what often gets called "real time," but which we will here call *system time*. System time is whatever time frame is natural to the system under study: work days, seasons, years of seniority, and so on. Laboratory experiments, on the other hand, are set within an *experimental time*, which is created for purposes of the study and usually involves much shorter intervals and durations. Sometimes, for example, an ad hoc group is given a "get acquainted" period of, say, 10 minutes; then they are given a task for a specific brief period (say 10 minutes), and then given a distracter task for 5 minutes, and then given a final questionnaire. Here, the cause–effect intervals are not determined by theory, nor by the timing of events in the "natural system" that the experimental system is in some sense intended to reflect. Rather, they are set within experimental time, usually in large part for experimental convenience. Experimental simulations do something similar, although they often reflect a more complicated sequencing of tasks and activities that reflects the sequencing (though not the durations) of tasks and activities of the system being simulated. However, experimental simulations do so in a much-truncated temporal frame. Sample surveys and judgment studies often are couched in terms that imply a timelessness; they ask for responses about hypothetical situations or about preferences among hypothetical alternatives. Mathematical models and verbal theories, as well as computer simulations and computational models, are cast in "conceptual time." Such strategies often postulate system processes in complex sequences that in some way are intended to reflect the sequences of the natural systems being simulated. But the processes "occur" in more or less instantaneous patterns. They preserve sequences but not intervals or durations.

Thus, various research strategies are set within different time frames. Our methodological paradigm has no algorithms by which we can translate temporal equivalences among them. How many minutes of laboratory time does it take to represent 1 hour of real or system time—or a month, a year, or three seasons? This seems a strange question to ask, and indeed we seldom seriously ask it of our empirical studies. But it is an essential question if we accept the idea that cause–effect relations have a finite temporal duration and that observation intervals shorter or longer than that may miss detecting those relations.

CONCLUDING REMARKS ABOUT TIME AND METHOD

The different timescales of different research strategies feed into and exacerbate the measurement problems as well as the problems of causality and validity discussed in earlier sections of the chapter. Suppose, for example, that we knew that it takes 3 months on the average for a new worker to become proficient on a particular job. Suppose we set out to test a hypothesis that requires participants to be beyond that initial learning period, and wished to test that hypothesis in a laboratory experiment. On what basis could we estimate how long in *experimental time* it would take participants, on average, to become proficient? That is, how many minutes of experimental time equals 3 months of time working in the real system?

This problem works in reverse, as well, and for translations between other research strategies. Suppose we learned that after twenty trials (of 5 minutes each) in a laboratory setting fatigue begins to drop efficiency for most people. How would we translate that back to real systems so as to improve the timing of rest periods and the arrangements of work tasks? Even more crucially, we have no procedures by which to translate between the conceptual times of theories (verbal theories, or formal models, or computer simulations or computational models) and either the system times of field studies or the experimental times of laboratory studies. That hinders us even further in any attempts we might make to build temporal factors into both our theoretical formulations and our empirical studies.

In social psychology we have dealt with these problems most frequently by regarding systems, and the values of all variables in them, as essentially stable over time (and often, stable across situations as well)—except, of course, that they can be changed by our experimental manipulations. That fits well with the classical theory of measurement and its idea of relatively static essences or true scores. It also fits well with the classical positivistic ideas about causality and validity. It does not fit well, however, with the ideas expressed in this book: That most human systems are dynamic rather than stable; that they change over time in complex and patterned ways; and that a full understanding of human systems and human behavior will require us to investigate those temporal patterns far more thoroughly than we have.

Social psychology could benefit by borrowing ideas from some sister disciplines that have attended more to these temporal matters because of the nature of their subject matter. For example, developmental psychology—both the portions focussed on infancy and early childhood and the portions focussed on aging processes—has had to deal with many of these substantive and methodological temporal issues (see, e.g., Adam, 1978, for a thoughtful discussion of problems involved in separating out history, cohort, generational, and aging effects). Studies of education and educational systems and some areas of cognitive psychology have also had to deal with these issues. Many of the models of fields such as operations research and human factors research—such as queueing theory and survival analysis (Cox & Oakes, 1984)—also give temporal factors a central role in their analyses of individual and collective human activity. Still another field, whose concepts are beginning to influence ours is dynamical systems analyses (e.g., Arrow & Burns, 2003; Arrow & Crosson, in press; Latané & Nowak, 1994; Vallacher & Nowak, 1994). Although these do not totally handle all of the temporal issues discussed in this chapter and elsewhere in this book, they represent a good beginning in attempting to deal directly with some of these temporal matters. We urge more attention to them by social psychological researchers of the future.

AFTERTHOUGHTS

Cause–Effect Sequence

Research in vivo offers gains,
But tangles up our causal chains.
If cause and outcome both run free
We're up an inferential tree!
Mere correlations we abhor.
The cause at least must come before!

Cause–Effect Intervals

We implement our "treatment" plan
Then measure outcome when we can.
If look too soon, no impact's made;
If wait too long, effects might fade.
Dare not observe too soon or late
But how do we know how long to wait?

Time Intervals and Threats to Validity

From cause till outcome doth arrive
Is time where plausible rivals thrive.
Some threats increase, and some get meager
As time 'twixt X and Y gets bigger.
To measure Y too soon, you see,
Enhances reactivity.
But longer times increase our bets
That into play will come some threats.
Yes, in Time's window, with a bang,
Comes History, and all that gang!

Measuring Temporal Patterns

Observing once will not arrange
Evidence for any change.
Observing twice a help 'twould be:
Results can now a difference see.
Observing thrice gives further yield:
Non-linear forms can be revealed.
But to see a cycle, *por favor*,
You need to measure four or more.

Time Frames of Different Research Strategies

The world puts on a real-time face
But labs unfold at quickened pace.
In lab-time, many things can't show:
No time to meditate, or grow,
No time to eat, or sleep, or stew;
No time for lovers' rendezvous!
What can we learn of human antic
From scenarios so frantic?
What can we learn of human ways
In labs with 15-minute days?

9

TIME AND THE FUTURE
OF SOCIAL PSYCHOLOGY

One main aim of this book has been to try to raise the consciousness of social psychologists about the importance of time in human lives and in our field. We have done so in a format that stressed, first, some conceptual issues we encounter in dealing with temporal matters; then several substantive areas in which temporal factors play an important role in the lives of individuals, groups, and collectivities; and finally, some serious methodological problems that arise because of the importance of time in our studies, problems that have been given little attention because of our past neglect of those temporal matters.

In this chapter, we will attempt the daunting task of suggesting how social psychology might try to take all of those temporal matters—conceptual, substantive, and methodological—into account in future social psychological theory and research. Some of our suggestions will seem problematic, both for conceptual and for practical reasons. They will be problematic and controversial also because in some sense we will be proposing "cultural changes" in our science: that is, changes in how we design and implement our studies, in how we construct and what we include in our theories, and even in what issues are important for study. That is a brash thing to do! No one—ourselves included—has the "standing" that gives them permission to dictate such cultural changes for a field. Yet at the same time, all serious scholars—ourselves included—have the duty to point out serious problems in their field and to try to propose potential remedies for them.

Moreover, we see hopeful signs that the field may be ready for such changes. As we have noted in several places throughout the book, other scholars have made suggestions that can help attain more incisive study of a wide range of temporal matters. We will note some of them again here.

In this chapter we will offer suggestions for needed changes in the field, knowing, as we do, that those suggestions will be extremely hard to implement, and that they would be imperfect fixes even if implemented. It is apparent, from the preceding eight chapters, that there is much to be done if social psychology is to begin to take temporal matters fully into account. In this chapter, we address three main areas in which we believe such changes are needed:

1. We need to incorporate temporal matters into our theoretical formulations. Until we do, we are unlikely to search for empirical information about them. Moreover, the logic of our positivist paradigm insists that the processes by which causes have their effects take specifiable amounts of time; so specification of such intervals is crucial to our attempts to test and confirm those theories. We comment on those matters in the first section of this chapter, noting two specific approaches that could aid us in this regard.
2. We need somehow to develop methods for collection, analysis, and interpretation of empirical evidence that allow us to ask and answer a range of temporal questions. In the second section of this chapter, we note some promising directions for such developments.
3. We need to focus much more of our empirical research than we have in the past on specifically temporal issues that are so ubiquitous in social psychological phenomena. The final section of this chapter lists some temporal topics that we think would be especially fruitful for empirical study.

MAKING TIME AN INTEGRAL PART OF THEORY

Even though social psychological and psychological theory have for the most part ignored temporal issues, social psychological phenomena nevertheless take time to occur, show temporal patterning as they unfold, and often are sensitive to temporal factors in the embedding contexts. It seems to us, therefore, that we need to express our hypotheses and formulate our theories in terms that reckon with the temporal features of the phenomena and their contexts. We also note some signs of movement in that direction in particular substantive domains. For example, both George and Jones (2000) and Mitchell and James (2001) have argued along similar lines regarding the formulation of theory in organizational research. Arrow, McGrath, and Berdahl (2000) have made a similar case for the small group research field.

Mitchell and James, for example, present a thorough analysis and discussion of temporal issues along with a meta-analysis of the frequency and forms of different types of causal relations postulated in the organizational research literature. They found that most of the causal relations postulated can be subsumed under eight temporal patterns:

1. X causes Y, but with no implication as to whether that (level of) Y persists. This is the most frequent pattern in the literature they reviewed.
2. X causes Y, and that (level of) Y is stable over time.
3. X causes Y, and Y changes (e.g., continues to increase) over time.
4. X causes Y, but over repeated exposure to X, Y changes.
5. X causes Y, and then a changed X causes a changed Y.
6. X causes Y, which causes a changed X which causes a changed Y.
7. X causes Y, which causes a different variable, Z, which may in turn cause a different variable Q.
8. X causes Z, but the strength of the relationship varies as a function of the level of Y.

These eight patterns include both time-limited and persistent X–Y relations, as well as patterns involving recurrent X–Y causality, reciprocal X–Y causal relations, and relations in which Y serves in the role of mediator or of moderator.

Mitchell and James then discuss the temporal requirements that each such pattern of proposed causal relations implies for our theoretical formulations, and suggest some means by which we can begin to deal with those requirements. For example, the most frequent form of causal relation presented in the literature that Mitchell and James reviewed, configuration 1, was X changes Y, with no implication as to whether the change in Y persists. Here, the researcher needs to know that X preceded Y, and what the time lag is at which the full effect of X on Y will be in force. Consider the more complex pattern 6: X causes Y, which causes a changed X, which causes a changed Y

(that is, recursive causation). Here, the theorist needs to know the time lag between initial X and changed Y, between that changed Y and later changed X, and between that later changed X and still later changed Y. Still other patterns require knowledge about rates of change of X and of Y, and about the time relations of "third variables" to both X and Y.

Mitchell and James propose a Moderation by Causal Cycle curve (MCC curve) as a technique for helping to map empirically such time lag relations. They assume (a) that any effect takes some finite time, however short, to occur and stabilize (a period that they refer to as the equilibriating period of the X–Y relation); (b) that this is followed by a period, perhaps lengthy, of equilibrium in the X–Y effect (their equilibrium period); and (c) that in principle, any X–Y effect will eventually vary, or lessen, or be confounded with other effects (a period they refer to as an entropic period). They argue, further, than any statistical test of the X–Y relation will vary depending on when the data were obtained with respect to those three periods. It will be underestimated during the equilibriating period—and the earlier the more so. It will be underestimated during the entropy pe-riod—the later the more so. It will be most accurately estimated during the equilibrium period.

Assuming that the X–Y relation is linear, if such relations are assessed for each of a series of X–Y intervals, and the sizes of those relations (not the values of X or of Y) are plotted against the time intervals, those analyses must show an increasing, then a stable, then a decreasing size of relation. Those relation sizes can be used to trace the pattern of those time lags. Mitchell and James also illustrate several ways in which variations of their MCC curve can be used to map more complex temporal patterns.

An alternative approach to this same set of concerns regarding tem-poral processes in our theoretical formulations has been offered by Arrow and colleagues (Arrow & Burns, 2003; Arrow & Crosson, in press; Arrow et al., 2000). The last work offers a theory of groups as complex systems that encompasses a logic of inquiry that contrasts with the logic of our currently dominant paradigm, and that would deal directly with temporal patterns of phenomena. (This set of ideas was already discussed in chapters 6,7, and 8). Our current dominant logic of inquiry is one by which we compare (a) the average value on specific local or microlevel variables, at one point in time, averaged over a set of cases treated alike, with (b) the average value on those same variables for one or more other sets of cases that have received different experimental or control treatments. The proposed new logic of inquiry would be one by which we trace the pattern over time of system-level variables for each case studied, and an accompanying logic by which we examine how the patterns over time traced by various cases fit with or contrast with one another (see Arrow et al., 2000, for an extended discussion of this logic of inquiry, by which we would trace the evolution of key system variables over time). Arrow and Crosson (in press) make use of several concepts from the complex systems theory approach to study group formation as a dynamic process. They examine changes in group membership over time, illustrating "attractors," effects of contextual conditions, the application of phase portraits, and the like (for illustrations of such approaches, see also Arrow & Burns, 2003; Baron, Amazeen, & Beek, 1994).

Both the Mitchell and James and the Arrow and colleagues approaches seem to offer promise as bases for formulating more temporally sensitive theory. Both of these formulations, however, make several strong assumptions, and still leave many unanswered questions about just how this can be carried out and what new methodological problems those methods, in turn, might give rise to. We think this is one of the crucial issues facing social psychological theory, and we hope that other social psychological scholars will take on these issues and add still more possibilities for their resolution.

DEVELOPING TIME-SENSITIVE TOOLS FOR SOCIAL PSYCHOLOGICAL RESEARCH

In the previous chapter, we noted some serious methodological issues that need to be dealt with if we are to develop a time-sensitive social psychology. They are all issues that were raised at various earlier points in the book. They are also all issues that must be dealt with if we are to carry out research on the temporal aspects of the substantive phenomena of our field. In this section, we note some recent developments that may help in these matters and, where we can, we offer suggestions for approaches that might be useful in dealing with them.

Time, Cause, and Research Strategies

We need somehow to develop methods and an accompanying "scientific rationale" by which to take into account forms of causal relation in addition to linear mechanical causes. One especially difficult challenge has to do with *intentionality*. There is an exceedingly difficult question of how to develop scientific ways to study the impact of intentionality on human action without at the same time abandoning both the goal of prediction and the goal of objectivity in that science. The positivistic rationale that is our dominant methodological paradigm seeks the prediction of events from formulation of general causal propositions, on the basis of "objective" observation. If we admit human intention as a legitimate "cause" of behavior, that poses at least two key problems for that paradigm: First, how can we obtain evidence about what causal forces are operating in any but "subjective" ways, if some of those causal forces are human intentions rather than external mechanical causal forces? Second, how can we predict behavior on any future occasion, as we cannot deliberately manipulate or control the pattern of intentions that will hold in that future?

A related problem for the development of a cumulative body of social psychological knowledge, noted in the previous chapter, is that research strategies vary in the time frames at which they operate, and in their adaptability with regard to temporal processes and intervals. Experiments run in experimental time; field studies have reference to real time or system time; surveys often refer to hypothetical blocks of past or future time; theories are formulated in conceptual time. We need some means by which to adjust, or map, their differing time frames to one another—some way to "scale up" from a given interval of experimental time, for example, to its appropriate interval of system time. This is an extremely intriguing, but extremely difficult, problem.

Time and Validity

In chapter 8, we discussed at some length the intertwining of temporal issues with various "threats to validity" of empirical findings. We also discussed the dual role that a system's own history and its maturation or development play, both as "threats to validity" in terms of conventional analysis techniques, and as legitimate substantive factors influencing the system's current and future behavior. In light of these discussions, we need to develop a rationale by which to integrate both the "threats to validity" arguments and the "history and development as substance" arguments into a single coherent rationale for scientific study. If we are going to deal with temporal issues at all, it seems to us necessary to take the impact of both history and anticipated futures into account. Yet doing so, on the face of it, seems to move us from a nomothetic toward an ideographic rationale.

Time-Sensitive Methods for Collection and Analysis of Data

It is obvious from all that has been said thus far that we think there is a need for continued development of methods for gathering, processing, and analyzing empirical data that will allow the exploration of a wide array of temporal factors. There is a need for much more frequent use of *research strategies* that permit a more effective treatment of temporal issues—strategies such as comparative field studies, field experiments, experimental simulations, and the use of time-based computational models.

But even if those strategies are used, researchers do not always take advantage of their potential for collecting data at multiple points in time. We think one of the most crucial needs for future research in our field is the establishment of strong norms favoring the use of *multiple measurement occasions*, spaced deliberately at time intervals reflecting theoretical considerations about the operation of various temporal processes. We must give much more emphasis to both the collection of data over extended periods of time, and the collection of multiple *waves* of measurements of crucial variables, if we are to begin to develop meaningful theoretical formulations that take time seriously.

There are some signs of progress in regard to methods for the analysis of data that allow consideration of temporal issues. McGrath and Altermatt (2000) provide a recent discussion of several data analysis methods that are available for analysis of temporal information in group interaction data, some of which are discussed later in this section. Those methods differ in terms of their data requirements, with some of those differences having to do with temporal aspects of the data. For example, some of these analysis techniques are applicable to qualitative or categorical data, others require quantitative data. Likewise, some of these techniques can be used if data have been aggregated into a few phases or measurement waves, whereas others can be applied to data that is an extended event-by-event (or observation-by-observation) sequence.

Categorical data that has been aggregated into a sequence of phases can be analyzed in either of two forms: in terms of frequencies via log linear models or in terms of proportions via logit models. For time-related analyses, these methods are used to determine whether the time-ordered intervals or waves of data are significantly different from each other in terms of the distribution of frequencies or proportions in the various categories of the dependent variables. One can introduce more powerful tests if there is a theoretical basis for prediction of a linear trend over time intervals (Agresti, 1996).

If such categorical data contains multiple waves and there is information about time ordering of those waves, then categorical data can be tested for *serial dependence*—that is, for the extent to which later events are dependent on the occurrence of earlier ones. McGrath and Altermatt (2000) discuss three types of such serial dependence analysis methods: lag-sequential analysis, applications of those lag-sequential analysis methods to interpersonal dominance relations, and Markov models.

For data expressing magnitude (i.e., quantitative rather than categorical data), McGrath and Altermatt (2000) discuss four approaches. One is repeated measures analyses, which provide tests of quantitative data that parallel those for categorical data that are not time-ordered. A second is analyses of linear or polynomial trends, which is a special case of repeated measures analyses if there is information about the time-ordering of the data waves. A third is the use of time-domain analyses of causal variables, of which Box and Jenkins' (1976) Autoregressive Integrated Moving Average (ARIMA) model is the best known. A fourth is the analyses of periodic trends, also known as harmonic or frequency-domain analyses (Pole, West, & Harrison, 1994). McGrath and Altermatt (2000) also discuss a fifth approach, Tuckerized growth curves (Brossart, Patton, & Wood, 1998; Tucker, 1966), which they characterize as permitting the analysis of multiple time series that "are not well behaved"—that is, temporal patterns that are nonlinear, are not fit well by polynomial models, and are aperiodic.

Note that although all of these methods for analysis of data can provide valuable information regarding temporal factors, each also involves constraints on what temporal factors can be explored. As already noted, the applicability of these various analysis models depends on the specific temporal (and other) features of the data. Moreover, each specific analysis method also contains additional assumptions, often ones affecting the analysis of temporal issues. For example, Markov models require two assumptions that make them problematic for much data on human action and interaction: the assumptions of stationarity and of path independence. In Markov models, stationarity assumes that the probability of a given sequence of events will remain the same throughout the entire period of observation. That assumption would not hold if there were any change over time in relations among acts or members, and we have argued throughout this book that such changes are ubiquitous in individual and collective human action. The path independence assumption holds that only the immediately preceding act (or the previous two acts for a three act analysis sequence) affects the target act, with all earlier events irrelevant to that target act. Such an assumption discounts all factors involved in both initial conditions and past history of the systems whose behavior is being analyzed.

Other methods of analysis similarly involve sets of assumptions that limit the kinds of temporal processes that they can be used to examine. So, although each of these analysis methods is a valuable addition to our technology, none of them can solve all of our needs for analysis methods regarding temporal processes. Other sources in which these and related methods are discussed in more detail are available: (Adam, 1978; Agresti, 1996; Arundale, 1980; Box & Jenkins, 1976; Brossart et al., 1998; Dillon, Madden, & Kumar, 1983; Faraone & Dorfman, 1987; Gardner & Griffin, 1989; Goldstein, 1995; Gottman, 1981; Gottman & Roy, 1990; Horne, Yang, & Ware, 1982; Jones, 1993; Kerr, 1981; Kraemer & Jacklin, 1979; Nesselroade, Stigler, & Baltes, 1980; Neter, Wasserman, & Kutner, 1990; Pole, West, & Harrison, 1994; Porges et al., 1980; Rogosa, Brandt, & Zimowski, 1982; Singer, 1998; Tucker, 1966; Wampold, 1984; Wasserman & Faust, 1994; Wasserman & Jacobucci, 1988; Wasserman & Pattison, 1996; Wilhelm, 2001).

Social psychological phenomena subsume a relatively extensive array of temporal parameters and temporal processes that must be reckoned with. Some of them were noted and defined elsewhere in this book. Moreover, if we are going to take the study of temporal matters seriously and if we are to extend our logic of inquiry to include approaches by which we trace the evolution of system-level variables over time (as discussed earlier), we will need to use multiple measurement waves rather than single static measures of our variables or simple before–after designs. Doing so, however, poses many practical problems and also some conceptual ones. For example, we will need to figure out "how long to wait" between measurements (or experimental implementations) of causal processes and outcomes, and also how long to persist in obtaining measurements of the evolution over time of those causal processes. The Mitchell and James Moderation by Causal Cycle conceptions, noted earlier in this chapter, may help with these questions. Moreover, if each measurement is to be regarded as a meaningful datum, as our proposed new logic of inquiry would hold, how then can we establish reliability (in the sense of stability over successive measurements) of our measures?

STUDYING TIME MATTERS WITHIN SOCIAL PSYCHOLOGICAL PHENOMENA: A SUBSTANTIVE AGENDA FOR FUTURE RESEARCH

The chapters of this book point to a host of temporal issues that are relevant to social psychological phenomena and that are amenable to empirical research. In this section we will list several key temporal issues that we think are especially ripe for and amenable to empirical investigation. We will list them in roughly the order in which we treated their underlying topics in this book. We think these need considerable attention in future social psychological theory and research. Moreover, the issues underlying many of these questions probably need to be conceptualized in new ways, for which we do not yet have an appropriate conceptual vocabulary. If so, that will doubtless open up whole new sets of empirical questions that will need to be pursued, questions we cannot yet conceive of nor articulate coherently at this time.

Time Use

Research on how people allot their time over activities is one of the more successful areas of study of temporal issues. We assume, and hope, that the strong interest in cross-time and cross-cultural studies of time use will continue. It would be very useful to develop less cumbersome and less subject-dependent methods by which to document people's distribution of time over activities. Major advances in electronic technology may help considerably in this regard: such things as handheld computers that could serve both as "beepers" and as the basis for entering responses that could be automatically processed, and sensors that identify who is where in relation to what other people. It would also be useful to develop standardized conceptual categories for classifying activities—perhaps at a relatively abstract level as proposed by Chalendar (1976)—in terms of which to characterize varieties of activities. This is a difficult task, because these will need to apply across cultures.

Human Experience of the Passage of Time

The study of how humans judge the passage of time is probably the longest established area of study of temporal matters. There continues to be active work on alternative models of both retrospective and prospective judgments of passage of time. We probably need more studies to help clear up differences in how different groups of people feel about passage of time in general, and about the speed of passage of time during various activities. One strong need in this area, we think, would be to examine more closely what consequences for human lives, if any, arise from differences ("biases") in estimations of passage of time. (See, also, Mitchell, Peterson, & Cronk, 1997).

The field could profit, as well, from a more concentrated empirical research effort on the phenomenon of *flow*. Some of the questions we need to examine include the following: When and how does flow occur? What is the range of situational features that affect its occurrence? We also need more research to explore the positive and negative effects of flow for those who experience it and their interaction partners.

Temporal Orientations and Human Motivation

This is a third area in which there has been considerable work on temporal matters, with most of it focussed on future temporal orientations. Much of that work, however, presupposes that temporal orientation is trait-like in that it persists for a given person over time and situations. It is not clear that such persistence has been established empirically. We need to investigate how persistent temporal orientations are for a given person over time and situations.

Human motivation is intertwined with these temporal orientations. Many features of motivation are temporal in character, such as a strong concern for and focus on the future that is characteristic of people with high achievement motivation. This notion is closely intertwined with the "persistent" (trait-like) pattern regarded as a future temporal orientation. We need to clear up, both empirically and conceptually, the relations of the temporal features of motivational states (which presumably wax and wane) and temporal orientations (which presumably persist over time and situations).

We also need to document more thoroughly how these temporal orientations vary among cultures, and how they vary over age, gender, race, ethnicity, and class within cultures. It would also be useful, we think, to examine more thoroughly how such variations arise, and what, if anything, can or should be done about (inducing or hindering) their development. Finally, we need to explore in what ways temporal orientations impact other human activities.

Time, Goals, and Individual Action

Goals and action are closely intertwined both at individual and group levels, and both involve myriad temporal features. There is still much empirical work to be done in exploring the temporal aspects of phases and cycles of individual action, and the role of planning in such action sequences. Multiple conceptual formulations—action theory, control theory, goal-setting theory, self-regulation theory, and complex systems theory—have been applied fruitfully to these issues, but there is not as yet a single widely accepted formulation. Conceptual as well as empirical progress is called for here.

Time and Decisions

Interest in temporal aspects of decision making seems to have gained impetus in recent years, particularly in regard to analysis of time from decision until its anticipated consequences. We need to continue to explore the consequences of temporal biases in decision processes and outcomes. In particular, we need a full consideration of how temporal aspects of the decision process can be managed in ways that are helpful to the decision makers. Time pressure, deadlines, and temporal features of the work setting (which we have treated under the topic of stress and coping) also play into decision making, and these relations need to be explored as well.

Waiting, Impatience, and Boredom

We need to explore more systematically the conditions under which people do and do not have strong negative affect with regard to waiting for a service or an activity. This ought to include examination of different kinds of waiting as discussed in chapter 4. We also need to continue to explore ways in which we could help people "suffer" waiting time less impatiently, and potentially recapture some of their waiting time to use for what they would regard as fruitful activities.

Examination of waiting, boredom, and impatience also needs to address the question of the extent to which impatience or boredom are persistent trait-like characteristics for which there are individual differences that persist over time and situations, or instead are closely tied to features of the contexts in which waiting occurs, or perhaps involve interactions of persons and situations.

Work, Time, and Stress

We need to examine more extensively the impact that several temporal features of work and nonwork settings (such as work load, time pressure, and the like) have both in creating stressful working and living environments and in offering opportunities to cope with otherwise stressful circumstances. We especially need to disentangle the various temporal levels and patterns at which stress operates, and how those levels and patterns are interconnected.

Time Features of Group Formation and Development

There has been relatively little work on group formation, although it is currently receiving some attention from Arrow and colleagues (e.g., Arrow & Crosson, in press; Arrow & McGrath, 1993, 1995). The topic of group development has received much attention in the past, and is experiencing new vitality in the form of work by Wheelan and colleagues (Wheelan, 1994; Wheelan & McKeage, 1993). We need to develop a broader understanding of when and how groups form, what types of groups there are or can be and how they differ in their formation. We also need to increase our understanding of when and how groups persist and flourish, and how this might vary for groups of different types. It would also be of great value if we could use such understanding to help people form more effective groups.

Change in Groups Over Time

It is remarkable how little study there has been of the relations between groups and their embedding contexts, and of how groups change over time in response to changes in those embedding systems. As we indicated earlier in the book, there are some signs of a recent increase in interest in those issues. It is crucial that we focus much more of our empirical and theoretical efforts toward understanding how groups adapt to actions and events (or anticipated actions and events) in their embedding contexts. If we can do that, we then need to find ways to put that knowledge to work to help groups flourish when they must deal with complex and dynamic embedding contexts.

Another formidable challenge is to develop a better understanding of how groups "learn"—that is, how they profit from their own and others' experience—and of where and how groups retain and make use of the results of that experience. Here, too, there is evidence of a recent increase in interest in these issues. One topic of interest in this area is the complex interplay among the group's developmental history, its record of and reputation for effective task performance, and its adaptation to changes in its environmental contexts.

Cycles, Phases, and Entrainment in Collective Action

We clearly need to develop a better understanding of the cyclical patterns of collective actions—how groups act, obtain feedback on results of their actions, and use that feedback to modify subsequent group action. Such knowledge is basic to any attempt to deliberately train groups for effective action, and to train them, as well, for effective structuring and scheduling of the task performance processes and of strategic planning.

We also need to explore further the conditions under which the behaviors of individuals engaged in collective action become entrained to one another's actions and to external pacers and cycles. We need to determine both the conditions under which entrainment occurs, and the consequences of such entrainment of behavior patterns for the individuals and groups involved. In that effort, it would be useful to explore the relations between deadlines and the setting of quantitative production goals, and hence to understand whether goal-setting phenomena are compatible with effects of deadlines and other entrainment phenomena.

Multiple Simultaneous Cycles and Cadences

One of the most complex temporal issues involved in all of these topics is the interweaving of simultaneously occurring multiple rhythms, cycles, and cadences in individual and collective behavior. Considering the action of groups, for example, different but overlapping temporal rhythms and cadences are involved in (a) the operations by which group members carry out group tasks and projects; (b) the developmental patterns by which those groups form and change over time; (c) the temporal patterns that characterize changes in the members' and groups' embedding contexts, and the groups' reactions to those changes. Add to these the different rhythms and cadences of individual member's behaviors, not to mention the ongoing temporal patterning of individual psychophysiological activity. One of the most demanding challenges for future research on temporal matters will be to disentangle these rhythms, cycles, and cadences; to articulate them in systematic and coherent ways; and then to understand how those multiple temporal patterns become coordinated or synchronized with one another in the everyday lives of individuals and groups.

CONCLUDING COMMENTS

To restate our opening thought: Time matters in social psychology, in myriad ways. We have discussed many of those matters in this book; and, of course, there are many others we did not consider or even identify. Moreover, we also identified several difficult methodological and conceptual issues that are raised when one tries to study those substantive temporal issues.

We believe that an increased concern with temporal matters is of extreme importance for the future of social psychological theory and research. At the same time, we recognize the difficulties such study entails. Although this book will not itself solve these difficult issues, we hope it will induce other scholars to seek their solution.

We end the book with one final set of rhyming "Afterthoughts."

AFTERTHOUGHTS

Studying Time, Redux

The point, dear friends, of all this rhyme
Is just that now's the time for time:
The time to take time seriously,
Not treat it so imperiously!
The time to make time's mysteries yield
In laboratory and field.
The time to make time fill our theories
Ere time's sharp arrow ends (h)our queries!

APPENDIX A:
PARAMETERS OF
TEMPORAL PATTERNING

Studies of time make use of several different parameters of time and of temporal patterning: rate, frequency, rhythms, trends, cycles, and so on. Sometimes those parameters are used in inconsistent ways. It would be useful if we had a relatively standardized set of definitions for those parameters, to clarify discussions of temporal matters in the literature.

In our view, parameters of temporal patterns include a relatively wide span of features of situations in which humans behave, not just the simple reckoning of clock time and calendar date. Of course, temporal matters do include features having to do with location of an event or action in *historical* time, as measured by some clock and calendar such as the Gregorian calendar date and Greenwich Mean Time. But they also involve the location of an event or action in one or more *situational* times (such as years of tenure in an organization, time before the end of some specific season, or time before some performance deadline).

Moreover, time matters also have to do with the *duration* of events or actions, and with the durations of *intervals* between successive recurrences of events or actions of a particular kind or between two or more notable events or actions of different kinds.

Time is also a component of rate and frequency—that is, of the number of repetitions of an event or action of a certain kind within a given total time interval. Time is also an aspect of the order relations (sequence or simultaneity) of two or more notable events or actions, of same or different kinds.

At a more complex level, time is reflected in the durations of successive intervals between multiple occurrences of events or actions of a certain type. That is a complicated way of saying that there are cyclical rhythms in the occurrence of events or actions. Finally, time is a key aspect of cause–effect relations—that is, of the regularity of occurrence, and the interval before occurrence, of events or actions of a given type, following the occurrence of an event of a specific different type.

In this appendix, we will attempt to lay out some fairly straightforward definitions of all of these temporal parameters (e.g., rate, frequency, periodicity, and so on). To make those parameter definitions clear, we need to begin by assuming some arbitrary units of time, and to state what we mean by events, observations, amplitudes, and the like. Those assumptions, and the definitions of temporal parameters, are given below, as a set of propositions.

ASSUMPTIONS

A. *Time Units:* Let us assume some minimum unit of time, t. For example, we might consider $t = 1$ sec, although it could equally well be a nanosecond, or a minute, or a day, or a year.

    1. Let us assume, also, that we can define a larger temporal period, T, as having n adjacent and successive ts, specified as $t1, t2, \ldots ti, \ldots tn$. If $t = 1$ sec, for example, and we chose to put T equal to 1 hour, then n would equal 60×60 or 3600.

    2. Together these assume also that time is, or can be treated as, "digital" rather than continuous, but that because they are adjacent there is no "time" or "space" between adjacent successive ts.

B. *Events:* Let us define an event, e, as an observed state or action of some concrete system or a component of such a system.

    1. A concrete system can be a human individual, a group, a human–machine system (such as a truck or a tank or an airplane), a machine system, or an ecological system (e.g., a weather front).

    2. A state is the "value" of one or more properties of any condition or component of such a system.

    3. An action is movement, behavior, or output of such a system or one of its components.

C. *Observations:* An observation is any record of a state or action of a concrete system—that is, a record of an event.

    1. Observations (i.e., records of events) may be made in words (which may later be converted to numerical values), in numerical values, or in any other symbol system (e.g., a coding schema using nonalphanumeric notations).

    2. Observations may be made with or without the aid of physical instruments—recording devices such as cameras, enhancing devices such as telescopes, or translating devices such as thermometers or pressure gauges.

D. *Sources of Observation:* Observations (that is, records of states or conditions or actions of a system) can be made by any of three classes of observers distinguished in terms of the relation of the observer to the system being observed:

    1. A human observer who is the system being observed, or is a part or component of such a system (or is the suprasystem within which the observed system is embedded, as in the observation that "my arm is itching"). This class of observer is designated as s (for self or subject).

2. A human observer who is "investigating" some questions having to do with the observed systems. This class of observer is designated as *r* (for researcher, or researcher surrogate). Instruments (e.g., stop watches, thermometers) can also serve as researcher surrogates.
3. A human observer who is external to the reference system, and not engaged in investigating it, but who is carrying out some function in interdependence with the observed systems, such as a customer, or a supplier, or a tax collector. This class of observer is designated as *o* (for outsider, or third-party recorder).

E. *Classes of Events:* Two events, *ei* and *ej*, are of the same class of events *E* if the recorder of those events (*s*, *r*, or *o*) sees them as sharing common features that define *E*.
   1. Those features-in-common can be virtually any one or more characteristics of the event *e*: that is, any feature of its *who, what, where, when, how much,* or *why*.
   2. Moreover, if an *r* later makes use of observations that were recorded earlier by an *s* or an *o* (or another *r*), he or she can aggregate or reassemble those events into new classes, *E*, on the basis of characteristics that the original *s*, *r*, or *o* did not use for classification but that are nonetheless available as information about the events. For example, all the acts by both member *a* and member *b*, previously kept separate, can be aggregated into a single class of events.

F. *Magnitude of Events:* Let us define the amplitude, intensity, or magnitude of a given event *e* as the value associated by the observer with the amount of some property of that *e* (e.g., its hardness, accuracy, color, extroversion, or any other denotable aspect of *e*). That value is regarded as a property of that event, *e*. Such values of amount can be expressed in numbers (using ratio, interval, or ordinal scales), or in terms of words (often using nominal scales).

Note that the units of time, *t* and *T*, are arbitrary. So is the definition of an event, *e*, and the classification of *es* as in a given event class *E*, "events that are alike." So, too, are the properties used to define the amplitude, intensity, or magnitude of an event. Given these assumptions, we can then formulate definitions of some useful temporal concepts.

TEMPORAL CONCEPTS

1. *Frequency:* Under these assumptions, we can define frequency of an event as the number of times, *f*, that a given event, *e*, of the event class *E*, occurs (that is, has an onset) within a given *T*.
2. *Rate:* Rate of an event, expressed in units of *t*, is f/T.

3. *Duration:* Duration of an event, *e*, is the number of units, *t*, between the observed onset and observed cessation of that event.

4. *Proportional Duration:* Duration can also be expressed as the proportion of time during which events of the class *E* are occurring, compared with no events of class *E* occurring (e.g., the percentage of time someone in a group is talking vs. silent); Proportional duration is the number of *t* in a period *T* during which an event *e* of class *E* is occurring, divided by *n* (i.e., by the number of *t* in *T*).

5. *Sequence:* Sequence refers to the order of onset of two events, *ei* and *ej* (of the same or different classes of *E*). Simultaneity of two events, *ei* and *ej*, occurs when and only when the onset of *ei* is the same *t* as the onset of *ej*.

6. *Sequence, simultaneity, and size of time unit:* It is apparent that simultaneity and sequence can be established only with reference to observations of events accurate to a given unit of time (our arbitrary value, *t*).

   (a). Two events that are simultaneous with reference to a given unit, *t*, may or may not still be simultaneous at any more micro unit of *t*.

   (b). Alternatively, a sequence of two events can be established only with reference to given sized units of time, and may or may not hold for more macro time units.

   (c). For example, if two events happened on Wednesday, one at 2 p.m. and one at 3 p.m., they are sequential if observation is accurate to the minute or to the hour, but simultaneous if observations are only taken "to the day" or "to the week."

7. *Temporal Location:* The temporal location of an event, *e*, is defined as the number associated with the *t* of its onset, when those numbers are considered within a total overall sequence of *t*s within a mega-period, *T*.

   (a). A mega-period *T* refers to a large block of time as reckoned on some clock or calendar.

   (b). Such a clock or calendar can be a generic one such as Greenwich Mean Time or the Gregorian calendar (i.e., a "G-clock").

   (c). It can be a clock or calendar that reckons time within a given specific situation, setting, or system. For example, the start of the "two minute warning" for the final two minutes of each half of a football game, or the "first day of instruction" of a semester at some university, or "three days before my 27th birthday" for the life of some specific person (i.e., an "S-clock").

   (d). Any given time *t* may be located at a point in, or referenced to a point in, either or both G and S clocks, with reference to each of multiple mega-*T* periods.

8. *Temporal Patterning:* The temporal patterning of a series of events, *ei*, *ej*, *ek*...(of the same class of events *E*) refers to the number of *t* between suc-

cessive occurrences of *es*, within a block of observed successive *ts* (that is, a *T*).

    (a). Temporal patterning is regular in period *T* if there is (approximately) the same number of *t* between each adjacent pair of *es*, throughout *T*. The periodicity of such a regular pattern of events can be expressed as the number of *t* between adjacent successive occurrences of the event.

    (b). An approximately regular pattern of events can be defined, with its periodicity expressed as the average number of *ts* between adjacent successive occurrences. Such an approximation can be defined to any given level of approximation expressed as some function of the variance among the *t* counts for all successive adjacent pairs of events.

    (c). An irregular pattern is defined as a set of successive *es* within a period *T* for which the variance in the number of *t* between adjacent successive pairs exceeds some arbitrary value set for the approximation, above. The degree of irregularity can be defined as the size of the variances (or some function of the variances) of the number of *ts* between all pairs of adjacent successive events, *e*, of the class *E*.

9. *Rhythms:* A rhythm or rhythmic pattern refers to a regular or approximately regular pattern of a series of events, *e*, of the same class *E*. It can be defined in terms of either periodicity (as above) or frequency or rate (see earlier definitions). That is, it can be defined in terms of number of evenly spaced occurrences of *e* within a given *T*, or in terms of the number (or average number) of "temporal spaces," *t*, between successive occurrences. (These are referred to as the frequency domain and the time domain.)

10. *Trends:* A trend is a temporal pattern of events, *e*, all of a given class *E* within a time period *T*, that shows a systematic directionality or pattern—not necessarily linear or even monotonic—in the amount of some property used to reference the amplitude, intensity, or magnitude of that event, *e*.

    (a). A linear trend is a temporal pattern showing a systematic equal increase (or decrease) in amount over successive units of time. The size of that linear trend can be expressed in units of amount (of a reference property) per unit of time.

    (b). A nonlinear trend is a temporal pattern showing a systematically increasing (or decreasing) amount of change in the value of the reference property of successive events, *es*, rather than a systematically unchanging amount of change in those values.

    (c). If those amounts of change shift in direction (from positive to negative, or vice versa) within the period under consideration, that becomes a nonmonotonic nonlinear trend. A cycle (see below) is a special case of a nonmonotonic nonlinear trend.

(d). Punctuated equilibrium refers to the pattern of operation of a system in which a given developmental pattern is rapidly stabilized, and remains so until a certain time at which it abruptly changes to another pattern, which then stabilizes. The timing of the changes depends on a variety of system and contextual conditions, and may itself be time linked (e.g., halfway to a deadline).

11. *Cycles:* A cycle is a temporal pattern showing a systematic and recurrent increase and then decrease (or vice versa) in amount of the property used to reference event *es* amplitude, intensity, or magnitude, such that it departs from and then returns to its initial value, recurrently. Any given point in any one recurrence of the cycle can be characterized in terms of its phase and magnitude.

(a). The phase of a cycle refers to the different regions of its cyclical progression: for example, its lowest point, ascending region, highest point, or descending region. The number of phases and the basis for division of a cycle into phases are arbitrary.

(b). The periodicity of a cycle can be specified either (i) in terms of the number of reoccurrences of a given phase of the cycle (say, its peak) per period of time T; or (ii) in terms of the number of units of time, t, between successive reoccurrences of a given phase of the cycle. These are referred to as the frequency domain and the time domain.

(c). Linear trends, nonlinear trends, nonmonotonic nonlinear trends, and cycles all assume regularity, or approximate regularity, of pattern. If the amount of time between successive *es* shows variation, but no discernable pattern of differences in amount (i.e., there are changes in values, but they do not approximate a regular linear, curvilinear, nonmonotonic, or cyclical pattern), that pattern is regarded as a temporal fluctuation. It is not appropriate, however, to assume that such fluctuations are necessarily random error.

12. *Coupled Series of Events:* As noted previously, the series of events, (*ei*, *ej*, ...), is part of an event class E because all of those *es* are related; that is, they all exhibit one or more properties in terms of which the event class E has been defined.

(a). One form of such relatedness can be that events in a particular set of events (a series of successive *es*) are regarded as functionally related to one another—that is, as one event in the sequence leading to, or setting the conditions for, or "causing," later events. For example, a series of stimuli to, and subsequent responses by, a given system may be regarded as a functionally related set of events.

(b). Hence, the occurrence, and the time of occurrence, of successive events in the sequence may be of interest. We can refer to this as a functionally related series. Some trends and some cycles are composed of occurrences of such functionally related sets of events.

13. *Functionally Coupled Sequences:* Sometimes such a functionally related series of events is composed of two (or more) subseries, each of which is emanating from different systems (or different subsystems of a larger embedding system). For example, one subseries may be the actions of subsystem *a*, and the other subseries may be the actions of subsystem *b* (e.g., a series of actions of person *a* and of person *b* who are in interaction with one another). If such is the case, there may be a temporally regular pattern to the times between occurrences of given acts of series *a* and occurrence of (functionally related) acts of series *b*, and vice versa. When this is the case, we can consider those two subseries as functionally coupled sequences. (When they are cyclical in form, they are sometimes referred to as coupled oscillators.) The implication is that the occurrence of acts in each of the subseries induces or establishes the conditions for occurrence of subsequent acts of the other subseries.

14. *Entrainment:* The term *entrainment* refers to the systematic synchronization, in phase and periodicity, of two or more cyclical patterns of events.

(a). Both cyclical patterns may be within one system (e.g., the mutual entrainment of different rhythmic processes in an individual's circadian system; cf. Brown & Graeber, 1982; Moore-Ede, Sulzman, & Fuller, 1982; Pittendrigh, 1972; Wever, 1981), or within separate but interacting systems (e.g., the entrainment of given processes in two or more interacting individuals; cf. Cappella, 1981; Jaffe & Feldman, 1970; Warner, 1979; Warner, Waggener, & Kronauer, 1983). Often, such entrainment is mutual entrainment in that the timing of the occurrence of events in each of the series induces or modifies the timing of events in the other series.

(b). The term *external entrainment* refers to the systematic temporal regulation of a cyclical pattern of events in a system by a stimulus, or signal, or cyclical pattern of stimulation or signals, from a source external to that system (e.g., Ancona & Chong, 1996; Hoagland, 1935; Kelly, Futoran, & McGrath, 1990; Kelly & Karau, 1993; Kelly & McGrath, 1985; Roth, Murnigham, & Schumaker, 1988). For example, the circadian rhythms in humans are externally entrained to the light–dark patterns associated with the rotation of the planet.

(c). To be synchronized does not necessarily mean to be simultaneous in time. Rather, it means to be in a fixed temporal relation one to the other. Two processes are synchronized if they are 180 degrees out of phase, or 90 degrees, or any other specifiable amount, so long as that relation persists.

(d). Entrainment and mutual entrainment have the effect of altering the phase and adjusting the periodicities of one or both of the sequences. External entrainment has the effect of resetting the phase, and adjusting the periodicity, of the sequence of events that is entrained. *Ceteris paribus*, both kinds of entrainment tend to persist.

APPENDIX B:
SLIFE'S ANALYSIS OF
TEMPORAL CONCEPTIONS

Slife (1993) presents a detailed analysis of several conceptions of time. He lays out five key themes regarding time that overlap a lot with the philosophical issues we noted in chapter 2. He then discusses the dominant Newtonian conception in terms of those themes, and lays out some anomalies that arise in psychological theory and evidence if that Newtonian position is adopted. He also compares the Newtonian position to two alternative conceptions of time, both in terms of those five basic themes and in relation to those anomalies for psychological study. He calls those alternative conceptions "organismic holism" and "hermeneutic temporality."

THEMES OF THE NEWTONIAN CONCEPTION

Slife argues that a Newtonian conception embodies a conception of time as well as space and mechanics, and that many aspects of the Newtonian conception as applied to time can be represented in five themes. Those five Newtonian themes are:

Theme 1: The *objectivity* of time. Basically, this holds that time is separate from and independent of objects, observers, and events.

Theme 2: The *continuity* of time. This means, basically, that time is both homogeneous and continuous, without lacunae between its parts.

Theme 3: The *universality* of time. This speaks to time's homogeneous rather than epochal nature, and expresses the idea that time is the same both every*where* and any*time*.

Theme 4: The *linearity* of time. This refers to the flow of time, forward and at a uniform rate.

Theme 5: The *reductivity* of time. This idea is related to time's linearity, and also to the question of whether it is discrete or continuous. It expresses the idea that complex processes, viewed at a microlevel, are distributed over time rather than present all at once.

Slife argues that if a Newtonian conception of time as well as of mechanics and space gets adopted and incorporated into the basic premises of a field—as it has been in psychology—such a conception carries with it several assumptions that in turn give rise to several anomalies in that field's theoretical and evidential treatments of its phenomena. He illustrates that idea extensively in terms of several subfields of psychology (developmental, cognitive, methodology, personality, family, and group therapy). Below, we will note briefly some of the main assumptions embedded in psychological theory, method, and evidence related to the Newtonian conception of time, and discuss some of the anomalies that they can give rise to.

Theme 1: The objectivity of time. Slife argues that the idea of objectivity of time carries with it the following assumptions for psychology:

1. There is an objective standard for the measurement of psychological events.
2. All psychological processes occur across time.
3. Humans store the past as an objective entity.

The idea of time's objectivity is called into question in psychological theory and evidence because time is context-bound. In a sense, psychological processes can be viewed as "outside" linear time. Moreover, the past is reconstructed psychologically from the vantage point of the present.

Theme 2: The continuity of time. According to Slife, the idea of continuity of time also carries with it certain assumptions:

1. All psychological processes are consistent with their pasts.
2. Psychological change is continuous (if not indeed linear) in nature.

These, too, need to be called into question, because psychological processes can be discontinuous from the past, and because change is often discontinuous in nature.

Theme 3: The universality of time. According to Slife, the universality of time, as that theme is used in psychological theory and research, assumes the following:

1. Universal principles are the most fundamental form of knowledge.
2. Researchers (do and should) seek conditions that will facilitate the discovery of universal laws or principles.

But universal principles turn out to be specific to contexts. Slife argues that researchers should study phenomena that are filled with context.

Theme 4: The linearity of time. According to Slife, the linearity of time as applied in psychological theory and research assumes:

1. Proper (or final) explanations require the antecedent determinants of a phenomenon.

2. The earlier an event occurs, the more significant it is for explanation.
3. Mind is a mediator between the environment and behavior.
4. Nonlinear theories and nonlinear constructs need to be linearized or else are considered unscientific.

The linearity of time poses problems because the present (without regard to the past) can determine processes, and so can (anticipations of) the future. Moreover, for many purposes one can reasonably regard the mind and the environment as simultaneously a part of a holistic context. Furthermore, humans are agents of their own actions and attitudes.

Theme 5: The reductivity of time. According to Slife, this position assumes the following:

1. Psychological processes are reduced to their separate parts as they occur across time.
2. Subject and object are separated in time.
3. The focus of psychological study and explanation is the individual.

Slife raises several arguments as to why reductivity needs to be questioned. He argues that psychological processes should be studied holistically, with subject and object understood as simultaneously parts of a whole. Moreover, individuals are to be understood in terms of their relations to that simultaneous context.

ORGANISMIC HOLISM

Slife offers two alternative paradigms that take different positions than the Newtonian one about the nature of time. In *organismic holism*, time is regarded as completely dependent on the holistic relations among events. Rather than being objective, time is *in* events. And it is events, not time, that provides the linearity: Events have a natural order. Moreover, there is discontinuous change (of events). For this position, only the "deep structure" of objects and events can be regarded as universal. And neither events nor psychological phenomena are necessarily reductive in time.

It is worth noting that this position invokes a broadened idea of causation. The Newtonian view deals exclusively with mechanical or efficient causality. The holistic position seems to invoke several more of the Aristotelian forms of causality, both formal cause and material cause. So the differences between them entail more than just their time orientation.

HERMENEUTIC TEMPORALITY

For his discussion of the second alternative conception of time, *hermeneutic temporality*, Slife draws heavily on Heidegger's ideas of an individual's "modes of engagement" with the world. Heidegger takes issue with the Newtonian conception in this regard. He argues that the mode of engagement that Newton treats as the fundamental form of knowledge—the "present at hand," a mode of engagement that is the abstract viewing of objects and events as separate from self—is not the fundamental mode of engagement. Rather, Heidegger regards as fundamental the "ready to hand": the direct, in-action mode of engagement, in which subject and object are all together in a unitary whole (*dasein* for Heidegger). In this view, time is embedded in the connectedness of meaning implicit in everyday activities. (Heidegger prefers to talk about "temporality," rather than about time, and that use of terms subtly emphasizes time's ephemeral status as well.)

In this view, knowledge is "situated," and neither independent nor universal. Temporality is *in* events, not separate from them (thus disputing the objective quality of time). It is not continuous, but rather has gaps. It is not universal but rather is situated. Rather than time being linear, the present *contains* both the past and the future in the now. And temporality is entirely holistic, rather than reductive.

CONCLUDING COMMENTS ABOUT SLIFE'S ANALYSIS

This presentation of Slife's analysis is necessarily quite brief. Slife elaborates and interconnects all of these ideas in considerably more detail, and we recommend a full examination of that extended treatment for readers interested in time and psychological processes. Our main purpose in presenting this condensed version here is to show some of the connections between the philosophical issues about time that were noted in chapter 2 of this volume and theory and research in psychology and social psychology. Slife's analysis shows both that the Newtonian position on time is not without serious philosophical questions, and that there are viable alternative conceptions that would deal with some of those questions—albeit raising other philosophical issues at the same time.

Slife's interest is in how these conceptions of temporal issues have had a major impact on the body of theory, evidence, and methodology in several areas of psychology. Appendix C presents another analysis of conceptions of time, one that focuses on the relation between time as conceptualized and time as experienced in the everyday social psychological experience of humans.

APPENDIX C:
MCGRATH AND KELLY'S TREATMENT
OF CONCEPTIONS OF TIME

McGrath and Kelly (1986) examined many of the issues described in chapter 2 of this volume, trying to tie them to alternative conceptualizations about time. They identified four clusters of temporal issues, each consisting of two "crossed" dichotomous issues. Those four clusters have to do with (a) the structure of time, (b) the flow of time, (c) the reality of time, and (d) the validity (of measurements) of time. They identify four quadrants within each cluster, and locate each of four major conceptions of time in a quadrant of each cluster. Those four conceptions of time are (a) a Newtonian view, (b) a view associated with the "new physics," (c) a conception characteristic of some Eastern mystical religions, and (d) a conception arising from transactional views of social psychological phenomena.

CLUSTER 1: THE STRUCTURE OF TIME

McGrath and Kelly define a cluster having to do with the structure of time by "crossing" the two dichotomous questions of (1) whether time is to be regarded as holistic or atomistic, and (2) whether time is to be regarded as homogeneous (i.e., undifferentiated) or differentiated. Please see Table 1 for a look at this cluster.

In that cluster, they characterized the quadrant in which time is regarded as homogeneous and atomistic as "Time as Succession." They labeled the quadrant that characterizes time as homogeneous but holistic as "Time as Duration." In the quadrant in which time is regarded as atomistic and differentiated they locate views that regard "Time as Epochal." The final quadrant, which treats time as holistic but differentiated, they label as "Time

TABLE 1
The Structure of Time

	Time as Homogeneous	Time as Differentiated
Time as Atomistic	SUCCESSION	EPOCHAL
Time as Holistic	DURATION	TRANSPOSABLE

as Transposable." This latter quadrant may or may not be a contradiction in terms, depending on one's view about singular versus multiple times.

CLUSTER 2: THE FLOW OF TIME

McGrath and Kelly define a cluster having to do with the flow of time by crossing the two questions of (3) whether time is to be regarded as reversible or irreversible, and (4) whether time is to be regarded as uniform in its passage (i.e., as linear) versus as phasic in its passage (i.e., as cyclical). Please see Table 2 for a representation of this cluster.

In this cluster, they identified the quadrant in which time is regarded as uniform and reversible in its flow as having a bidirectional flow (as both Newton and Einstein regarded it). They labeled the quadrant in which time is regarded as flowing uniformly and irreversibly—as our current dominant conception has it—as "Linear Time." They characterized the quadrant in which time is regarded as phasic and reversible in its flow as "Recurrent Time," and suggest that some mystical religions make use of such a conception. They characterized the quadrant in which time is regarded as phasic and irreversible in its flow as "Developmental Time." This is the kind of time that supports ideas about "stages of development" of organisms (which are discussed extensively in chapter 6 of this volume).

CLUSTER 3: THE REALITY OF TIME

McGrath and Kelly define a cluster having to do with the reality of time by crossing the two questions of (5) whether time is to be regarded as abstract or concrete (with real effects), and (6) whether time is to be regarded as absolute (independent of objects) or relational (inherent in relations among objects). Please see Table 3 for a representation of this cluster.

TABLE 2
The Flow of Time

	Time as Uniform in Passage	Time as Phasic in Passage
Time as Reversible	BIDIRECTIONAL	RECURRENT
Time as Irreversible	LINEAR	DEVELOPMENTAL

TABLE 3
The Reality of Time

	Time as Abstract	Time as Concrete
Time as Absolute	MATHEMATICAL	NEUMONAL/REAL
Time as Relational	RELATIVITY TIME	EXPERIENTIAL TIME

In this cluster, they identified the quadrant in which time is regarded as abstract and absolute as "Mathematical Time," which of course characterizes the Newtonian view. They identified the quadrant in which time is regarded as abstract but relational as "Relativity Time," and suggest that in it time is regarded as *constrained* by location of the observer. They characterized the quadrant in which time is regarded as absolute and concrete as "Neumonal Time" or "Real Time." They characterized the quadrant in which time is regarded as concrete and relational as "Experiential Time," and suggest that in it time is *determined* by the observer.

CLUSTER 4: THE VALIDITY (OF MEASURES) OF TIME

Finally, McGrath and Kelly define a cluster having to do with the validity (of measures) of time by crossing the two questions of (7) whether time should be regarded as being singular or as being multiple, and (8) whether time is to be regarded as independent of space, or as an inherent part of a space–time continuum. Please see Table 4 for a representation of this cluster.

TABLE 4
The Validity of Measures of Time

	Time as Singular	Time as Multiple
Time & Space Independent	HIGH CONVERGENT & DISCRIMINANT VALIDITY	LOW CONVERGENT HIGH DISCRIMINANT VALIDITY
Time Part of Space–Time Continuum	HIGH CONVERGENT LOW DISCRIMINANT VALIDITY	LOW CONVERGENT & DISCRIMINANT VALIDITY

McGrath and Kelly considered those two questions in terms familiar within the methodology of social psychology, namely, convergent and discriminant validity of measures. They identified the quadrant in which time is regarded as independent and singular as one in which measures of time are expected to have both high convergent and high discriminant validity. They identified the quadrant in which time is regarded as part of a space–time continuum, though singular, as one in which measures are expected to have low discriminant validity with regard to measures of space, but high construct validity among measures of time. They label this as a "Unified Space–Time Continuum." They characterized the quadrant in which time is regarded as encompassing multiple constructs, each an independent dimension, as being expected to have high discriminant validity (with respect to measures of other features, such as space) although having low convergent validity (for measures of other time constructs). They characterize the quadrant in which time is regarded as encompassing multiple constructs confounded with space (and perhaps other constructs) as being a view in which measures of time are expected to have both low discriminant validity and low convergent validity in traditional senses. They also label this quadrant as "Time as Illusion," and associate it with the time-views of some mystical religions.

SUMMARY

Together, these eight dichotomous dimensions generate 256 possibilities, but are, as described above, treated as four clusters consisting of crossed pairs of those dimensions. Summarized, these sixteen quadrants are

Time is structured as Succession, Duration, Epochal, or Transposable.

Time flows as Bidirectional, Linear, Recurrent, or Developmental.

Time's existential status is Mathematical, Relational, Neumonal (or Real), or Experiential.

The validity status of measures of time is Singular Independent Dimension, Space–Time Continuum, Multiple Constructs, or Illusory.

McGrath and Kelly locate each of four major conceptions of time within one or another of the four quadrants of each cluster. They argue that the Newtonian position treats time as having to do with Succession, as Bidirectional in its flow, as Mathematical, and as a Singular Independent Dimension. They indicate that the temporal conception of the "new physics" treats time as Transposable, Linear, Relative, and as part of a Unified Space–Time Continuum. They identify the time conception of some mystical religions as having to do with time as "pure" Duration, as Recurrent, as Experiential, and as perhaps Illusory. Their fourth conception, which they term *Transactional*, treats time as Epochal, Developmental, Experiential, and Multiple.

REFERENCES

Adam, J. (1978). Sequential strategies and the separation of age, cohort, and time-of-measurement estimations in developmental data. *Psychological Bulletin, 95,* 1309–1316.

Agnew, C. R., & Loving, T. J. (1998). Future time orientation and condom use: Attitudes, intentions, and behavior. *Journal of Social Behavior and Personality, 13,* 755–764.

Agresti, A. (1996). *An introduction to categorical data analysis.* New York: Wiley.

Allmendinger, J., & Hackman, J. R. (1996). Organizations in changing environments: The case of East German symphony orchestras. *Administrative Science Quarterly, 41,* 337–369.

Ancona, D. G., & Caldwell, D. F. (1988). Beyond task and maintenance: External roles in groups. *Group and Organization Studies, 13,* 468–494.

Ancona, D. G., & Caldwell, D. F. (1990). Information technology and new product teams. In J. Galegher, R. Kraut, & C. Egido (Eds.), *Intellectual teamwork: Social and technological foundations of cooperative work* (pp. 173–190). Hillsdale, NJ: Erlbaum.

Ancona, D. G., & Chong, C. (1996). Entrainment: Pace, cycle, and rhythm in organizational behavior. In B. Staw & L. L. Cummings (Eds.), *Research in organizational behavior* (Vol. 18, pp. 251–284). New York: JAI Press.

Andorka, R. (1987). Time budgets and their uses. *Annual Review of Sociology, 13,* 149–164.

Angrilli, A., Cherubini, P., Pavese, A., & Manfredini, S. (1997). The influence of affective factors on time perception. *Perception and Psychophysics, 59,* 972–982.

Annett, J., & Duncan, K. D. (1967). Task analysis and training design. *Occupational Psychology, 41,* 211–221.

Argote, L. (1999). *Organizatonal learning: Creating, retaining and transferring knowledge.* Norwell, MA: Kluwer Academic.

Argote, L., Gruenfeld, D., & Naquin, C. (1996). Group learning in organizations. In M. E. Turner (Ed.), *Groups at work: Advances in theory and research* (pp. 369–411). Hillsdale, NJ: Erlbaum.

Argote, L., & McGrath, J. E. (1993). Group processes in organizations: Continuity and change. *International Review of Industrial and Organizational Psychology, 8,* 333–389.

Argyle, M., & Henderson, M. (1985). The rules of relationships. In D. Perlman (Ed.), *Understanding personal relationships* (pp. 63–84). London: Sage.

Arrow, H., & Burns, K. L. (2003). Self-organizing culture: How norms emerge in small groups. In M. Shaller & C. Crandall (Eds.), *The psychological foundations of culture* (pp. 171–199). Mahwah, NJ: Erlbaum.

Arrow, H., & Crosson, S. B. (2003). Musical chairs: Membership dynamics in self-organized group formation. *Small Group Research, 34.*

Arrow, H., & McGrath, J. E. (1993). Membership matters: How member change and continuity affect small group structure, process, and performance. *Small Group Research, 24,* 354–361.

Arrow, H., & McGrath, J. E. (1995). Membership dynamics in groups at work: A theoretical framework. *Research in Organizational Behavior, 17,* 373–411.

Arrow, H., McGrath, J. E., & Berdahl, J. L. (2000). *Small groups as complex systems: Formation, coordination, development, and adaptation.* Thousand Oaks, CA: Sage.

Arundale, R. B. (1980). Studying change over time: Criteria for sampling from continuous variables. *Communication Research, 7,* 227–263.

Atkinson, J. W., & Birch, D. (1970). *A dynamic theory of action.* New York: Wiley.

Aveni, A. (1989). *Empires of time.* New York: Basic Books.

Baker, J., & Cameron, M. (1996). The effect of the service environment on affect and consumer perception of waiting time: An integrative review and research propositions. *Journal of the Academy of Marketing Science, 24,* 338–349.

Bales, R. F. (1950). *Interaction process analysis: A method for the study of small groups.* Cambridge, MA: Addison Wesley.

Bales, R. F., & Strodtbeck, F. L. (1951). Phases in group problem solving. *Journal of Abnormal and Social Psychology, 46,* 485–495.

Bandura, A., & Schunk, D. H. (1981). Cultivating competence, self-efficacy, and intrinsic interest through proximal motivation. *Journal of Personality and Social Psychology, 41,* 586–598.

Barak, Y., Achiron, A., Rotstein, Z., Elizur, A., & Noy, S. (1998). Stress associated with asbestosis: The trauma of waiting for death. *Psycho-Oncology, 7,* 126–128.

Barling, J., & Boswell, R. (1995). Work performance and the achievement-strivings and impatience–irritability dimensions of Type A behavior. *Applied Psychology: An International Review, 44,* 143–153.

Barnett, R. C., & Hyde, J. S. (2001). Women, men, work, and family: An expansionist theory. *American Psychologist, 56,* 781–796.

Baron, R. M., Amazeen, P. G., & Beek, P. J. (1994). Local and global dynamics in social relations. In R. R. Vallacher & A. Nowak (Eds.), *Dynamical systems in social psychology* (pp. 111–138). New York: Academic Press.

Baumeister, R. F., Faber, J. E., & Wallace, H. M. (1999). Coping and ego depletion. In C. R. Snyder (Ed.), *Coping: The psychology of what works* (pp. 50–69). New York: Oxford University Press.

Beckmann, J., & Kuhl, J. (1984). Altering information to gain action control: Functional aspects of human information processing in decision making. *Journal of Research in Personality, 18,* 224–237.

Beehr, T. A. (1995). Social support as a form of treatment. In T. A. Beehr (Ed.), *Psychological stress in the workplace* (pp. 182–210). New York: Routledge.

Beehr, T. (1998). An organizational psychology meta-model of occupational stress. In G. L. Cooper (Ed.), *Theories of organizational stress* (pp. 6–27). Oxford: Oxford University Press.

Bennett, J. B. (2000). *Time and intimacy: A new science of personal relationships*. Mahwah, NJ: Erlbaum.

Benson, L., & Beach, L. R. (1996). The effects of time constraints on the prechoice screening of decision options. *Organizational Behavior and Human Decision Processes, 67*, 222–228.

Berglas, S., & Iones, E. E. (1978). Drug choice as a self-handicapping strategy in response to noncontingent success. *Journal of Personality and Social Psychology, 36*, 405–517.

Betsch, T., Fiedler, K., & Brinkmann, J. (1998). Behavioral routines in decision making: The effects of novelty in task presentation and time pressure on routine maintenance and deviation. *European Journal of Social Psychology, 28*, 861–878.

Bettenhausen, K. L., & Murnigham, J. K. (1985). The emergence of norms in competitive decision-making groups. *Administrative Science Quarterly, 30*, 350–372.

Bion, W. R. (1961). *Experience in groups and other papers*. New York: Basic Books.

Bittman, M., & Goodin, R. E. (2000). An equivalence scale for time. *Social Indicators Research, 52*, 291–311.

Block, R. A. (1990a). Models of psychological time. In R. A. Block (Ed.), *Cognitive models of psychological time* (pp. 1–35). Hillsdale, NJ: Erlbaum.

Block, R. A. (Ed.). (1990b). *Cognitive Models of Psychological Time*. Hillsdale, NJ: Erlbaum.

Block, R. A., & Zakay, D. (1997). Prospective and retrospective duration judgments: A meta-analytic review. *Psychonomic Bulletin and Review, 4*, 184–197.

Bluedorn, A. C., & Denhardt, R. B. (1987). Time and organizations. *Journal of Management, 14*, 299–320.

Blunt, A., & Pychyl, T. A. (1998). Volitional action and inaction in the lives of undergraduate students: State orientation, procrastination, and proneness to boredom. *Personality and Individual Differences, 24*, 837–846.

Boos, M., & Meier, F. (1993). *Die Regulation des Gruppenprozesses bei der Enscheidungsfindung* [The regulation of group processes in decision making]. *Zeitschrift für Sozialpsychologie, 24*, 3–14.

Box, G. E. P., & Jenkins, G. (1976). *Time series analysis: Forecasting and control*. San Francisco: Holden-Day.

Bray, D. H. (1970). Extent of future time orientation: A cross-ethnic study among New Zealand adolescents. *British Journal of Educational Psychology, 40*, 200–208.

Brilhart, J. K., & Jochem, L. M. (1964). Effects of different patterns on outcomes of problem-solving discussion. *Journal of Applied Psychology, 48*, 175–179.

Brossart, D. F., Patton, M. J., & Wood, P. K. (1998). Assessing group process: An illustration using Tuckerized growth curves. *Group Dynamics: Theory, Research and Practice, 2*, 3–17.

Brown, F. M., & Graeber, R. C. (Eds.). (1982). *Rhythmic aspects of behavior*. Hillsdale, NJ: Erlbaum.

Brown, V., & Paulus, P. B. (1996). A simple dynamic model of social factors in group brainstorming. *Small Group Research, 27*, 93–114.

Burnstein, E., & Berbaum, M. L. (1983). Stages in group decision making: The decomposition of historical narratives. *Political Psychology, 4*, 531–561.

Buunk, B. P. (1990). Affiliation and helping interactions within organizations: A critical analysis of the role of social support with regard to occupational stress. In M. Hewstone (Ed.), *European review of social psychology* (Vol. 1, pp. 293–322). Chichester, England: Wiley.

Buunk, B. P., de Jonge, J., Ybema, J. F., & de Wolff, C. J. (1998). Psychosocial aspects of occupational stress. In C. J. de Wolff (Ed.), *Handbook of work and organizational psychology: Vol. 2. Work psychology* (2nd ed., pp. 145–182). East Sussex, England: Psychology Press.

Buunk, B. P., & Schaufeli, W. B. (1999). Reciprocity in interpersonal relationships: An evolutionary perspective on its importance for health and well-being. In M. Hewstone (Ed.), *European Review of Social Psychology* (Vol. 10, pp. 259–291). Chichester, England: Wiley.

Campbell, D. T., & Stanley, J. C. (1966). *Experimental and quasi-experimental designs for research*. Chicago: Rand McNally.

Cantor, N., Norem, J. K., Niedenthal, P. M., Langston, C. A., & Brower, A. M. (1987). Life tasks, self-concept ideals, and cognitive strategies in a life transition. *Journal of Personality and Social Psychology, 53*, 1178–1191.

Cantor, N., & Sanderson, C. A. (1999). Life task participation and well-being: The importance of taking part in daily life. In N. Schwarz (Ed.), *Well-being: The foundations of hedonic psychology* (pp. 230–243). New York: Russell Sage Foundation.

Cappella, J. N. (1981). Mutual influence in expressive behavior: Adult–adult and infant–adult interaction. *Psychological Bulletin, 89*, 101–132.

Carver, C. S., & Scheier, M. F. (1999). Themes and issues in the self-regulation of behavior. In R. S. Wyer (Ed.), *Perspectives on behavioral self-regulation* (Vol. 12, pp. 1–105). Mahwah, NJ: Erlbaum.

Carver, C. S., Scheier, M. F., & Pozo, C. (1992). Conceptualizing the process of coping with health problems. In H. S. Friedman (Ed.), *Hostility, coping, and health* (pp. 167–188). Washington, DC: American Psychological Association.

Chalendar, J. de (1976). *Lifelong allocation of time*. Paris: OECD.

Chapple, E. D. (1970). *Culture and biological man: Explorations in behavioral anthropology*. New York: Holt.

Chubick, J. D., Boland, C. S., Witherspoon, A. D., Chaffin, K. L., & Long, C. K. (1999). Relation of functioning with beliefs about coping, and future time perspective. *Psychological Reports, 85*, 947–953.

Cohen, M. S., Freeman, J. T., & Wolf, S. (1996). Meta-recognition in time-stressed decision making: Recognizing, critiquing, and correcting. *Journal of the Human Factors and Ergonomics Society, 38*, 206–219.

Cohen, S. G., & Denison, D. R. (1990). Flight attendant teams. In J. R. Hackman (Ed.), *Groups that work (and those that don't)* (pp. 382–397). San Francisco, CA: Jossey-Bass.

Colquhoun, W. P., Blake, M. J. F., & Edwards, R. S. (1968). Experimental studies of shift work. I: A comparison of "rotating" and "stabilized" 4-hour shift systems. *Ergonomics, 11,* 437–453.

Conte, J. M., Landy, F. J., & Mathieu, J. E. (1995). Time urgency: Conceptual and construct development. *Journal of Applied Psychology, 80,* 178–185.

Conte, J. M., Mathieu, J. E., & Landy, F. J. (1998). The nomological and predictive validity of time urgency. *Journal of Organizational Behavior, 19,* 1–13.

Conte, J. M., Ringenbach, K. L., Moran, S. K., & Landy, F. J. (2001). Criterion–validity evidence for time urgency: Association with burnout, organizational commitment, and job involvement in travel agents. *Applied HRM Research, 6,* 129–134.

Converse, P. E. (1972). Country differences in time use. In A. Szalai (Ed.), *The use of time: Daily activities of urban and suburban populations in twelve countries* (pp. 145–177). The Hague: Mouton.

Cook, T. D., & Campbell, D. T. (1979). *Quasi-experimentation: Design and analysis for field settings.* Chicago, IL: Rand McNally.

Cox, D. R., & Oakes, D. (1984). *Analyisis of survival data.* London: Chapman and Hall.

Cranach, M. von (1996). Toward a theory of the acting group. In E. Witte & J. H. Davis (Eds.), *Understanding group behavior: Small group processes and interpersonal relations* (pp. 147–187). Hillsdale, NJ: Erlbaum.

Cranach, M. von, Kalbermatten, U., Indermuehle, K., & Gugler, B. (1982). *Goal-directed action.* London: Academic Press.

Cseh-Szombathy, L. (1972). International differences in the types and frequencies of social contacts. In A. Szalai (Ed.), *The use of time: Daily activities of urban and suburban populations in twelve countries* (pp. 307–316). The Hague: Mouton.

Csikszentmihalyi, M. (1997). *Finding flow: The psychology of engagement with everyday life.* New York: Basic Books.

Csikszentmihalyi, M., & LeFevre, J. (1989). Optimal experience in work and leisure. *Journal of Personality and Social Psychology, 56,* 815–822.

Dabbs, J. M., Jr. (1982, August). *Fourier analysis and the rhythm of conversation.* Presentation at the annual meeting of the American Psychological Association, Washington, DC.

Darden, D. K., & Marks, A. H. (1999). Boredom: A socially disvalued emotion. *Sociological Spectrum, 19,* 13–37.

Darr, E., Argote, L., & Epple, D. (1995). The acquisition, transfer and depreciation of knowledge in service organizations: Productivity in franchises. *Management Sciences, 41,* 1750–1762.

Das, T. K. (1991). Time: The hidden dimension in strategic planning: Long range planning. *International Journal of Strategic Management, 24,* 49–57.

Das, T. K. (1993). Time in management and organizational studies. *Time and Society*, 2, 267–274.

Dewey, J. (1933). *How we think*. Boston, MA: D. C. Heath.

Dillon, W. R., Madden, W. J., & Kumar, A. (1983). Analyzing sequential categorical data on dyadic interaction: A latent structure approach. *Psychological Bulletin*, 94, 584–593.

Doob, L. W. (1971). *Patterning of time*. New Haven, CN: Yale University Press.

Dormann, C., & Zapf, D. (1999). Social support, social stressors at work, and depressive symptoms: Testing for main and moderating effects with structural equations an a three-wave longitudinal study. *Journal of Applied Psychology*, 84, 874–884.

Dunckel, H. (1985). *Mehrfachbelastungen am Arbeitsplatz und psychosoziale Gesundheit* [Multiple strains at work and psychosocial health]. Frankfurt am Main: Peter Lang Publishing.

Edmondson, A. C., Bohmer, R. M., & Pisano, G. P. (2001). Disrupted routines: Team learning and new technology implementation in hospitals. *Administrative Science Quarterly*, 46, 685–715.

Eisenhardt, K. M. (1989). Making fast strategic decisions in high-velocity environments. *Academy of Management Journal*, 32, 543–576.

Eisenhardt, K. M., & Sull, D. N. (2001). Strategy as simple rules. *Harvard Business Review*, 19, 107–116.

Eisenhardt, K. M., & Tabrizi, B. N. (1995). Accelerating adaptive processes: Product innovation in the global computer industry. *Administrative Science Quarterly*, 40, 84–100.

Elfering, A., Semmer, N. K., Schade, V., Grund, S., & Boos, N. (2002). Supportive colleague, unsupportive supervisor: The role of provider-specific constellations of social support at work in the development of lower back pain. *Journal of Occupational Health Psychology*, 7, 130–140.

Emmons, R. A., King, L. A., & Sheldon, K. M. (1993). Goal conflict and the self-regulation of action. In J. W. Pennebaker (Ed.), *Handbook of mental control* (pp. 528–551). Englewood Cliffs: Prentice Hall.

Epstein, S. (1998). Cognitive-experiential self-theory. In D. F. Barone, M. Hersen, & V. B. Van Hasselt (Eds.), *Advanced personality* (pp. 211–238). New York: Plenum Press.

Ericsson, K. A., & Lehmann, A. C. (1996). Expert and exceptional performance : Evidence of maximal adaptation to task constraints. *Annual Reviews of Psychology*, 47, 273–305.

Faraone, S. V., & Dorfman, D. D. (1987). Lag sequential analysis: Robust statistical methods. *Psychological Bulletin*, 101, 312–323.

Fisher, B. A. (1970). Decision emergence: Phases in group decision making. *Speech Monographs*, 37, 53–66.

Fisher, B. A., & Stutman, R. K. (1987). An assessment of group trajectories: analyzing developmental breakpoints. *Communication Quarterly*, 35, 105–124.

Fletcher, B. C. (1988). The epidemiology of occupational stress. In C. L. Cooper & R. Payne (Eds.), *Causes, coping and consequences of stress at work* (pp. 3–50). Chichester, England: Wiley.

Folkman, S. (1993). Psychosocial effects of HIV infection. In L. Goldberger & S. Breznis (Eds.), *Handbook of stress. Theoretical and clinical aspects* (2nd ed., pp. 658–681). New York: Free Press.

Folkman, S., & Lazarus, R. S. (1988). *Manual for the ways of coping questionnaire*. Palo Alto, CA: Consulting Psychologists Press.

Ford, C. E., & Brehm, J. W. (1987). Effort expenditure following failure. In C. E. Ford (Ed.), *Coping with negative life events: Clinical and social psychological perspectives* (pp. 81–104). New York: Plenum.

Fraisse, P. (1963). *The psychology of time*. New York: Harper & Row.

Fraisse, P. (1984). Perception and estimation of time. *Annual Reviews of Psychology, 35,* 1–36.

Francis-Smythe, J., & Robertson, I. (1999). Time-related individual differences. *Time and Society, 8,* 273–292.

Fraser, J. T. (1975). *Time, passion, and knowledge*. Princeton, NJ: Princeton University Press.

Frederick, J. A., & Fast, J. E. (2001). Enjoying work: An effective strategy in the struggle to juggle? *Statistics Canada* (Catalogue No. 11-008). Retrieved January 3, 2003, from http://www.statcan.ca/english/indepth/11-008/feature/star2001061000s2a02.pdf

Frese, M., & Semmer, N. (1986). Shiftwork, stress, and psychosomatic complaints: A comparison between workers in different shiftwork schedules, non-shiftworkers, and former shiftworkers. *Ergonomics, 29,* 99–114.

Frese, M., & Zapf, D. (1988). Methodological issues in the study of work stress: Objective vs. subjective measurements of work stress and the question of longitudinal studies. In R. Payne (Ed.), *Causes, coping, and consequences of stress at work* (pp. 375–411). Chichester, England: John Wiley & Sons.

Frese, M., & Zapf, D. (1994). Action as the core of work psychology: A German approach. In H. C. Triandis, M. D. Dunnette, & L. Hough (Eds.), *Handbook of industrial and organizational psychology* (Vol. 4, pp. 271–340). Palo Alto, California: Consulting Psychologists Press.

Friedman, M., & Rosenman, R. H. (1974). *Type A behavior and your heart*. New York: Alfred A. Knopf.

Friedman, W. J. (1990). *About time: Inventing the fourth dimension*. Cambridge, MA: MIT Press.

Funder, D. C., & Block, J. (1989). The role of ego-control, ego-resiliency, and IQ in delay of gratification in adolescence. *Journal of Personality and Social Psychology, 57,* 1041–1050.

Gardner, W., & Griffin, W. A. (1989). Methods for the analysis of parallel streams of continuously recorded social behaviors. *Psychological Bulletin, 105,* 446–455.

Garst, H., Frese, M., & Molenaar, P. C. M. (2000). The temporal factor of change in stressor–strain relationships: A growth curve model on a longitudinal study in East Germany. *Journal of Applied Psychology, 85,* 417–438.

Gasparini, G. (1995). On waiting. *Time and Society, 4,* 29–46.

George, J. M., & Jones, G. R. (2000). The role of time in theory and theory building. *Journal of Management, 26,* 657–684.

Gersick, C. A. G. (1988). Time and transition in work teams: Toward a new model of group development. *Academy of Management Journal, 31,* 9–41.

Gersick, C. A. G. (1989). Marking time: Predictable transitions in task groups. *Academy of Management Journal, 32,* 274–309.

Gersick, C. A. G., & Hackman, J. R. (1990). Habitual routines in task performing groups. *Organizational Behavior and Human Decision Processes, 47,* 65–97.

Gililand, A. R., Hofeld, J., & Eckstrand, G. (1946). Studies in time perception. *Psychological Bulletin, 43,* 162–176.

Goldstein, H. (1995). *Multilevel statistical models* (2nd ed.). London: Edward Arnold.

Golembiewski, R. T., & Munzenrieder, R. F. (1988). Phases of burnout: Developments in concepts and applications. New York: Praeger Publishers.

Gollwitzer, P. M. (1990). Action phases and mind-sets. In E. T Higgins & R. M. Sorrentino (Eds.), *Handbook of motivation and cognition, Vol. 2.: Foundations of social behavior* (pp. 53–93). New York: Guilford Press.

Gollwitzer, P. M., Heckhausen, H., & Steller, B. (1990). Deliberative and implemental mind-sets: Cognitive tuning towards congruous thoughts and information. *Journal of Personality and Social Psychology, 59,* 1119–1127.

Gollwitzer, P. M., & Moskowitz, G. B. (1996). Goal effects on action and cognition. In A. W. Kruglanski (Ed.), *Social psychology: Handbook of basic principles* (pp. 361–399). New York: Guilford Press.

Gonzales, A., & Zimbardo, P. G. (1985, March). Time in perspective. *Psychology Today,* 21–26.

Gottman, J. M. (1981). *Time-series analysis: A comprehensive introduction for social scientists.* New York: Cambridge University Press.

Gottman, J. M., & Roy, A. K. (1990). *Sequential analysis: A guide for behavioral researchers.* New York: Cambridge University Press.

Gould, S. J. (1987). *Time's arrow time's cycle: Myth and metaphor in the discovery of geological time.* Cambridge, MA: Harvard University Press.

Greenberg, J. (1989). The organizational waiting game: Delay as a status-asserting or status-neutralizing tactic. *Basic and Applied Social Psychology, 10,* 13–26.

Greenblatt, E. L. (2001). *A paradox in paradise: Depletion and restoration of personal resources, emotional labor, and burnout in an idyllic total institution.* Unpublished doctoral dissertation, Harvard University.

Greenglass, E. R., Fiksenbaum, L., & Burke, R. J. (1995). The relationship between social support and burnout over time in teachers. In P. L. Perrevé (Ed.), *Occupational stress: A handbook* (pp. 239–248). Washington, DC: Taylor & Francis.

Gundlach, W., & Schultz, G. (1987). *Ist die Effektivitaet von Problemloesungen aus Diskussionen voraussagbar?* [Predicting problem solving effectiveness from discussions?] *Psychologie fuer die Praxis, 4,* 350–368.

Hacker, W. (1998). *Allgemeine Arbeitspsychologie. Psychische Regulation von Arbeit-stätigkeiten* [General work psychology: Regulation of work-tasks]. Bern: Hans Huber.

Hackman, J. R. (1969). Nature of the task as a determiner of the job behavior. *Personnel Psychology, 22,* 435–444.

Hackman, J. R. (1986). The psychology of self-management in organizations. In M. S. Pallak & R. O. Perloff (Eds.), *Psychology and work: Productivity, change, and employment.* Washington, DC: American Psychological Association.

Hackman, J. R. (1990). *Groups that work and those that don't.* San Francisco: Jossey-Bass.

Hackman, J. R. (1993). Teams, leaders, and organizations: New directions for crew-oriented flight training. In E. L. Wiener, B. G. Kanki, & R. L. Helmreich (Eds.), *Cockpit resource management* (pp. 47–69). San Diego: Academic Press.

Hackman, J. R. (1999). Thinking differently about context. In R. Wageman (Ed.), Research on managing groups and teams: Vol. 2. Groups in context (pp. 233–243). Stamford, CT: JAI Press.

Hackman, J. R. (2002). *Leading teams: Setting the stage for great performances.* Boston, MA: Harvard Business School Press.

Hackman, J. R., Brousseau, K. R., & Weiss, J. A. (1977). The interaction of task design and group performance strategies in determining group effectiveness. *Organizational Behavior and Human Performance, 16,* 350–365.

Hackman, J. R., & Morris, C. H. (1975). Group tasks, group interaction process, and group effectiveness: A review and proposed integration. In L. Berkowitz (Ed.), *Advances in experimental social psychology* (Vol. 8, pp. 45–99). New York: Academic Press.

Hall, E. T. (1983). *The dance of life: The other dimension of time.* NY: Doubleday.

Halpern, J., & Isaacs, K. (1980). Waiting and its relation to status. *Psychological Reports, 48,* 351–354.

Hancock, P. A. (1993). Body temperature influence on time perception. *Journal of General Psychology, 120,* 197–207.

Havighurst, R. J. (1972). *Human development and education* (3rd ed.). New York: McKay.

Heath, L. R. (1956). *The concept of time.* Chicago, IL: The University of Chicago Press.

Heckhausen, H. (1991). *Motivation and action.* New York: Springer.

Hesse, B. W., Werner, C. M., & Altman, I. (1987). Temporal aspects of computer mediated communication. *Computers in Human Behavior, 4,* 147–165.

Higgins, E. T. (1996). Emotional experiences: The pains and pleasures of distinct regulatory systems. In S. Fein (Ed.), *Emotion: Interdisciplinary perspectives* (pp. 203–241). Mahwah, NJ: Erlbaum.

Hill, O. W., Block, R. A., & Buggie, S. E. (2000). Culture and beliefs about time: Comparisons among black Americans, black Africans, and white Americans. *The Journal of Psychology, 134,* 443–461.

Hill, W. F., & Gruner, L. (1973). A study of development in open and closed groups. *Small Group Behavior, 4,* 355–381.

Hinz, A. (2000). *Psychologie der Zeit. Umgang mit Zeit, Zeiterleben und Wohlbefinden* [Psychology of time]. Muenster: Waxmann Verlag.

Hirokawa, R. Y. (1983). Group communication and problem solving effectiveness: An investigation of group phases. *Human Communication Research, 9,* 231–305.

Hirokawa, R. Y. (1985). Discussion procedures and decision-making performance: A test of a functional perspective. *Human Communications Research, 12,* 203–224.

Hirway, I. (2000). *Tabulation and analysis of the Indian time use survey data for improving measurement of paid and unpaid work.* Expert group meeting on methods for conducting time-use surveys, New York, 23–27 October 2000. Retrieved January 3, 2003, from http://unstats.un.org/unsd/methods/timeuse/xptgrpmeet/hirway.pdf

Hoagland, H. (1935). *Pacemakers in relation to aspects of behavior.* New York: Macmillan.

Hobfoll, S. E. (2001). The influence of culture, community, and the nested-self in the stress process: Advancing conservation of resources theory. *Applied Psychology: An International Review, 50,* 337–421.

Holahan, C. J., Moos, R. H., Holahan, C. K., & Cronkite, R. C. (1999). Resource loss, resource gain, and depressive symptoms: A 10-year model. *Journal of Personality and Social Psychology, 77,* 620–629.

Horne, G. P., Yang, M. C. K., & Ware, W. B. (1982). Time series analysis for single-subject designs. *Psychological Bulletin, 91,* 178–189.

Houston, M. B., Bettencourt, L. A., & Wenger, S. (1998). The relationship between waiting in a service queue and evaluation of service quality: A field theory perspective. *Psychology and Marketing, 15,* 735–753.

Hui, M. K., Dubé, L., & Chebat, J. C. (1997). The impact of music on consumers' reactions to waiting for services. *Journal of Retailing, 73,* 87–104.

Hui, M. K., & Zhou, L. (1996). How does waiting duration information influence customers' reaction to waiting for services? *Journal of Applied Social Psychology, 26,* 1702–1717.

Jaffe, J., & Feldman, S. (1970). *Rhythms of dialogue.* New York: Academic Press.

James, W. (1981). *The principles of psychology.* Cambridge, MA: Harvard University Press. (Original work published 1890)

Janis, I. L., & Mann, L. (1977). *Decision making.* New York: Free Press.

Jarboe, S. (1988). A comparison of input–output, process–output, and input–process–output models of small group problem solving effectiveness. *Communication Monographs, 55,* 121–142.

Jarboe, S. (1996). Procedures for enhancing group decision making. In R. Y. Hirokawa & M. S. Poole (Eds.), *Communication and group decision making* (2nd ed., pp. 345–383). Thousand Oaks, CA: Sage.

Jason, L. A., Schade, J., Furo, L., Reichler, A., & Brickman, C. (1989). Time orientation: Past, present, and future perceptions. *Psychological Reports, 64,* 1199–1205.

Jones, K. (1993). Using multilevel models for survey analysis. *Journal of the Market Research Society, 35,* 249–265.

Jones, M. R. (1985). Structural organization of events in time: A review. In J. A. Michon & J. L. Jackson (Eds.), *Time, mind, and behavior* (pp. 192–214). Heidelberg: Springer-Verlag.

Jones, M. R. (1986). Attentional rhythmicity in human perception. In J. R. Evans & M. Clynes (Eds.), *Rhythm in psychological, linguistic, and music processes* (pp. 13–40). Springfield, IL: Charles C Thomas.

Jones, M. R., & Boltz, M. (1989). Dynamic attending and responses to time. *Psychological Review, 96,* 459–491.

Kahn, R. L., & Byosiere, P. (1992). Stress in organizations. In M. D. Dunnette & L. Hough (Eds.), *Handbook of industrial and organizational psychology* (Vol. 3, pp. 551–650). Palo Alto, CA: Consulting Psychologists Press.

Kanki, B. G., & Foushee, H. C. (1989). Communication as group process mediator of aircrew performance. *Aviation, Space, and Environmental Medicine, 4,* 402–410.

Kanner, A. D., Coyne, J. C., Schaefer, C., & Lazarus, R. S. (1981). Comparison of two modes of stress management: Daily hassles and uplifts versus major life events. *Journal of Behavioral Medicine, 4,* 1–37.

Karasek, R., & Theorell, T. (1990). *Healthy work: Stress, productivity, and the reconstruction of working life.* New York: Basic Books.

Karau, S. J., & Kelly, J. R. (1992). The effects of time scarcity and time abundance on group performance quality and interaction process. *Journal of Experimental Social Psychology, 28,* 542–571.

Kellaris, J. J., & Kent, R. J. (1992). The influence of music on consumers' temporal perceptions: Does time fly when you're having fun? *Journal of Consumer Psychology, 1,* 365–376.

Kelly, J. R., Futoran, G. C., & McGrath, J. E. (1990). Capacity and capability: Seven studies of entrainment of task performance rates. *Small Group Research, 21,* 283–314.

Kelly, J. R., & Karau, S. J. (1993). Entrainment of creativity in small groups. *Small Group Research, 24,* 179–198.

Kelly, J. R., & Karau, S. J. (1999). Group decision making: The effects of initial preferences and time pressure. *Personality and Social Psychology Bulletin, 25,* 1342–1354.

Kelly, J. R., & McGrath, J. E. (1985). Effects of time limits and task types on task performance and interaction of four-person groups. *Journal of Personality and Social Psychology, 49,* 395–407.

Kelly, J. R., & McGrath, J. E. (1988). *On time and method.* Newbury Park, CA: Sage.

Kennedy, Q., Fung, H., & Carstensen, L. L. (2001). Aging, time estimation, and emotion. In S. H. McFadden & R. C. Atchley (Eds.), *Aging and the meaning of time* (pp. 51–74). New York: Springer.

Keough, K. A., Zimbardo, P. G., & Boyd, J. N. (1999). Who's smoking, drinking, and using drugs? Time perspective as a predictor of substance use. *Basic and Applied Social Psychology, 21,* 149–164.

Kerr, N. L. (1981). Social transition schemes: Charting the group's road to agreement. *Journal of Personality and Social Psychology, 41*, 684–702.

Kerstholt, J. (1994). The effect of time pressure on decision-making behavior in a dynamic task environment. *Acta Psychologica, 86*, 89–104.

Kirby, K. N., Petry, N. M., & Bickel, W. K. (1999). Heroin addicts have higher discount rates for delayed rewards than non-drug-using controls. *Journal of Experimental Psychology: General, 128*, 78–87.

Klinger, E. (1996). Emotional influences on cognitive processing, with implications for theories of both. In P. M. Gollwitzer & J. A. Bargh (Eds.), *The psychology of action: Linking cognition and motivation to behavior* (pp. 168–189). New York: Guilford.

Knulst, W., & Kraaykamp, G. (1997). The decline of reading: Leisure reading trends in the Netherlands (1955–1995). *Netherlands' Journal of Social Sciences, 33*, 30–150.

Kraemer, H. C., & Jacklin, C. N. (1979). Statistical analysis of dyadic social behavior. *Psychological Bulletin, 86*, 217–224.

Kruglanski, A. W. (1996). A motivated gatekeeper of our minds. Need-for-closure effects on interpersonal and group processes. In R. M. Sorrentino & E. T. Higgins (Eds.), *Handbook of motivation and cognition, Vol. 3: The interpersonal context* (pp. 465–496). New York: Guilford Press.

Kuhl, J. (1984). Volitional mediators of cognition-behavior consistency: Self-regulatory processes and action versus state orientation. In J. Beckmann (Ed.), *Action control: From cognition to behavior* (pp. 101–128). New York: Springer.

Kuhl, J. (1992). A theory of self-regulation: Action versus state orientation, self-discrimination, and some applications. *Applied Psychology: An International Review, 41*, 95–173.

Kuhl, J., & Goschke, T. (1994). A theory of action control: Mental subsystems, modes of control, and volitional conflict resolution strategies. In J. Beckmann (Ed.), *Volition and personality: Action versus state orientation* (pp. 93–124). Goettingen, Germany: Hogrefe & Huber.

Lacey, R., & Gruenfeld, D. H. (1999). Unwrapping the work group: How extra-organizational context affects group behavior. In R. Wageman (Ed.), *Research on managing groups and teams: Groups in context* (Vol. 2, pp. 157–177). Stamford, CT: JAI Press.

Lamm, H., Schmidt, R. W., & Trommsdorff, G. (1976). Sex and social class as determinants of future orientation (time perspective) in adolescents. *Journal of Personality and Social Psychology, 34*, 317–326.

Landes, D. S. (1983). *Revolution in time: Clocks and the making of the modern world.* Cambridge, MA: Harvard University Press.

Landy, F. J., Rastegary, H., Thayer, J., & Colvin, C. (1991). Time urgency: The construct and its measurement. *Journal of Applied Psychology, 76*, 644–657.

Lane, C., & Hobfoll, S. E. (1992). How loss affects anger and alienates potential supporters. *Journal of Consulting and Clinical Psychology, 60*, 935–942.

Lang, F. R. (1998). *Einsamkeit, Zärtlichkeit und subjektive Zukunftsorientierung im Alter: Eine Untersuchung zur sozioemotionalen Selektivitätstheorie* [Loneliness, tenderness, and subjective future orientation in old age]. *Zeitschrift für Klinische Psychologie, 27,* 98–104.

Larson, J. R., & Schaumann, L. J. (1993). Group goals, group coordination, and group member motivation. *Human Performance, 6,* 49–69.

Larson, R., & Verma, S. (1999). How children and adolescents around the world spend time: Work, play, and developmental opportunities. *Psychological Bulletin, 125,* 701–736.

Latané, B., & Nowak, A. (1994). Attitudes as catastrophes: From dimensions to categories with increasing involvement. In R. R. Vallacher & A. Nowak (Eds.), *Dynamical systems in social psychology* (pp. 219–249). New York: Academic Press.

Lawton, M. P., Moss, M., & Duhamel, L. M. (1995). The quality of daily life among elderly care receivers. *Journal of Applied Gerontology, 14,* 150–171.

Lazarus, R. S. (1999). *Stress and emotion. A new synthesis.* New York: Springer.

Lazarus, R. S., & Folkman, S. (1998). *Stress, appraisal, and coping* (10th ed.). New York: Springer.

Lee, R. T., & Ashford, B. E. (1996). A meta-analytic examination of the correlates of the three dimensions of job burnout. *Journal of Applied Psychology, 81,* 123–133.

Leitner, M. B. (1991). Coping patterns as predictors of burnout: The function of control and escapist coping patterns. *Journal of Organizational Behavior, 12,* 123–144.

Lennings, C. J. (2000). Optimism, satisfaction and time perspective in the elderly. *International Journal of Aging and Human Development, 51,* 167–181.

Levine, J. M., & Moreland, R. L. (1991). Culture and socialization in work groups. In L. B. Resnick, J. M. Levine, & S. D. Teasly (Eds.), *Perspectives on socially shared cognition* (pp. 257–279). Washington, DC: American Psychological Association.

Levine, R. V. (1988). The pace of life across cultures. In J. McGrath (Ed.), *The social psychology of time: New perspectives* (pp. 39–59). Beverly Hills, CA: Sage.

Levine, R. V. (1997). *A geography of time: The temporal misadventures of a social psychologist, or how every culture keeps time just a little bit differently.* NY: Basic Books.

Levine, R. V., & Bartlett, K. (1984). The pace of life, punctuality, and coronary heart disease in six countries. *Journal of Cross Country Psychology, 15,* 233–255.

Levine, R. V., West, L., & Reis, H. (1980). Perceptions of time and punctuality in the United States and Brazil. *Journal of Personality and Social Psychology, 38,* 541–550.

Levine, R. V., & Wolff, E. (1985, March). Social time: The heartbeat of culture. *Psychology Today,* pp. 28–35.

Levitt, B., & March, J. G. (1988). Organizational learning. *Annual Reviews of Sociology, 14,* 319–340.

Liberman, N., & Trope, Y. (1998). The role of feasibility and desirability consider-ations in near and distant future decisions: A test of temporal construal theory. *Journal of Personality and Social Psychology, 75,* 5–19.

Little, B. R. (1983). Personal projects: A rationale and method for investigation. *Environment and Behavior, 15,* 273–290.

Locke, E. A., & Latham, G. P. (1990). *A theory of goal setting and task performance.* Englewood Cliffs, NJ: Prentice Hall.

Loewenstein, G., Weber, E., Hsee, C., & Welch, E. (2001). Risk as feelings. *Psycho-logical Bulletin, 127,* 267–286.

Lord, R. G., & Rowzee, M. (1979). Task interdependence, temporal phase, and cognitive heterogeneity as determinants of leadership behavior and behavior-performance relations. *Organizational Behavior and Human Performance, 23,* 182–200.

Maes, S., Leventhal, H., & de Ridder, D. T. D. (1996). Coping with chronic diseases. In N. S. Endler (Ed.), *Handbook of coping: Theory, research, applications* (pp. 221–251). New York: John Wiley & Sons.

Mak, A. S., & Mueller, J. (2000). Job insecurity, coping resources and personality dispositions in occupational strain. *Work & Stress, 14,* 312–328.

Malmberg, L. E., & Trempala, J. (1997). Future planning both at school and in other contexts: The case of Finnish and Polish general-secondary and vocational-school students. *Scandinavian Journal of Educational Research, 42,* 207–226.

Mann, J. B. (2001). *Time for a change: The role of internal and external pacing mecha-nisms in prompting the midpoint transition.* Unpublished honors thesis, Harvard University.

Martin, L. L., Tesser, A., & McIntosh, W. D. (1993). Wanting but not having: The effects of unattained goals on thoughts and feelings. In J. W. Pennebaker (Ed.), *Handbook of mental control* (pp. 552–572). Englewood Cliffs, NJ: Prentice Hall.

Maslach, C., Schaufeli, W. B., & Leitner, M. B. (2001). Job burnout. *Annual Reviews of Psychology, 52,* 397–422.

Maule, A., Hockey, G. R. J., Bdzola, L. (2000). Effects of time pressure on decision making under uncertainty: Changes in affective state and information process-ing strategy. *Acta Psychologica, 104,* 283–301.

McCabe, K. M., & Barnett, D. (2000). The relation between familial factors and the future orientation of urban, African American sixth graders. *Journal of Child and Family Studies, 9,* 491–508.

McEwen, B. S. (1998). Protective and damaging effects of stress mediators. *New England Journal of Medicine, 338,* 171–179.

McGrath, J. E. (1976). Stress and behaviour in organizations. In M. D. Dunette (Ed.), *Handbook of industrial and organizational psychology* (pp. 1351–1395). Chicago: Rand McNally.

McGrath, J. E. (1991). Time, interaction, and performance (TIP): A theory of groups. *Small Group Research, 22,* 147–174.

McGrath, J. E., & Altermatt, T. W. (2000). Observation and analysis of group inter-action over time: Some methodological and strategic choices. In M. A. Hogg & R. S. Tindale (Eds.), *Handbook of social psychology, Vol. 3: Group processes* (pp. 525–556). London: Blackwell.

McGrath, J. E., & Argote, L. (2000). Group processes in organizational contexts. In M. A. Hogg & R. S. Tindale (Eds.), *Handbook of social psychology, Vol. 3: Group processes* (pp. 603–627). London: Blackwell.

McGrath, J. E., & Beehr, T. A. (1990). Time and the stress process: Some temporal issues in the conceptualization and measurement of stress. *Stress Medicine, 6*, 93–104.

McGrath, J. E., & Berdahl, J. R. (1998). Groups, technology, and time: Use of computers for collaborative work. In R. Scott Tindale, L. Heath, J. Edwards, E. J. Posovac, F. B. Bryant, Y. Suarez-Balcazr, et al. (Eds.), *Theory and research on small groups* (pp. 205–228). New York: Plenum Press.

McGrath, J. E., & Hollingshead, A. B. (1994). *Groups interacting with technology.* Newbury Park, CA: Sage.

McGrath, J. E., & Kelly, J. R. (1986). *Time and human interaction.* New York: Guilford Press.

McGrath, J. E., Kelly, J. R., & Machatka, D. E. (1984). The social psychology of time: Entrainment of behavior in social and organizational settings. In S. Oskamp (Ed.), *Applied social psychology annual* (Vol. 5, pp. 21–44). Beverly Hills, CA: Sage.

McGrath, J. E., & O'Connor, K. M. (1996). Temporal issues in work groups. In M. A. West (Ed.), *Handbook of work group psychology* (pp. 25–52). NY: Wiley.

McGrath, J. E., & Rotchford, N. L. (1983). Time and behavior in organizations. In L. Cummings & B. Staw (Eds.), *Research in organizational behavior* (Vol. 5, pp. 57–101). New York: JAI Press.

McGrath, J. E., & Tschan, F. (in press). Dynamics in groups and teams. In M. S. Poole & A. H. Van de Ven (Eds.), *Handbook of organizational change and innovation.* New York: Oxford University Press.

Metcalfe, J., & Mischel, W. (1999). A hot/cool system analysis of delay of gratification: Dynamics of willpower. *Psychological Review, 106*, 3–19.

Michon, J. A. (Ed.). (with Pouthas, V., & Jackson, J. L.). (1988). *Guyau and the idea of time.* Amsterdam: North-Holland Publishing Company.

Mikulincer, M., & Florian, V. (1996). Coping and adaptation to trauma and loss. In N. S. Endler (Ed.), *Handbook of coping: Theory, research, applications* (pp. 554–572). New York: John Wiley & Sons.

Milgram, S., Liberty, H. J., Toledo, R., & Wackenhut, J. (1986). Response to intrusion into waiting lines. *Journal of Personality and Social Psychology, 51*, 683–689.

Miller, G. A., Galanter, E., & Pribram, K. H. (1960). *Plans and the structure of behavior.* New York: Holt, Rinehart, & Winston.

Mintzberg, H., Raisinghani, D., & Théorêt, A. (1976). The structure of "unstructured" decision processes. *Administrative Science Quarterly, 21*, 246–275.

Mischel, W. (1974). Processes in delay of gratification. In L. Berkowitz (Ed.), *Advances in experimental social psychology* (Vol. 7, pp. 249–292). New York: Academic Press.

Mischel, W., Shoda, Y., & Peake, P. K. (1988). The nature of adolescent competencies predicted by preschool delay of gratification. *Journal of Personality and Social Psychology, 54,* 687–696.

Mitchell, T. R., & James, L. R. (2001). Building better theory: Time and the specification of when things happen. *Academy of Management Review, 26,* 530–547.

Mitchell, T. R., Peterson, E., & Cronk, R. (1997). Temporal adjustment in the evaluation of events: The "rosy" view. *Journal of Experimental Social Psychology, 33,* 421–448.

Moore, W. E. (1963). *Man, time and society.* New York: John Wiley & Sons.

Moore-Ede, M. C., Sulzman, F. M., & Fuller, C. A. (1982). *The clocks that time us.* Cambridge, MA: Harvard University Press.

Moreland, R. L., & Levine, J. M. (1982). Socialization in small groups: Temporal changes in individual-group relations. In L. Berkowitz (Ed.), *Advances in experimental social psychology* (Vol. 15, pp. 137–192). New York: Academic Press.

Murrell, A. J., & Mingrone, M. (1994). Correlates of temporal perspective. *Perceptual and Motor Skills, 78,* 1331–1334.

Nesselroade, J. R., Stigler, S. M., & Baltes, P. B. (1980). Regression toward the mean and the study of change. *Psychological Bulletin, 88,* 622–637.

Neter, J., Wasserman, S., & Kutner, M. H. (1990). *Applied linear statistical models* (3rd ed.). Boston, MA: Irwin.

Neuringer, C., & Harris, R. M. (1974). The perception of the passage of time among death-involved patients. *Life Threatening Behavior, 4,* 240–254.

Nurmi, J. E. (1989). Development of orientation to the future during early adolescence: A four-year longitudinal study and two cross-sectional comparisons. *International Journal of Psychology, 24,* 195–214.

Nurmi, J. E. (1991). How do adolescents see their future? A review of the development of future orientation and planning. *Developmental Review, 11,* 1–59.

Nurmi, J. E., & Pulliainen, H. (1991). The changing parent–child relationship, self-esteem, and intelligence as determinants of orientation to the future during early adolescence. *Journal of Adolescence, 14,* 35–51.

Nutt, P. C. (1984). Types of organizational decision processes. *Administrative Science Quarterly, 29,* 414–450.

Ochberg, F. M. (1993). Gift from within: Posttraumatic therapy. In J. P. Wilson & B. Raphael (Eds.), *International handbook of traumatic stress syndromes* (pp. 773–783). New York: Plenum Press.

Oesterreich, R. (1981). *Handlungsregulation und Kontrolle* [The regulation of actions and control]. München: Urban & Schwarzenberg.

Orasanu, J. M. (1993). Decision-making in the cockpit. In E. L. Wiener, B. G. Kanki, R. L. Helmreich (Eds.), *Cockpit resource management* (pp. 137–172). San Diego, CA: Academic Press.

Orasanu, J. M. (1994). Shared problem models and flight crew performance. In N. Johnston, N. McDonald, & R. Fuller (Eds.), *Aviation psychology in practice* (pp. 255–285). Hants, England: Avebury Technical.

Ornstein, R. E. (1969). *On the experience of time*. London: Penguin.

Osuna, E. E. (1985). The psychological cost of waiting. *Journal of Mathematical Psychology, 29*, 82–105.

Palinkas, L. A. (2001). Psychosocial issues in long-term space flight: Overview. *Gravitational and Space Biology Bulletin, 14*, 25–33.

Pandey, R. N. (2000). *Conducting the time use survey: Indian experience.* Expert Group Meeting on Methods for Conducting Time-Use Surveys 23–27 October 2000 New York. Retrieved January 3, 2003, from http://unstats.un.org/unsd/methods/timeuse/xptgrpmeet/india.pdf

Payne, J. W., Bettman, J. R., & Johnson, E. J. (1993). The use of multiple strategies in judgment and choice. In N. J. Castella (Ed.), *Individual and group decision making* (pp. 19–39). Hillsdale, NJ: Erlbaum.

Peeters, M. C. W., Buunk, B. P., & Schaufeli, W. B. (1995). Social interactions, stressful events, and negative affect at work: A micro-analytic approach. *European Journal of Social Psychology, 25*, 349–401.

Peterson, C., & Park, C. (1998). Learned helplessness and explanatory style. In V. B. Van Hasselt (Ed.), *Advanced personality* (pp. 287–310). New York: Plenum Press.

Petry, N. M. (2001). Pathological gamblers, with and without substance abuse disorders, discount delayed rewards at high rates. *Journal of Abnormal Psychology, 116*, 482–487.

Piaget, J. (1927). *Le developpement de la notion de temps chez l'enfant* [The child's conception of time]. Paris: Presses Universitaires de France.

Pisano, G. P., Bohmer, R. M., & Edmondson, A. C. (2001). Organizational differences in rates of learning: Evidence from the adoption of minimally invasive cardiac surgery. *Management Science, 47*, 752–768.

Pittendrigh, C. S. (1972). On temporal organization in living systems. In H. Yaker, H. Osmond, & F. Cheek (Eds.), *The future of time*. NY: Anchor Books.

Pole, A., West, M., & Harrison, P. J. (1994). *Applied Bayesian forecasting and time series analysis*. New York: Chapman & Hall.

Poole, M. S. (1981). Decision development in small groups I: A test of two models. *Communication Monographs, 48*, 1–24.

Poole, M. S. (1983). Decision development in small groups III: A multiple sequence model of group decision making. *Communication Monographs, 50*, 321–344.

Poole, M. S., & Baldwin, C. L. (1996). Developmental processes in group decision making. In R. Y. Hirokawa & M. S. Poole (Eds.), *Communication and group decision making* (2nd ed., pp. 215–268). Thousand Oaks, CA: Sage.

Poole, M. S., & Roth, J. (1989a). Decision development in small groups IV: A typology of decision paths. *Human Communication Research, 15*, 323–356.

Poole, M. S., & Roth, J. (1989b). Decision development in small groups V: Test of a contingency model. *Human Communication Research, 15*, 549–589.

Pöppel, E. (1989). *Gegenwart psychologisch gesehen* [A psychological view on the present]. In R. Wendorff (Ed.), *Im Netz der Zeit* [In the Web of Time] (pp. 11–16). Stuttgart: Wissenschaftliche Verlagsgesellschaft.

Porges, S. W., Bohrer, R. E., Cheung, M. N., Drasgow, F., MacCabe, P. M., & Keren, G. (1980). New time-series statistic for detecting rhythmic co-occurrence in the frequency domain: The weighted coherence and its applicability to psychophysiological research. *Psychological Bulletin, 88,* 589–587.

Pruessner, J. C., Hellhammer, D. H., & Kirschbaum, C. (1999). Burnout, perceived stress, and cortisol responses to awakening. *Psychosomatic Medicine, 61,* 197–204.

Psathas, G. (1960). Phase movement and equilibrium tendencies in interaction process in psychotherapy groups. *Sociometry, 23,* 177–194.

Pulkkinen, L., & Rönkä, A. (1994). Personal control over development, identity formation, and future orientation as components of life orientation: A developmental approach. *Developmental Psychology, 30,* 260–271.

Putnam, L. L. (1981). Procedural messages and small group work climates: A lag sequential analysis. In M. Burgoon (Eds.), *Communication yearbook* (pp. 331–350). New Brunswick, NY: Transaction Publishers.

Pynoos, R. S., Sorenson, S. B., & Steinberg, A. M. (1993). Interpersonal violence and traumatic stress reactions. In L. Goldberger & S. Breznis (Eds.), *Handbook of stress: Theoretical and clinical aspects* (2nd ed., pp. 573–590). New York: Free Press.

Reason, J. (1990). *Human error.* New York: Cambridge University Press.

Reicherts, M. (1999). *Comment gérer le stress? Le concept des règles cognitivo-comportementales* [How to deal with stress? The concept of cognitive-behavioral rules]. Fribourg: Edition Universitaires Fribourg Suisse.

Reicherts, M., & Perrez, M. (1992). Adequate coping behavior: The behavior rules approach. In M. Reicherts (Ed.), *Stress, coping and health: A situation-behavior approach: Theory, methods, applications* (pp. 161–177). Bern: Hogrefe & Huber.

Reicherts, M., & Pihet, S. (2000). Job newcomers coping with stressful situations: A micro-analysis of adequate coping and well-being. *Swiss Journal of Psychology, 59,* 303–316.

Robinson, J. P., Converse, P. E., & Szalai, A. (1972). Everyday life in twelve countries. In A. Szalai (Ed.), *The use of time: Daily activities of urban and suburban populations in twelve countries* (pp. 113–144). The Hague: Mouton.

Robinson, J. P., & Godbey, G. (1997). *Time for life: The surprising ways Americans use their time.* University Park, PA: Pennsylvania State University Press.

Rodriguez, M. L., Mischel, W., & Shoda, Y. (1989). Cognitive person variables in the delay of gratification of older children at risk. *Journal of Personality and Social Psychology, 57,* 358–367.

Rogosa, D., Brandt, D., & Zimowski, M. (1982). A growth curve approach to the measurement of change. *Psychological Bulletin, 92,* 726–748.

Roth, A. E., Murnigham, J. K., & Schumaker, F. (1988). The deadline effect in bargaining: Some empirical evidence. *The American Economic Review, 78,* 806–824.

Rothbaum, F., Weisz, J., & Snyder, S. (1982). Changing the world and changing the self: A two process model of perceived control. *Journal of Personality and Social Psychology, 42*, 5–37.

Ruback, R. B., & Juieng, D. (1997). Territorial defense in parking lots: Retaliation against waiting drivers. *Journal of Applied Social Psychology, 27*, 821–834.

Ruback, R. B., Pape, K. D., & Doriot, P. (1989). Waiting for a phone: Intrusion on callers leads to territorial defense. *Social Psychology Quarterly, 52*, 232–241.

Russo, J. E., & Dosher, B. A. (1983). Strategies for multiattribute binary choice. *Journal of Experimental Psychology: Learning, Memory, and Cognition, 9*, 676–696.

Ryan, R. M., & Deci, E. L. (2000). Self-determination theory and the facilitation of intrinsic motivation, social development, and well-being. *American Psychologist, 55*, 68–78.

Sambamurthy, V., Poole, M. S., & Kelly, J. (1993). The effects of variations in GDSS capabilities on decision-making processes in groups. *Small Group Research, 24*, 523–546.

Sapolsky, R. M. (1998). *Why zebras don't get ulcers: An updated guide to stress, stress-related diseases, and coping.* New York: Freeman.

Schallberger, U., & Pfister, R. (2001). *Flow-Erleben in Arbeit und Freizeit* [Flow-experience in work and leisure]. *Zeitschrift für Arbeits- und Organisationspsychologie, 45*, 176–187.

Schaufeli, W. B., & Enzmann, D. (1998). *The burnout companion to study and practice: A critical analysis.* London: Taylor and Francis.

Schmidt, R. W., Lamm, H., & Trommsdorff, G. (1978). Social class and sex as determinants of future orientation (time perspective) in adults. *European Journal of Social Psychology, 8*, 71–90.

Schmitt, B. H., Dubé, L., & Leclerc, F. (1992). Intrusions into waiting lines: Does the queue constitute a social system? *Journal of Personality and Social Psychology, 63*, 806–815.

Schoenpflug, W., & Battmann, W. (1988). Costs and benefits of coping. In S. Fisher & J. Reason (Eds.), *Handbook of health, stress, cognition, and coping* (pp. 701–715). New York: Wiley.

Schriber, J. B., & Gutek, B. A. (1987). Some time dimensions of work: Measurement of an underlying aspect of organization culture. *Journal of Applied Psychology, 72*, 642–650.

Schwarzer, R. (1995). Modelling health behavior change: The health action process approach. *The Canadian Health Psychologist/Le Psychologue Canadien de la Santé, 3*, 49–51.

Schwarzer, R., & Schwarzer, C. (1996). A critical survey of coping instruments. In N. S. Endler (Ed.), *Handbook of coping: Theory, research, applications* (pp. 107–132). New York: John Wiley & Sons.

Schweizerische Depeschen Agentur. (2001). *Höhlendrama in Goumois: Überlebenschancen der Eingeschlossenen sinken* [Cave accident in Goumois: Decreased chances to survive]. Retrieved August 22, 2002, from http://www.espace.ch/cgi-bin/art_parse.pl?file=/news/artikel/08279/artikel.html

Seligman, M. E. P. (1975). *Helplessness*. San Francisco: Freeman.

Semmer, N. K. (1992). One man's meat, another man's poison? Stressors and their cultural backgrounds. In M. Cranach, G. Mugny, & W. Doise (Eds.), *Social representations and the social bases of knowledge* (pp. 152–157). Bern: Huber.

Semmer, N. K. (in press). Individual differences, work stress, and health. In M. J. Schabraq, H. A. Winnubst, & C. L. Cooper (Eds.), *Handbook of work and health psychology* (2nd ed.). Chichester, England: Wiley.

Semmer, N., Zapf, D., & Dunckel, H. (1995). Assessing stress at work: A framework and an instrument. In O. Svane & C. Johansen (Eds.), *Work and health: Scientific basis of progress in the working environment.* (pp. 105–113). Luxembourg: European Commission.

Shannon, L. (1976). Age change in time perception in native Americans, Mexican Americans, and Anglo-Americans. *Journal of Cross-cultural Psychology, 7,* 117–122.

Shaw, S. M., Caldwell, L. L., & Kleiber, D. K. (1996). Boredom, stress and social control in the daily activities of adolescents. *Journal of Leisure Research, 28,* 274–292.

Shepherd, A. (1998). HTA as a framework for task analysis. *Ergonomics, 41,* 1537–1552.

Shoda, Y., Mischel, W., & Peake, P. K. (1990). Predicting adolescent cognitive and social competence from preschool delay of gratification: Identifying diagnostic conditions. *Developmental Psychology, 26,* 978–986.

Shupe, E. I., & McGrath, J. E. (1998). Stress and the sojourner. In C. L. Cooper, (Ed.), *Theories of organizational stress* (pp. 86–100). Oxford: Oxford University Press.

Shure, G. H., Rogers, M. S., Larsen, I. M., & Tassone, J. (1962). Group planning and task effectiveness. *Sociometry, 25,* 263–282.

Siegrist, J. (1998). Adverse health effects of effort-reward imbalance at work. In C. L. Cooper (Ed.), *Theories of organizational stress* (pp. 190–204). New York: Oxford University Press.

Silver, S. D., Cohen, B. P., & Rainwater, J. (1988). Group structure and information exchange in innovative problem solving. *Advances in Group Processes, 5,* 169–194.

Simon, H. A. (1955). A behavioral model of rational choice. *The Quarterly Journal of Economics, 69,* 99–118.

Singer, J. D. (1998). Using SAS PROC MIXED to fit multilevel models, hierarchical models, and individual growth models. *Journal of Educational and Behavioral Statistics, 23,* 323–355.

Singleton, J. F. (1999). Lessons from leisure-time budget research. Implications for practice. In E. Wendy, A. S. Harvey, M. P. Lawton, & M. A. McColl (Eds.), *Time Use Research in the Social Sciences* (pp. 245–259). New York: Kluwer Academic/Plenum.

Skorzynski, Z. (1972). The use of free time in Torun, Maribor and Jackson. In A. Szalai (Ed.), *The use of time: Daily activities of urban and suburban populations in twelve countries* (pp. 265–289). The Hague: Mouton.

Slife, B. D. (1993). *Time and psychological explanation*. Albany, NY: State University of New York Press.

Slovic, P., Fischhoff, B., & Lichtenstein, S. (1982). Facts versus fears: Understanding perceived risk. In A. Tversky (Ed.), *Judgment under uncertainty: Heuristics and biases* (pp. 463–489). Cambridge, England: Cambridge University Press.

Smyth, J. M., & Pennebaker, J. W. (1999). Sharing one's story. Translating emotional experiences into words as a coping tool. In C. R. Snyder (Ed.), *Coping: The psychology of what works* (pp. 70–89). New York: Oxford University Press.

Sommer, J., & Vodanovic, S. J. (2000). Boredom proneness: Its relationship to psychological and physical health symptoms. *Journal of Clinical Psychology, 56,* 149–155.

Sommerfield, M. R., & McCrae, R. R. (2000). Stress and coping research. Methodological challenges, theoretical advances, and clinical applications. *American Psychologist, 55,* 620–625.

Sonnentag, S., & Frese, M. (2003). Stress in organizations. In W. C. Borman, D. R. Ilgen, & J. R. Klimoski (Eds.), *Handbook of psychology, Vol. 12: Industrial and organizational psychology* (pp. 453–291). Hoboken, NJ: Wiley.

Sonnentag, S., & Schmidt-Brasse, U. (1998). Expertise at work: Research perspectives and practical interventions for ensuring excellent performance at the workplace. *European Journal of Work and Organizational Psychology, 7,* 449–454.

Spector, P. E., & Jex, S. M. (1998). Development of four self-report measures of job stressors and strain: Interpersonal conflict at work scale, organizational constraints scale, quantitative workload inventory, and physical symptoms inventory. *Journal of Occupational Health Psychology, 3,* 356–367.

Spence, J. T., Helmreich, R. L., & Pred, R. S. (1987). Impatience versus achievement strivings in the type A pattern: Differential effects on student's health and academic achievement. *Journal of Applied Psychology, 72,* 522–528.

Spendlove, D. C., Rigdon, M. A., Jenson, W. N., & Udall, K. S. (1987). Effects of waiting on patient mood and satisfaction. *Journal of Family Practice, 24,* 200–202.

Staw, B. M., Sandelands, L. E., & Dutton, J. E. (1981). Threat-rigidity effects in organizational behavior: A multilevel analysis. *Administrative Science Quarterly, 26,* 501–524.

Stech, E. L. (1975). An analysis of interaction structure in the discussion of a ranking task. *Speech Monographs, 37,* 249–256.

Stein, G. L., Kimiecik, J. C., Daniels, J., & Jackson, S. A. (1995). Psychological antecedents of flow in recreational sport. *Personality and Social Psychology Bulletin, 21,* 125–135.

Stone, P. J. (1972). Models of everyday time allocations. In A. Szalai (Ed.), *The use of time: Daily activities of urban and suburban populations in twelve countries* (pp. 179–189). The Hague: Mouton.

Strathman, A., Gleicher, F., Boniger, D. S., & Edwards, C. S. (1994). The consideration of future consequences: Weighting immediate and distant outcomes of behavior. *Journal of Personality and Social Psychology, 66,* 742–752.

Stroebe, M., Stroebe, W., Schut, H., Zech, E., & van den Bout, J. (2002). Does disclosure of emotions facilitate recovery from bereavement? Evidence from two prospective studies. *Journal of Consulting and Clinical Psychology, 70,* 169–178.

Suzuki, H., Hashimoto, Y., & Ishii, K. (1997). Measuring information behavior: A time budget survey in Japan. *Social Indicators Research, 42,* 151–169.

Talland, G. A. (1955). Tasks and interaction process: Some characteristics of therapeutic group discussions. *Journal of Abnormal and Social Psychology, 50,* 105–189.

Tasto, D. L., Colligan, M. J., Skjei, E. W., & Polly, S. J. (1978). *Health consequences of shift work.* Cincinnati, OH: U.S. Department of Health and Human Services.

Taylor, S. (1994). Waiting for service: The relationship between delays and evaluations of service. *Journal of Marketing, 58,* 56–69.

Taylor, S. (1995). The effects of filled waiting time and service provider control over the delay on evaluations of service. *Journal of the Academy of Marketing Science, 23,* 38–48.

Tennen, H., Affleck, G., Armeli, S., & Carney, M. A. (2000). A daily process approach to coping. *American Psychologist, 55,* 626–636.

Tesser, A., Martin, L. L., & Cornell, D. P. (1996). On the substitutability of self-protective mechanisms. In J. A. Bargh (Ed.), *The psychology of action: Linking cognition and motivation to behavior* (pp. 48–68). New York: Guilford Press.

Thayer, R., & Schiff, W. (1975). Eye-contact facial expression, and the experience of time. *The Journal of Social Psychology, 95,* 117–124.

Thoits, P. A. (1994). Stressors and problem-solving: The individual as psychological activist. *Journal of Health and Social Behavior, 35,* 143–159.

Tice, D. M. (1991). Esteem protection or enhancement? Self-handicapping motives and attributions differ by trait self-esteem. *Journal of Personality and Social Psychology, 60,* 711–725.

Tom, G., & Lucey, S. (1997). A field study investigating the effect of waiting time on customer satisfaction. *Journal of Psychology, 131,* 655–660.

Trommsdorff, G. (1983). Future orientation and socialization. *International Journal of Psychology, 18,* 381–406.

Tschan, F. (1995). Communication enhances small group performance if it conforms to task requirements: The concept of ideal communication cycles. *Basic and Applied Social Psychology, 17,* 371–393.

Tschan, F. (2002). Ideal cycles of communication (or cognition) in triads, dyads, and individuals. *Small Group Research, 33,* 615–643.

Tschan, F., & Cranach, M. (1996). Group task structure, processes, and outcome. In M. A. West (Ed.), *Handbook of work group psychology* (pp. 92–121). Chichester, England: Wiley.

Tschan, F., Semmer, N. K., Nägele, C., & Gurtner, A. (2000). Task adaptive behavior and performance in groups. *Group Processes and Intergroup Relations, 3,* 367–386.

Tucker, L. R. (1966). Learning theory and multivariate experiment: Illustration by determination of generalized learning curves. In R. B. Cattell (Ed.), *Handbook of multivariate experimental psychology* (pp. 476–501). New York: Rand McNally.

Tuckman, B. W. (1965). Developmental sequences in small groups. *Psychological Bulletin, 65,* 384–399.

Tuckman, B. W., & Jenson, M. A. C. (1977). Stages of small group development revisited. *Group and Organizational Studies, 2,* 419–427.

Turner, R. J., & Avison, W. R. (1992). Innovations in the measurement of life stress: Crisis theory and the significance of event resolution. *Journal of Health and Social Behavior, 33,* 36–50.

Tversky, A. (1969). Intransitivity of preferences. *Psychological Review, 76,* 31–48.

Vagg, P. R., & Spielberger, C. D. (1998). Occupational stress: Measuring job pressure and organizational support in the workplace. *Journal of Occupational Health Psychology, 3,* 294–305.

Vallacher, R. R., & Nowak, A. (Eds.). (1994). *Dynamical systems in social psychology.* New York: Academic Press.

Vallacher, R. R., & Wegner, D. M. (1989). Levels of personal agency: Individual variation in action identification. *Journal of Personality and Social Psychology, 57,* 660–671.

Verdi, A. F., & Wheelan, S. A. (1992). Developmental patterns in same sex and mixed sex groups. *Small Group Research, 23,* 356–378.

Wageman, R. (Ed.). (1999). *Research on managing groups and teams, Vol. 2: Groups in context.* Stamford, CT: JAI Press.

Waller, M. J. (2000). All in the timing: Team pacing behavior in dynamic conditions. In C. L. Cooper & D. M. Rousseau (Eds.), *Trends in organizational behavior* (Vol. 7, pp. 37–43). Chichester, England: Wiley.

Waller, M. J., Conte, J. M., Gibson, C. B., & Carpenter, M. A. (2001). The effect of individual perceptions of deadlines on team performance. *Academy of Management Review, 4,* 586–600.

Wampold, B. E. (1984). Testing of dominance in sequential categorical data. *Psychological Bulletin, 96,* 424–429.

Warner, D. J., & Block, R. A. (1984). Type A behavior and temporal judgment. *Bulletin of the Psychonomic Society, 22,* 163–166.

Warner, R. M. (1979). Periodic rhythms in conversational speech. *Language and Speech, 22,* 381–396.

Warner, R. M., Waggener, T. R., & Kronauer, R. E. (1983). Synchronized cycles in ventilation and vocal activity during spontaneous conversational speech. *Applied Physiology: Respiratory, Environmental, and Exercise Physiology, 34,* 1324–1334.

Wasserman, S., & Faust, K. (1994). *Social network analysis: Methods and applications.* Cambridge, England: Cambridge University Press.

Wasserman, S., & Jacobucci, D. (1988). Sequential social network data. *Psychometrika, 53,* 261–282.

Wasserman, S., & Pattison, P. (1996). Logit models and logistic regression for social networks: I. An introduction to Markov graphs and p*. *Psychometrika, 61,* 401–425.

Watt, J. D. (1991). Effect of boredom proneness on time perception. *Psychological Reports, 69,* 323–327.

Watt, J. D., & Blanchard, M. J. (1994). Boredom proneness and the need for cognition. *Journal of Research in Personality, 28,* 44–51.

Watt, J. D., & Vodanovic, S. J. (1999). Boredom proneness and psychological development. *Journal of Psychology, 133,* 303–314.

Webb, J. T., & Mayers, B. S. (1974). Developmental aspects of temporal orientation in adolescents. *Journal of Clinical Psychology, 30,* 504–507.

Webb, W. B. (1985). Sleep in industrialized settings in the northern hemisphere. *Psychological Reports, 57,* 591–598.

Weingart, L. (1992). Impact of group goals, task component complexity, effort, and planning on group performance. *Journal of Applied Psychology, 77,* 682–693.

Weinstein, L., Xie, X., & Cleanthous, C. C. (1995). Purpose in life, boredom, and volunteerism in a group of retirees. *Psychological Reports, 76,* 482.

Wells, J. D., Hobfoll, S. E., & Lavin, J. (1999). When it rains, it pours. The greater impact of resource loss compared to gain on psychological distress. *Personality and Social Psychology Bulletin, 25,* 1172–1182.

Wendorff, R. (Ed.). (1989). *Im Netz der Zeit* [In the web of time]. Stuttgart, Germany: S. Hirzel Wissenschaftliche Verlagsgemeinschaft.

Wensauer, M., & Grossmann, K. E. (1998). *Bindungstheoretische Grundlagen subjektiver Lebenszufriedenheit und individueller Zukunftsorientierung im hoeheren Erwachsenenalter* [Subjective satisfaction with life and future orientation in elderly people]. *Zeitschrift für Gerontologie und Geriatrie, 31,* 362–370.

West, M. A. (1996). Reflexivity and work group effectiveness: A conceptual integration. In M. A. West (Eds.), *Handbook of work group psychology* (pp. 555–579). Chichester, England: Wiley.

Wever, R. A. (1981). On varying work–sleep schedules: The biological rhythm perspective. In L. C. Johnson, D. I. Tepas, W. P. Colquhoun, & M. J. Colligan, (Eds.), *The twenty-four hour work-day: Proceedings of a symposium on variations in work–sleep schedules.* Cincinnati, OH: U.S. Department of Health and Human Services.

Wheelan, S. A. (1994). *Group processes: A developmental perspective.* Sydney: Allyn & Bacon.

Wheelan, S. A., & McKeage, R. L. (1993). Developmental patterns in small and large groups. *Small Group Research, 2,* 460–483.

Wilhelm, P. (2001). A multilevel approach to analyze ambulatory assessment data: An examination of family members' emotional states in daily life. In J. Fahrenberg & M. Myrteck (Eds.), *Progress in ambulatory assessment: Computer assisted psychological and psychophysiological methods in monitoring and field studies* (pp. 173–189). Goettingen, Germany: Hogrefe & Huber.

Wills, T. A. (1987). Help-seeking as a coping mechanism. In C. E. Ford (Ed.), *Coping with negative life events: Clinical and social psychological perspectives* (pp. 19–50). New York: Plenum Press.

Wittenbaum, G. M., & Stasser, G. (1996). Management of information in small groups. In J. L. Nye & A. M. Brower (Eds.), *What's social about social cognition? Social cognition in small groups* (pp. 2–29). Thousand Oaks, CA: Sage.

Worchel, S. (1996). Emphasizing the social nature of groups in a developmental framework. In J. L. Nye & A. M. Brower (Eds.), *What's social about social cognition? Social cognition in small groups* (pp. 261–284). Thousand Oaks, CA: Sage.

Worchel, S., & Coutant, D. (2001). It takes two to tango: Relating group identity to individual identity within the framework of group development. In M. A. Hogg & R. S. Tindale (Eds.), *Blackwell handbook of social psychology: Group processes* (pp. 461–481). Oxford, England: Blackwell.

Worchel, S., Coutant-Sassic, D., & Grossman, M. (1992). A developmental approach to group dynamics: A model and illustrative research. In S. Worchel, W. Wood, & J. Simpson (Eds.), *Group process and productivity* (pp. 181–202). Newbury Park, CA: Sage.

Young, M., & Schuller, T. (1988). (Eds.). *The rhythms of society*. London: Routledge.

Zakay, D. (1989). Subjective time and attentional resource allocation: An integrated model of time estimation. In I. Levin & D. Zakay (Eds.), *Time and human cognition: A life-span approach* (pp. 365–387). Amsterdam, The Netherlands: Elsevier.

Zakay, D. (1990). The evasive art of subjective time measurement: Some methodological dilemmas. In R. A. Block (Ed.), *Cognitive models of psychological time* (pp. 59–84). Hillsdale, NJ: Erlbaum.

Zapf, D., & Semmer, N. (in press). *Stress am Arbeitsplatz* [Stress at work]. In H. Schuler (Ed.), *Organisationspsychologie* [Organizational Psychology]. Goettingen, Germany: Hogrefe & Huber.

Zeigarnik, B. (1927). *Uber das Behalten erledigter und unerledigter Handlungen* [On remembering finished and unfinished tasks]. *Psychologische Forschung, 9*, 1–85.

Zerubavel, E. (1981). *Hidden rhythms: Schedules and calendars in social life*. Berkeley, CA: University of California Press.

Zimbardo, P. G., & Boyd, J. N. (1999). Putting time in perspective. A valid, reliable individual-difference metric. *Journal of Personality and Social Psychology, 77*, 1271–1288.

Zimbardo, P. G., Keough, K. A., & Boyd, J. N. (1997). Present time perspective as a predictor of risky driving. *Personality and Individual Differences, 23*, 1007–1023.

AUTHOR INDEX

Achiron, A., 92
Adam, J., 153, 162
Affleck, G., 83
Agnew, C. R., 42
Agresti, A., 161, 162
Allmendinger, J., 110
Altermatt, T. W., 161
Altman, I., 4
Amazeen, P. G., 148, 159
Ancona, D. G., 110, 125, 133,175
Andorka, R., 29
Angrilli, A., 36
Annett, J., 49
Argote, L., 100, 107, 110, 117, 118, 125, 126
Argyle, M., 90
Armeli, S., 83
Arrow, H., 100, 107, 110, 123, 124, 148, 153, 157, 158, 159, 166
Arundale, R. B., 162
Ashford, B. E., 94
Atkinson, J. W., 54
Aveni, A., 15, 18
Avison, W. R., 91, 95

Baker, J., 61
Baldwin, C. L., 103
Bales, R. F., 101, 130, 134
Baltes, P. B., 162
Bandura, A., 49
Barak, Y., 92
Barling, J., 65
Barnett, D., 41, 42
Barnett, R. C., 86
Baron, R. M., 148, 159
Bartlett, K., 32
Battmann, W., 88
Baumeister, R. F., 89
Bdzola, L., 59
Beach, L. R., 59
Beckmann, J., 55
Beehr, T. A., 70, 73, 74, 75, 76, 78, 79, 80, 81, 82, 85, 89, 90, 112, 144

Beek, P. J., 148, 159
Bennett, J. B., 4
Benson, L., 59
Berbaum, M. L., 135
Berdahl, J. L., 100, 107, 110, 148, 157
Berglas, S., 83
Betsch, T., 60
Bettencourt, L. A., 61
Bettenhausen, K. L., 127
Bettman, J. R., 59
Bickel, W. K., 56
Bion, W. R., 103
Birch, D., 54
Bittman, M., 29, 30
Blake, M. J. F., 4
Blanchard, M. J., 63
Block, J., 56
Block, R. A., 4, 33, 34, 35, 40, 65
Bluedorn, A. C., 4, 59
Blunt, A., 63
Bohmer, R. M., 118
Boland, C. S., 42
Boltz, M., 34, 132
Boniger, D. S., 39, 43
Boos, M., 127
Boos, N., 90
Boswell, R., 65
Box, G. E. P., 161, 162
Boyd, J. N., 38, 39, 40, 42, 43
Brandt, D., 162
Bray, D. H., 40
Brehm, J. W., 90
Brickman, C., 40
Brilhard, J. K., 137
Brinkmann, J., 60
Brossart, D. F., 161, 162
Brousseau, K. R., 126
Brower, A. M., 50
Brown, F. M., 175
Brown, V., 4
Buggie, S. E., 40
Burke, R. J., 94
Burns, K. L., 153, 158
Burnstein, E., 135

Buunk, B. P., 89, 90
Byosiere, P., 70

Caldwell, D. F., 110, 125
Caldwell, L. L., 63
Cameron, M., 61
Campbell, D. T., 145, 146, 147
Cantor, N., 50
Cappella, J. N., 175
Carney, M. A., 83
Carpenter, M. A., 65
Carstensen, L. L., 90
Carver, C. S., 48, 49, 50, 76, 90
Chaffin, K. L., 42
Chalendar, J. de, 163
Chapple, E. D., 133
Chebat, J. C., 61
Cherubini, P., 36
Chong, C., 125, 133, 175
Chubick, J. D., 42
Cleanthous, C. C., 63
Cohen, B. P., 137
Cohen, M. S., 60
Cohen, S. G., 115
Colligan, M. J., 4
Colquhoun, W. P., 4
Colvin, C., 64
Conte, J. M., 64, 65
Converse, P. E., 29, 30, 31
Cook, T. D., 145, 146, 147
Cornell, D. P., 50
Coutant, D., 104
Coutant-Sassic, D., 104
Cox, D. R., 153
Coyne, J. C., 75
Cranach, M., von, 48, 53, 100, 107, 123
Cronk, R., 164
Cronkite, R. C., 91
Crosson, S. B., 153, 158, 159, 166
Cseh-Szombathy, L., 29
Csikszentmihalyi, M., 37

Dabbs, J. M., Jr., 4
Daniels, J., 37
Darden, D. K., 63
Darr, E., 118
Das, T. K., 4, 59
Deci, E. L., 50
de Jonge, J., 90
Denhardt, R. B., 4, 59

Denison, D. R., 115
de Ridder, D. T. D., 96
Dewey, J., 134
de Wolff, C. J., 90
Dillon, W. R., 162
Doob, L. W., 3, 18, 33
Dorfman, D. D., 162
Doriot, P., 62
Dormann, C., 92
Dosher, B. A., 57
Dubé, L., 61, 62
Duhamel, L. M., 31
Duncan, K. D., 49
Dunckel, H., 77, 85
Dutton, J. E., 59

Eckstrand, G., 34
Edmundson, A. C., 118
Edwards, C. S., 39, 43
Edwards, R. S., 4
Eisenhardt, K. M., 60, 126, 127
Elfering, A., 90
Elizur, A., 92
Emmons, R. A., 49
Enzmann, D., 93, 94
Epple, D., 118
Epstein, S., 78
Ericsson, K. A., 128

Faber, J. E., 89
Faraone, S. V., 162
Fast, J. E., 31
Faust, K., 162
Feldman, S., 175
Fiedler, K., 60
Fiksenbaum, L., 94
Fischhoff, B., 82
Fisher, B. A., 101, 103, 126, 128, 134
Fletcher, B. C., 88
Florian, V., 96
Folkman, S., 70, 73, 81, 95
Ford, C. E., 90
Foushee, H. C., 128
Fraisse, P., 33, 37, 61
Francis-Smythe, J., 64
Fraser, J. T., 3
Frederick, J. A., 31
Freeman, J. T., 60
Frese, M., 48, 53, 72, 87, 91, 92, 97, 123
Friedman, M., 64

Sapolsky, R. M., 70, 92, 93
Schade, J., 40
Schade, V., 90
Schaefer, C., 75
Schallberger, U., 37
Schaufeli, W. B., 90, 93, 94
Schaumann, L. J., 126
Scheier, M. F., 48, 49, 50, 76
Schiff, W., 36
Schmidt, R. W., 39, 41, 42
Schmidt-Brasse, U., 128
Schmitt, B. H., 62
Schoenpflug, W., 88
Schriber, J. B., 66
Schuller, T., 4
Schumaker F., 175
Schultz, G., 131
Schunk, D. H., 49
Schut, H., 96
Schwarzer, C., 83
Schwarzer, R., 83, 84
Schweizerische Depeschen Agentur, 125
Seligman, M. E. P., 90
Semmer, N. K., 70, 74, 77, 90, 92, 127
Shannon, L., 34
Shaw, S. M., 63
Sheldon, K. M., 50
Shepherd, A., 49
Shoda, Y., 55, 56
Shupe, E. I., 70, 74, 86, 87, 91
Shure, G. H., 126
Siegrist, J., 72
Silver, S. D., 137
Simon, H. A., 57
Singer, J. D., 162
Singleton, J. F., 30, 31
Skjei, E. W., 4
Slife, B. D., 4, 13, 15, 16, 142, 177
Slovic, P., 82
Smyth, J. M., 96
Snyder, S., 83
Sommer, S. J., 63
Sommerfield, M. R., 87
Sonnentag, S., 72, 128
Sorenson, S. B., 95
Spector, P. E., 77, 85
Spence, J. T., 64, 65
Spendlove, D. C., 61
Spielberger, C. D., 77
Stanley, J. C., 145, 147
Stasser, G., 127
Staw, B. M., 59

Stech, E. L., 130, 131
Stein, G. L., 37
Steinberg, A. M., 95
Stellar, B., 58
Stigler, S. M., 162
Stone, P. J., 31
Strathman, A., 38, 39, 42, 43
Strodtbeck, F. L., 101, 134
Stroebe, M., 96
Stroebe, W., 96
Stutman, R. K., 103, 126, 128
Sull, D. N., 127
Sulzman, F. M., 175
Suzuki, H., 31
Szalai, A., 29, 31

Tabrizi, B. N., 126
Talland, G. A., 135
Tassone, J., 126
Tasto, D. L., 4
Taylor, S., 61, 62
Tennen, H., 83
Tessor, A., 50, 51
Thayer, J., 64
Thayer, R., 36
Theorell, T., 77
Théorêt, A., 137
Thoits, P. A., 86, 91
Tice, D. M., 83
Toledo, R., 62
Tom, G., 61
Trempala, J., 42
Trommsdorff, G., 39, 40, 42
Trope, Y., 58
Tschan, F., 53, 100, 107, 110, 123, 127, 131
Tucker, L. R., 161, 162
Tuckman, B. W., 102
Turner, R. J., 91, 95
Tversky, A., 57

Udall, K. S., 61

Vagg, P. R., 77
Vallacher, R. R., 52, 148, 153
van den Bout, J., 96
Verdi, A. F., 103
Verma, S., 29, 30
Vodanovich, S. J., 63

Wachenhut, J., 62
Wageman, R., 110
Waggener, T. R., 133, 175
Wallace, H. M., 89
Waller, M. J., 65, 129, 133
Wampold, B. E., 162
Ware, W. B., 162
Warner, D. J., 65
Warner, R. M., 133, 175
Wasserman, S., 162
Watt, J. D., 63
Webb, J. T., 41
Webb, W. B., 31
Weber, E., 59
Wegner, D. M., 52
Weingart, L., 126, 127
Weinstein, L., 63
Weiss, J. A., 126
Weisz, J., 83
Welch, E., 59
Wells, J. D., 84, 89
Wendorff, R., 40
Wenger, S., 61
Wensauer, M., 41
Werner, C. M., 4
West, L., 32
West, M., 161, 162

West, M. A., 128
Wheelan, S. A., 103, 166
Wilhelm, P., 162
Wills, T. A., 89
Witherspoon, A. D., 42
Wittenbaum, G. M., 127
Wolf, S., 60
Wolff, E., 32
Wood, P. K., 161
Worchel, S., 104, 105

Xie, X., 63

Yang, M. C. K., 162
Ybema, J. E., 90
Young, M., 4

Zakay, D., 33, 34, 35
Zapf, D., 48, 53, 77, 87, 91, 92, 97, 123
Zech, E., 96
Zeigarnik, B., 50, 51
Zerubavel, E., 4
Zhou, L., 61
Zimbardo, P. G., 38, 39, 40, 41, 42, 43
Zimowski, M., 162

SUBJECT INDEX

in experimental simulations, 151–152
in future-time orientation, 39
perception/estimation of, 33–36
stress events, 75–76, 78
Dynamic accumulation model, 92
Dynamic coping, 83–84, 112
Dynamical systems analyses, 153, 159

Eastern mystical religions, 182, 184
Einsteinian view, 15
Elasticity of time, and task performance, 129
Electronic communication, in groups,
        129–130
Emergent project planning, 127
Emotion-oriented coping, 83–84
Emotions, in time estimation, 35–36
Entrainment
    and coordinated action, 133
    definition, 175–176
    group task performance, 131–134
    research agenda for, 166–167
Epochal time
    collective action scheduling, 129
    conceptual issues, 16, 18–20, 181
    experience of, 18–20
    functions, 21–22
Events, 170–171
Experience of time, 18–20
"Experiential time," 183. *See also* Learning
        process
Experimental paradigms. *See* Research
        process
Experimental simulations, time frames,
        151–152, 160
Expert decision makers, 60
Explicit project planning, 127
External synchronization, 133–134,
        175–176
External validity, 148

Families, time use, 30–31
"Fast" decisions, 60
Feelings, about passage of time, 36–37
Field studies, time frame, 151–152, 160
Fitness landscape, groups, 110–111
Flow experiences, 16, 37, 164, 182
Frequency-domain analyses, 161
Frequency parameter
    definition, 7, 171
    stressor events, 75

Functionally coupled sequences, 175
Future-oriented perspective, 38–44
    behavioral correlates, 42–43
    conceptual aspects, 39
    cultural/ethnic differences, 40
    and duration estimation, 35
    life span influences, 40–42
    measures, 39
    motivation interaction, 164
    rating scale discriminative validity, 43
    research agenda for, 164
    time urgency interactions, 65

Gender differences
    time orientation, 41
    time use, 30–31
Generalizability, research findings, 145,
        148
Goals, 48–56
    and action process, 48–56
        phases, 51–53
    hierarchy of, 48–49, 53
    obstacles to attainment, dynamics,
        53–54
    sequential organization, 48–49
    and time orientation, 42–43
    volitional control strategies, 54–56
Grief process, 96–97
Groups
    adaptation and change in, 110–120, 166
    collective action, 121–139
    Complex Action System Theory,
        107–115, 123–131
    developmental forces, 99–110, 166
    embedded context effects, 111–115
    learning/experiential factors, 117–118,
        166
    member socialization stages, 104–106
    operational planning, 126–128
    problem-solving phases, 134–138
    research agenda for,166
    research methodology issues, 106–107
    role transitions, 105
    strategic planning, 124–126
    task performance, 123–139
        sequence of phases, 134–138

Harmonic analysis, 161
Heidegger's ideas, 180
Hermeneutic temporality, 16, 180

Work groups, 115–117
  formation of, 125
  types of, 108
Work stress. *See* Occupational stress
Work time
  cross-national differences, 29–31
  perception of, 36–37
  time use studies, 29–31
Written discussion technique, grief work,
        96

ABOUT THE AUTHORS

Joseph E. McGrath, PhD, is Professor Emeritus of psychology and women's studies at the University of Illinois at Urbana–Champaign. He earned his MA in psychology at the University of Maryland in 1951, and his PhD in social psychology at the University of Michigan in 1955 with T. M. Newcomb. His areas of research interest are in small group processes and performance, including the impact of electronic technology on groups, social and psychological factors in stress, research methodology, gender issues in social psychology, and temporal factors in social psychological theory and research.

Franziska Tschan, PhD, is a professor of social psychology and work psychology at the University of Neuchâtel, Switzerland. She earned her PhD in psychology in 1990 and completed her habilitation in social psychology and work psychology in 1999, both with Mario von Cranach at the University of Berne, Switzerland. Her research interests include small-group and team performance in computer-supported as well as face-to-face groups and teams, social relationships at work, action theory as applied to group performance, and temporal patterns in collective action.